Windows 98 Hints & Hacks

Dean Andrews

SAMS
PUBLISHING

201 West 103rd Street
Indianapolis, IN 46290

Windows 98 Hints & Hacks

Copyright © 1998 by Que Corporation

International Standard Book Number: 0-7897-1750-6

Library of Congress Catalog Card Number: 98-85720

Printed in the United States of America

First Printing: December, 1998

00   4   3

Trademarks

Warning and Disclaimer

Executive Editor
Brad Koch

Acquisitions Editor
Dustin Sullivan

Development Editor
Tom Dinse

Managing Editor
Brice Gosnell

Project Editor
Kevin Laseau

Copy Editor
Molly Schaller

Indexer
Charlotte Clapp

Proofreader
Benjamin Berg

Technical Editor
Eric White

Interior Design
Gary Adair

Cover Design
Anne Jones

Layout Technician
Marcia Deboy

Overview

Contents

Appendix

About the Author

Dean Andrews is a freelance writer and computer analyst. He has authored over 350 articles in a variety of national publications, including *PC World, Macworld, The Web Magazine*, and *Boston.com*, the online hub of the *Boston Globe*. Dean is a contributing author to *Peter Norton's Guide to Upgrading and Repairing PCs, Special Edition Using Windows 98*, and *Windows 98 Installation & Configuration Handbook*. He has also developed hundreds of computer benchmark and performance tests, usability studies, and test plans, used to evaluate computer products and technology. Dean has worked as a manager in the *PC World* Test Center, a senior test developer at *InfoWorld*, and a software developer at IBM. He has a bachelor's degree in Computer Science from the University of California at Berkeley. Currently, Mr. Andrews lives with his wife, Jane, in Boston.

Dedication

This book is dedicated to my mother and father. Thanks for the life-long encouragement.

Acknowledgments

Undoubtedly, you've heard that a book is never truly the work of just one person. I'll verify this as fact. Several people helped make this book a reality.

I would like to thank David Fugate, my agent at Waterside Productions, for signing me on to this book project and handling the reams of paperwork.

My trusty editors at Macmillan, Dustin Sullivan and Tom Dinse, who kept the project on-track whenever it started to veer off course. They deserve a lot of credit.

I would like to send a special thanks to Larry Passo, Kyle Bryant, Michael Desmond, and Jerry Honeycutt. These Macmillan authors shared some of their hints and hacks with me and I've included them in this book.

You would be reading a much shorter book if it weren't for the shareware/freeware developers who are mentioned throughout these pages. We should all thank them.

Finally, and most importantly, I want to thank my wonderful wife Jane. Without her inspiration, feedback, and support, this book would not be in your hands.

—Dean Andrews

Tell Us What You Think!

As the reader of this book, *you* are our most important critic and commentator. We value your opinion and want to know what we're doing right, what we could do better, what areas you'd like to see us publish in, and any other words of wisdom you're willing to pass our way.

As the Executive Editor for the Operating Systems team at Macmillan Computer Publishing, I welcome your comments. You can fax, email, or write me directly to let me know what you did or didn't like about this book—as well as what we can do to make our books stronger.

Please note that I cannot help you with technical problems related to the topic of this book, and that due to the high volume of mail I receive, I might not be able to reply to every message.

When you write, please be sure to include this book's title and author as well as your name and phone or fax number. I will carefully review your comments and share them with the author and editors who worked on the book.

Fax: 317-817-7070

E-mail: opsys@mcp.com

Mail: Jeff Koch
        Operating Systems
        Macmillan Computer Publishing
        201 West 103rd Street
        Indianapolis, IN 46290 USA

Introduction

What are "hints and hacks?" Hints and hacks are tips—but "tips" doesn't really describe the sexy, untold, forbidden knowledge you'll find in these pages. I could have used "the untold story," "forbidden knowledge," "sexy sinful secrets," or some other catchy phrase, but those all seemed a bit sensational. And hints and hacks is, I think, a more accurate description of what you'll find in these pages. As presented here, a "hint" is an action you can perform by adjusting Windows 98's settings or by using a special utility; a "hack" requires you to edit the Windows 98 Registry, which I explain in the section "Editing the Registry" later in this introduction.

The idea behind this book is simple—I wanted to deliver all the most useful but least obvious tips for users of the new Windows 98 operating system. I wanted readers to be able to turn to just about any page and say to themselves, "I didn't know I could do that!" And, after it's all written and done, I believe Windows 98 Hints and Hacks achieves this goal. Try out that little test for yourself right now, if you like. I'll meet you back here.

If you figured out some neat customization or optimization trick after using Windows 98 for five minutes, you probably won't find it in these pages. I considered that an obvious tip. You're spending good money for this book, so I worked hard to make it worth every dime. In these pages, you'll find the very best Windows hints. Most would have taken you weeks, if not months, to find on your own. And, because of their undocumented nature, I've included some hacks you might never have discovered on your own.

This book walks you through each hint and hack in plain language. No steps are skipped. Most pages include notes, tips, and cautions, all related to the current topic. Novices can follow along step by step. Intermediate and advanced users should scan through and stop when they find the startling revelations, which come every few paragraphs.

Don't be a Windows 98 drone. Installing and running Windows 98 with its defaults is like letting Microsoft control your desktop. Use these hints and hacks to customize, optimize, and manage your operating system. Make it yours.

The rest of the introduction describes who should read this book and how it's organized. It also walks you through the installation of the software tools (available on the Windows 98 CD) that you'll need to perform these hints and hacks.

Who Will Get the Most from This Book?

The main reason you didn't see the words "Idiot" or "Dummy" in the title of this book is because I don't consider you to be one. Congratulations! Another reason is that those complete novice guides use very structured formats, some would say formulaic, that really don't suit a tips book like this.

Beginners *are* welcome here, however. So are intermediate and advanced Windows users. These hints and hacks cover a lot of information that even many experienced PC users don't know, but they are written so that curious novices can take advantage of them as well.

All I assume is that you have some basic understanding of any Microsoft Windows operating system, meaning that you know how to start up and shut down your computer, click and double-click icons, move and size windows, drag files and folders, and so forth.

It doesn't really matter which Windows version you know—3.x, 95, or 98. The basic methods of using each are similar enough that anyone who knows these methods will understand the instructions in this book. You don't need to be an expert, but even if you are, you'll find new insights into how Windows 98 works and how to make it work for you.

What Windows 98 Adds to Your System

Despite plenty of controversy, negative publicity, even the involvement of the U.S. Department of Justice, Windows 98 has arrived. I'm not a lawyer, so I'll let others fight over the legal issues. Politics and anti-trust lawsuits aside, Microsoft has delivered a powerful new operating system.

As a follow-up to Windows 95, Windows 98 delivers enhancements in both software features and hardware support. With Windows 98 you'll be able to do more, work faster, add new types of hardware, and just have more fun with your computer.

On the software side, Windows offers several new components. With WebTV for Windows, for example, you can download your local TV program schedules and search them. Outlook Express, another new module, enables you to manage your contacts, schedules, and email. And, with the Active Desktop scheme and Internet

Explorer 4.0, you can seamlessly integrate the World Wide Web with the files on your hard disk.

In terms of hardware compatibility, Windows 98 beats all contenders. You can now install DVD-ROM drives for movies, games, and PC titles. You can also add Advanced Graphic Port (AGP) video boards for improved 3D graphics. And you can instantly Plug and Play a wide variety of Universal Serial Bus (USB) and Firewire (IEEE 1394) devices—such as scanners, printers, mouse pointers, and joysticks—without even turning off your computer.

Due in part to its power, Windows 98 can't meet every user's needs straight out of the box. With an audience of millions of people, Win98 couldn't hope to be all things to all users with one generic installation. You need to customize and optimize the software to get it to work to its full potential for your specific tasks. That's where these hints and hacks will come in handy.

Windows 98 is powerful, but not perfect. I don't work for Microsoft, so I'll tell you about the areas where Windows 98 stumbles or falls short. I'll also describe how to fix known bugs and get help from freeware and shareware utilities available on the World Wide Web.

How This Book is Organized

This book is divided into four sections—Look and Feel, Productivity, Performance, and Administration. Here's a quick breakdown of what the different sections cover:

Look and Feel

Need some clues on how to modify the Windows 98 user interface? Whether it's changing the startup and shutdown procedures, altering the Start menu and Taskbar, or livening up the Active Desktop or background, these chapters show you the details.

Productivity

With these tips, you'll be able to perform some of your most common tasks with fewer mouse clicks and fewer keystrokes. This section focuses on working smarter and running faster by streamlining the Windows 98 desktop and utilities. We'll also discuss troubleshooting hints, so you'll spend less time calling for tech support.

Performance

Inherently, Windows 98 contains some performance improvements over Windows 95. For example, starting up and shutting down your computer generally happens more quickly in the new operating system than it does using Windows 95. However, with the optimization and tuning tips you'll find here, you can speed up your overall system performance.

Administration

Whether you're responsible for all the PCs in your department or just your own family's system, the hints and hacks in this section will help you do the job effectively. You also find out how to deal with security issues and multiple users as well as fixing Windows 98's known bugs.

Many of the tips in this book show more than one way to customize or optimize your system. In these cases I'll always point out which method works best for novices. Intermediate and advanced users can gain greater insight into how Windows 98 works by exploring the alternative approaches.

Preparing to Use This Book

In addition to the basic operating system tools, the Windows 98 CD-ROM includes several utilities that enable you to manipulate, tune, and control the operating system. But guess what? The Windows 98 Setup program does not copy these tools to your hard drive during a normal installation.

Microsoft wanted to include the power of flexibility to these added tools for those who wanted to take advantage of them. They did not, however, want to confuse beginners or take up unnecessary hard disk space by loading these special programs during a standard installation.

One group—the Sample Resource Kit utilities—includes configuration utilities such as TweakUI, Batch98, ClipTray, The Time Zone Editor, and many other tools. You'll also find tools such as Policy Editor, which you can use for administration and security purposes.

To perform some of the hints and hacks I describe, you'll need to install these extra tools onto your hard drive. If you're short on disk space, you might first pick the tips you want to use and install only the tools required for them.

Installing the Windows 98 Sample Resource Kit

Microsoft sells a book and CD combo pack called the Windows 98 Resource Kit. It features instructions and tools targeted at Corporate Information Systems (CIS) managers. The Resource Kit describes, in gory technical detail, how Windows 98 works under the covers. The book is over 1500 pages long and makes a great cure for insomnia.

As a little teaser, Microsoft packed the Windows 98 CD with 25 of the utilities that you'll find in the Resource Kit. Most users don't need the expensive Resource Kit, but the sample tools on the Windows CD can benefit everyone. You'll find these tools used throughout this book.

To install the sample Resource Kit utilities, follow these steps:

1. Insert your Windows 98 CD into your CD-ROM drive.

2. Click the Start button on the Windows 98 Taskbar, then choose the Run item.

3. In the Run dialog box, enter the following path and filename into the Open text-entry field: **[[YOUR CD-ROM DRIVE LETTER]]:tools\ reskit\setup.exe.**

4. Windows will first display the Software License Agreement. Click the Accept button to move to the next screen.

5. The Microsoft Windows 98 Resource Kit Tools Sampler Setup screen tells you that you must only install the kit onto a single computer. Click the Continue button to move to the next screen.

6. The Name and Organization Information screen displays the user information you entered when you installed Windows 98. Click the OK button to move to the next screen.

7. On the new screen, click OK to confirm your information.

8. On the next screen, Windows asks if you want to change the destination folder for the Resource Kit files. I recommend that you do not change the destination folder. Click the OK button to continue.

9. Finally, Windows asks if you'd like to begin the installation (see Figure I.1). Click the Install button to begin. On the front of the button is a graphic of a computer.

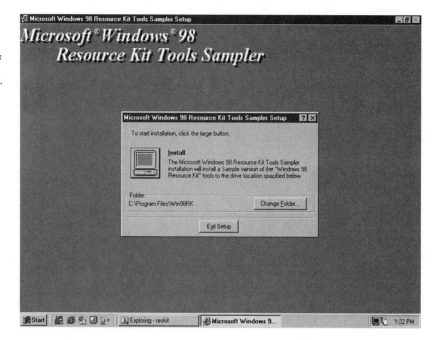

Figure I.1

*After five "get-
ready, get set"
screens, Windows
lets you install
the Resource Kit.*

10. After copying over the system files, Windows displays a message box
    telling you the setup is complete. Click the OK button to exit.

You'll find a Windows 98 Resource Kit item under Start | Programs in the Start
menu. This folder includes release notes, a small online book, help files, and the
Tools Management Console—which is the interface to the kit's utilities.

Using the Windows 98 Sample Resource Kit

Microsoft uses the Microsoft Management Console (MMC) program as a
"toolbox" for the Resource Kit's utilities. Through the MMC program, administrators manage networked computers. Microsoft and other companies write
additional "snap-in" programs that you can install into the MMC to add more
features and functions to your network. In this case, Microsoft wrote a Resource
Kit snap-in that lets you run the special utilities they included on the Windows 98 CD.

In each of the sections of this book, you'll see Resource Kit utilities that are
mentioned, so you'll need to know how to launch them. Each hint that discusses
a particular utility also describes exactly how to use the tool. Here I'll give you a
general overview.

To access the Sample Resource Kit utilities, follow these steps:

1. From the Start menu, choose Start | Programs | Windows 98 Resource Kit | Tools Management Console. These actions launch the Console with the Resource Kit Sampler snap-in already loaded (see Figure I.2).

Figure I.2

The Microsoft Management Console provides access to the Sample Resource Kit utilities.

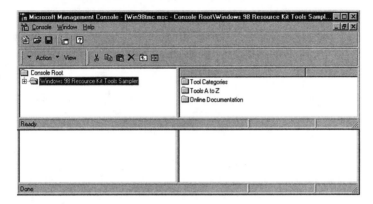

2. The folders of the MMC work just like folders under the Windows Explorer. When you select a folder, you open it, and the MMC program will display all the subfolders and files contained within the folder.

   Under the MMC, the top folder (root) is called the Console Root. With the Resource Kit Sampler loaded (as it is if you accessed the MMC through the method described in step 1 above) the subfolder beneath the Console Root is called Windows 98 Resource Kit Tools Sampler. This folder holds the utilities in the sample kit, as well as documentation on how to use them.

   Open the Windows 98 Resource Kit Tools Sampler folder by clicking on it. This action displays the three subfolders: Tool Categories, Tools A to Z, and Online Documentation.

3. The two folders—Tool Categories and Tools A to Z—let you access the same utilities either by topic or alphabetically. Open both of these folders by selecting them, and quickly examine the subfolders beneath them.

4. To close the MMC, go to the menu at the top of the screen, just under the title bar and choose Console, Exit.

Use the Windows 98 Resource Kit item on the Start | Programs menu if you want sample kit's "snap-in" program preloaded into the MMC.

Installing the TweakUI Utility

Microsoft originally created the TweakUI utility for Windows 95. They released it as a so-called power toy and made it available on their corporate Web site. TweakUI was aptly named. It lets you "tweak" the Windows 95 desktop with all sorts of settings that you can't access by regular means.

With Windows 98, Microsoft enhanced the TweakUI utility, packing in more features and customization options. And, helpfully, they included the utility right on the Windows 98 CD. So you don't need to battle Web traffic to get your hands on it.

TweakUI is officially part of the Resource Kit Sampler. You'll find it mentioned in the Microsoft Management Console (MMC) under Console Root | Windows 98 Resource Kit Tools Sampler | Desktop Tools and under Console Root | Windows 98 Resource Kit Tools Sampler | Tools A to Z | S to T (if you launch the MMC with the Resource Kit Sampler snap-in). But installing the Resource Kit Sampler does not install TweakUI. TweakUI is a special utility. Unlike the other sample kit utilities, TweakUI installs itself into your system's Control Panel.

Follow these steps to install TweakUI:

1. Insert your Windows 98 CD into your computer's CD-ROM drive.

2. Launch the Windows Explorer by choosing Start | Programs | Windows Explorer from the Start menu.

3. Navigate to the following folder on your Windows 98 CD: [[*YOUR CD-ROM DRIVE LETTER*]]:TOOLS\RESKIT\POWERTOY.

4. Right-click on the file called TWEAKUI.INF. Then choose the Install item from the pop-up menu.

5. Windows will display a Windows 98 Setup message box and run through the installation steps. When it gets to Introducing TweakUI, it will display a help window with some notes about the utility. To continue with the installation choose File | Exit from the help window's menus.

This process loads a TweakUI icon into your Control Panel folder.

Using the TweakUI Utility

Think of TweakUI as Windows 98's customization genie. Just tell it your wishes, and the utility will bestow them upon you. The tool enables you to change the speed of your mouse and Start menu, it enables you to alter the desktop's special icons, it restricts access to the Control Panel, and much more.

You'll find TweakUI mentioned in hints throughout this book. If I described all it can do in just one chapter, you'd end up confused and probably overwhelmed.

The hints that use TweakUI will step you through the utility's options, but here, I'll just show you how to launch it.

Follow these steps to launch TweakUI:

1. From the Start menu, choose Start | Settings | Control Panel.

2. Select the TweakUI icon from the list of Control Panel objects. This action launches the TweakUI utility (see Figure I.3)

Figure I.3

Use TweakUI to customize many aspects of Windows 98.

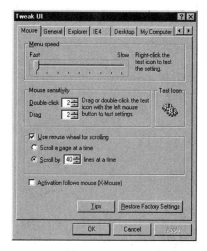

3. TweakUI has 13 tabs that divide up its features by Windows 98 component. Select a few of the tabs and examine some of the settings. But don't change anything yet! Wait until you read the hints that reference TweakUI.

WARNING   Unless you're an expert user, don't make any changes in TweakUI without first reading through the hints. You might alter your operating system in a way you didn't intend.

4. Click the little arrows in the upper right-hand corner of the window (below the Close [X] button). With these scroll arrows, you can move back and forth through all the 13 tabs.

5. To exit TweakUI without saving any changes, click the Cancel button at the bottom of the screen.

What is the Windows Registry?

The Registry is a core component of the Windows operating system, but most users never see it. The Registry acts like an internal database, tracking your software setup, your hardware device settings, and your preferences for the user interface, though it tracks this information behind the scenes. When you install new software onto your system, upgrade your hardware, or adjust settings in the Control Panel, Windows stores whatever information it needs about these changes in the Registry.

From an evolutionary standpoint, the Windows Registry is the latest version of the configuration files (.INI, .SYS, .BAT) used by the old Windows 3.1 operating system. Microsoft now asks hardware manufacturers and software developers to use the efficient Windows Registry, instead of these potentially messy configuration files, when creating products compatible with Windows 98. In Windows 3.1, configuration and setup information was stored in different files dispersed throughout your hard drive—and it wasn't very organized. Under Windows 98, all your PC's vital data is centrally located in the Registry.

As a user, you don't need to access the Registry directly, but doing so gives you more power and flexibility to customize and optimize your computer. Within the Registry, you can alter your computer in ways that you can't change by modifying the Control Panel or using other setup software. This is why the Registry hacks in this book will come in handy.

Be Cautious When Modifying the Windows Registry

Above all, take care when altering the Windows Registry. An erroneous Registry entry can cripple your computer. A mistake might generate a recurring error message, or, in the worst case, your PC might not boot correctly on the next restart.

You don't need to fear the Registry, however. If you follow the steps in this book's hacks, you won't have any problems. None of the Registry edits in these pages will wreak havoc with your computer.

Even if you do make a mistake while editing the Registry, it's not the end of the world. Windows 98 makes a backup copy of the Registry every time you boot up your PC, so you can always restore a "good" copy of the Registry if you encounter trouble. For instructions on restoring a previous version of your Registry read Chapter 2.9, "Smart Troubleshooting," hint 2.9.9, "Access a Previous Windows Registry to Recover from a Crash."

Editing the Registry

Windows provides a utility called the Registry Editor (REGEDIT.EXE) that lets you manually update the Registry database. The Registry Editor looks and acts similarly to the Windows Explorer, but instead of files and folders, the Registry Editor displays Registry keys and their values.

A Registry key contains values of three different types: string, binary, and DWORD. A string is a word, phrase, or filename such as "true" or "C:\Windows\System." Binary and DWORD (meaning Double Word-length) values are numbers stored in a hexadecimal format.

> **NOTE** The Windows Registry acts like one large database file, but it's actually made up of three separate files—USER.DAT, SYSTEM.DAT, and POLICY.POL.
>
> The USER.DAT file contains all the user-specific information, such as the Start menu profile, the Control Panel settings, logon IDs and passwords, and so on.
>
> The SYSTEM.DAT file holds all the details about your computer hardware, including interrupt allocation, device status, hardware profiles, and more.
>
> The POLICY.POL file stores "policies" defined by a system administrator that limit the rights and privileges of the PC's users.
>
> Fortunately, you don't need to ponder these separate files. Through the Registry Editor, the System Policy Editor, and other tools, you can interact with the Windows Registry as if it were one large logical file.

The best way to learn how to edit the Registry is to dive right in and do it. In this example, we'll add some new keys and values and then remove them. In the end, your system will emerge unchanged.

Follow these steps to edit the Windows Registry:

1. Choose Start | Run from the Start menu. Then, in the Run prompt text field, type the word **regedit** and press the Enter key. This launches the Registry Editor (see Figure I.4).

2. The My Computer key rests at the top of the entire Registry structure. To open or expand this key, double-click on it or click the plus sign (+) in front of it. This action displays the six root keys mentioned in the note above.

Figure I.4

To launch the Registry Editor (shown here), enter regedit at the Start | Run prompt.

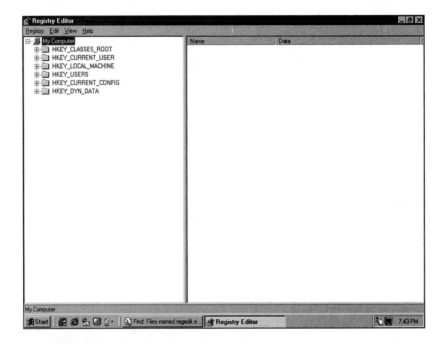

> **NOTE** In the Registry Editor, the first six keys you see beneath My Computer are called Registry root keys. Here are brief descriptions of what each of these keys contains.
>
> **HKEY_CLASSES_ROOT:** This root key contains all data on your system's registered file types, Quick View templates, ActiveX object properties, and other system "class" objects. HKEY_CLASSES_ROOT points to the Registry subkey HKEY_LOCAL_MACHINE\SOFTWARE\Classes.
>
> **HKEY_CURRENT_USER:** This root key stores all the profile data on the user who is currently logged on to the PC.
>
> **HKEY_LOCAL_MACHINE:** This root key holds hardware device configuration and device driver data. It also stores the computer's port details and network logon ID and security information.
>
> **HKEY_USERS:** This root key contains the profile data for all users who have ever logged on to this computer system.
>
> **HKEY_CURRENT_CONFIG:** This root key stores all the device information for the current computer configuration. All hardware profiles are stored here. Subkeys list all available printers and screen resolution and available fonts.
>
> **HKEY_DYN_DATA:** This root key holds the system's dynamic data and because this key is extremely volatile, it is held in RAM, not on the hard drive. Subkeys list which devices are currently active in the PC.

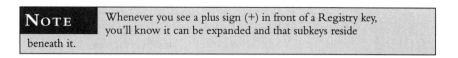

> **NOTE**   Whenever you see a plus sign (+) in front of a Registry key, you'll know it can be expanded and that subkeys reside beneath it.

3. Expand the HKEY_LOCAL_MACHINE root key by selecting it or by choosing the plus sign in front of it.

4. Expand the SOFTWARE key below the HKEY_LOCAL_MACHINE key.

5. Find the Microsoft key below the SOFTWARE key and expand it.

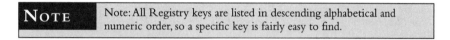

> **NOTE**   Note: All Registry keys are listed in descending alphabetical and numeric order, so a specific key is fairly easy to find.

6. Find the Windows key below the Microsoft key and expand it.

7. Find the CurrentVersion key below the Windows key and expand it. At this point, you should see the following Registry path displayed in the status bar at the bottom of the Regedit window: My Computer\ HKEY_LOCAL_MACHINE\SOFTWARE\Microsoft\Windows\ CurrentVersion. The Regedit status bar always shows you current location within the Registry (see Figure I.5).

Figure I.5

Check the Regedit status bar at the bottom of the Regedit window to track your current location within the Registry.

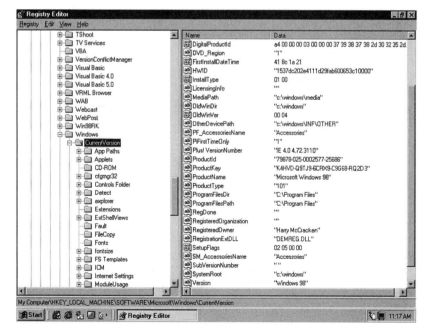

8. Beneath the CurrentVersion key, we'll add a new key. Right-click on the CurrentVersion key. Then select New | Key from the pop-up menu (see Figure I.6). Regedit will insert a new key at the end of the list below CurrentVersion in the left-hand pane of Regedit. The temporary name is "New Key #1." On the keyboard, enter the new name **WinHack**. Then press the Enter key to set it.

Figure I.6

To add a new key below the current key, right-click on the current key, then choose New | Key from the pop-up menu.

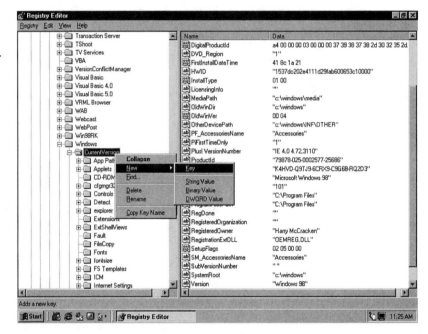

> **TIP**   You can also use the Edit menu to add keys and values. To do this, highlight the key where you want to insert a new key or value. Then choose Edit | New menu and pick the type of item you want to add from the pop-up list.

9. Now, we'll add a new string value to the WinHack key. Right-click on the WinHack key and select New | String Value from the pop-up list (see Figure I.7). Regedit will display the new string value in the right-hand pane with the temporary name "New Value #1." On the keyboard, enter the name **mystring** and press the Enter key to set it.

10. At this point, we'll add data to the new string value. To do this, double-click on mystring or highlight it and choose Edit | Modify from Regedit's menus. This action displays the Edit String dialog box. In the Value Data field, enter the phrase **This is my new string** (see Figure I.8). Click the OK button to close the Edit String dialog box.

Figure I.7

To add a new string value to the current key, right-click on the current key, then choose New | String Value from the pop-up menu.

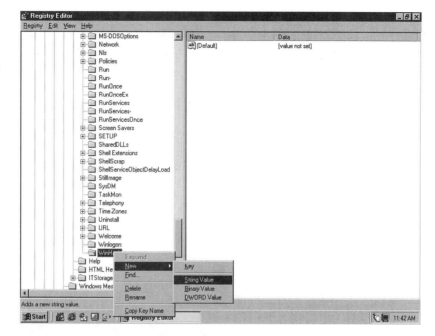

Figure I.8

Use the Edit String dialog box to modify a string value's data.

> **NOTE**   In Regedit, all your changes are saved automatically. You don't need to specify "save" when you exit. In fact, Regedit provides no "save" option on its menus.

11. Now we'll add a binary value to the WinHack key (the processes for adding Binary and DWORD values are very similar). To do this, right-click on the WinHack key and choose New | Binary Value from the pop-up menu (see Figure I.9). Regedit will display the new value with the temporary name "New Value #1" in the right-hand pane. Type in the new name **mybinary**. Then press the Enter key to set it.

12. Set a value for mybinary by double-clicking it or by right-clicking on it and selecting Modify from the pop-up menu. This action displays the Edit Binary Value dialog box.

Figure I.9

*Adding new
Binary and
DWORD values
is very similar to
adding a new
string value.*

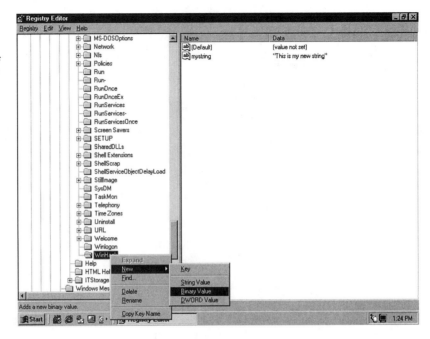

13. Enter the following value **01 01 00 10**. Don't worry about the spaces.
    Regedit will format everything automatically for you. Just type the
    numbers in sequence. The result will look like Figure I.10. Click the OK
    button to set the value.

Figure I.10

*Regedit formats
the binary values
automatically for
you. Just enter the
numbers in
sequence.*

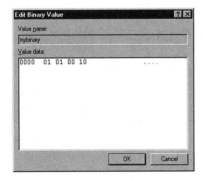

If you've followed all the above steps, you should have a new WinHack Registry
key that stores three values: (Default), mystring, and mybinary. Your Regedit
screen should look similar to Figure I.11.

Figure I.11

*Success! You've
added a key and
two new values
to the Windows
Registry.*

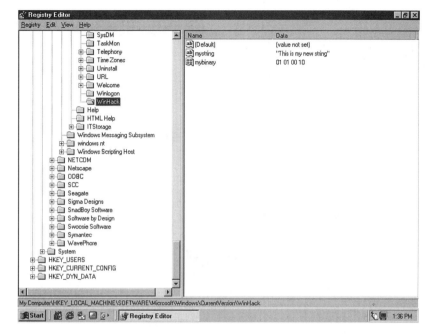

These new Registry entries won't effect your system in any way. Nonetheless, we
don't want to leave these examples sitting around in the Registry.

Follow these steps to remove the examples from the Registry:

1. Right-click on the WinHack key and choose Delete from the pop-up
   menu (see Figure I.12).

2. Regedit will display a confirmation dialog box. Click the Yes button.

3. From Regedit's menus, choose Registry | Exit to close the application.

As you can see, hacking the Registry isn't very difficult. Just make sure to follow
the steps outlined in this book's hacks carefully. You won't have any problems.

Installing the System Policy Editor

Microsoft created the System Policy Editor (POLEDIT.EXE) to help administrators manage PCs. In the System Policy Editor, you can create policies and apply
them to individual users or groups of users. These policies can restrict access to
areas of the operating system, control software setups, and limit users network
privileges.

Figure I.12

Delete the sample key to leave the Registry as you found it.

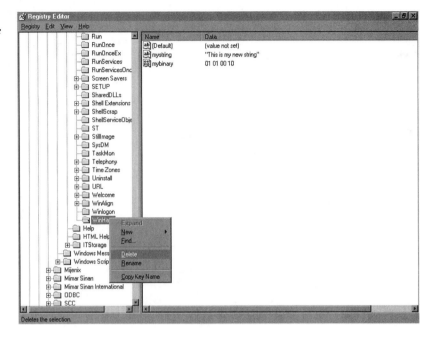

Like the tools above, the System Policy Editor is not loaded onto your computer during the Windows 98 installation. You must install it manually.

Follow these steps to install the System Policy Editor:

1. Insert the Windows 98 CD into your CD-ROM drive.

2. From the Start menu, choose Start | Settings | Control Panel.

3. Select the Add/Remove Programs object from the list in the Control Panel.

4. Pick the Windows Setup tab.

5. Click the Have Disk button at the bottom of the Windows Setup sheet.

6. On the Install From Disk dialog box, click the Browse button. This action displays an Open dialog box.

7. Click the drop-down arrow below the word "Drives" and choose your CD-ROM drive letter from the list. This drive should already contain your Windows 98 CD.

8. In the Folders box, navigate to the following Windows 98 CD folder: [*YOUR CD-ROM DRIVE LETTER*]:\TOOLS\RESKIT\ NETADMIN\POLEDIT.

9. Under the File Name heading of the Open dialog box, select POLEDIT.INF. Then click the OK button.

10. Back on the Install From Disk dialog box, click the OK button.

11. On the Have Disk dialog box, choose System Policy Editor (see Figure I.13). Then click the Install button.

Figure I.13

Choose the System Policy Editor on the Have Disk dialog box.

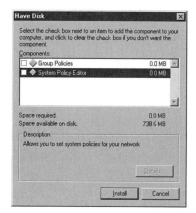

12. Click the OK button to close the Add/Remove Programs object.

Windows 98 installs the POLEDIT.EXE file to the C:\Windows directory of your hard drive. It also places a System Policy Editor item on your Start menu under Start | Programs | Accessories | System Tools.

Using the System Policy Editor

The System Policy Editor edits the Registry as does the Registry Editor, but it uses a different interface. Instead of keys and values, the System Policy Editor stores policies.

The hints that require the System Policy Editor describe exactly how to create new policies. In this introduction, I'll just show you how to launch the Policy Editor and navigate through its controls.

Follow these steps to launch and use the System Policy Editor:

1. On the Start menu, choose Start | Programs | Accessories | System Tools | System Policy Editor. The Policy Editor opens to a blank screen.

2. From the menus, select File | Open Registry. This action displays the two main policy roots: Local Computer and Local User (see Figure I.14).

Figure I.14

The System Policy Editor accesses the Registry differently from the Registry Editor.

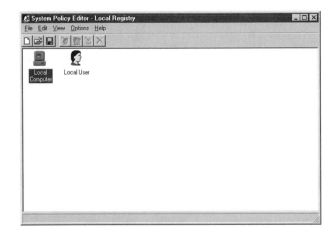

3. Select the Local User object. This action opens the Local User Properties sheet (see Figure I.15). The two main policy controls are labeled Windows 98 Network and Windows 98 System.

Figure I.15

The Local User Properties sheet displays the two main policy controls of the Registry.

4. As with the Registry Editor's keys, you can expand policies either by double-clicking them or by clicking on the plus sign (+) in front of the policy. Expand the Windows 98 System policy.

TIP Press the first letter of a policy and the System Policy Editor will highlight the first policy that begins with that letter. For example, press the C key to highlight Control Panel.

5. Expand the Control Panel policy.

6. Expand the Passwords policy.

7. Place a check in front of Restrict Passwords Control Panel. This action displays the settings for this policy in the box at the bottom of the window (see Figure I.16).

Figure I.16

Putting a check in front of a policy displays that policy's settings at the bottom of the window.

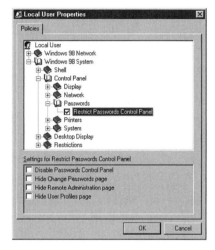

8. With the settings in the Passwords policy, you can hide or disable elements of the Control Panel's Password object from other users. In this example, we won't set any restrictions. Remove the check in front of Restrict Passwords Control Panel.

9. Click the Cancel button to close the Local User Properties sheet.

> **NOTE**   Unlike with the Registry Editor, you must save your changes in the System Policy Editor. You'll find the Save option under the File menu. In this example, we won't save any changes.

10. From the menus, choose File | Exit to close the System Policy Editor.

In a corporate environment, you should ask your Information Systems (IS) manager before modifying any policies on your PC. Generally, IS managers like to maintain control of all polices.

For a home PC, you should designate one family member as the system administrator.

Using Shareware and Freeware from the Web

Certain hints in this book cite shareware and freeware tools available from the World Wide Web. Individuals, companies, and universities have created hundreds (if not thousands) of software tools that can help optimize and customize your Windows 98 system, so I felt it would be useful to point out some of the best.

Freeware utilities are, as their name suggests, free. In most cases, you don't even need to register with anyone that you've downloaded a freeware tool.

However, shareware tools usually cost some nominal fee, generally less than $50 and typically around $20. Some shareware utilities cease functioning after their trial period (30 days or so) expires. Others use the honor system and simply ask that you send in money if you plan to continue using the software. Please do pay for any shareware tools you plan to keep; it's in everyone's best interests.

Here are some rules of thumb for using shareware and freeware utilities:

- If you use a slow Internet connection—28.8kbps (kilobits per second) or slower—try to download large files at off hours. All of the downloads mentioned in this book cite the file sizes on their Web pages. Files over 1MB might take several minutes to download over slow Internet connections. Generally, there is less Internet traffic at night. However, in most cases, the Web tools listed in this book are very small and will only take a minute or two to download.

- Check for viruses. Just like files you receive via floppy disk and CD-ROM, Web downloads might contain computer viruses. To be safe, virus scan any file downloads, with your own anti-virus software, before installing the utilities. The shareware/freeware Web sites mentioned in this book have good reputations as virus-free software repositories. Nonetheless, it's always better to be safe than sorry.

- Read the "readme" files. Most utilities include a text file called README.TXT in their download packages. These files contain the latest information about the tool, including any known problems, helpful instructions, trial period restrictions and much more. Open this file in Windows 98's Notepad editor (under Start | Programs | Accessories) and learn more about your utility.

- Try before you buy. I've installed and tested every Web download mentioned in this book. However, I can't make any claims about the ongoing stability of these Web tools. I didn't create them. Please take advantage of any shareware tool's trial period and determine if the tool works on your system with your software setup without any bugs or problems. When you are satisfied the tool works as you expect, then you can register and/or pay for a licensed copy.

Don't let the above tips scare you away from using Web downloads. These tools offer an incredible array of features, most of which you can't get anywhere else.

How to Read This Book

Finally, don't read this book like a novel (unless you'd like to read it like a novel). Each hint and hack stands alone as a separate element and contains all the information you need to know about that particular topic. Feel free to scan the table of contents, skip around, flip through the pages, and find the tips that interest you most. Have fun!

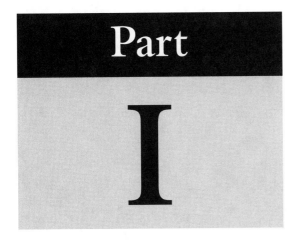

Part

I

Look and Feel

Are you tired of staring at the basic Windows 98 desktop? Who isn't? After a few days, it's about as aesthetically pleasing as a toaster. Sure, you know about changing the Wallpaper background and adding screen savers to spice things up, but those are the easy tricks you learn after your first half-hour touring through the operating system. Fortunately, you can customize Windows 98 more than you've ever imagined. And, with only minimal effort, you'll end up with a personalized computer interface that better suits your home or work environment.

In this section, we'll cover all the components of the Windows interface: the Start menu and Task bar, background, shortcuts, Active Desktop, the MS-DOS window, Internet Explorer, and Outlook Express, as well as starting up and shutting down the operating system. We'll discuss removing or modifying the annoying elements and adding in new stuff of your own design.

Think of the Windows desktop as a blank canvas, and let your creative juices flow. Operating systems don't have to be boring. Experiment with the hints and hacks that spark your interest, and leave your own imprint on Windows. If you don't like the result, you can quickly change back to the default settings.

Chapter

1.1

Change Startup and Shutdown

Booting up takes quite a while, even on a fast computer. So does shutting down. Why not make these "dead" periods more interesting and useful? In this chapter, I'll show you how to customize the Windows startup and shutdown with your own screens and menus. You can even remove the Windows login screen or boot to a different operating system.

1.1.1 Replace the Startup and Shutdown Screens

Every time you power up and power down your computer, you see the same old "splash" screens with the Windows 98 logo. Did you know that you can replace these Microsoft ads with your own artwork?

Windows 98 stores the startup and shutdown graphics in standard bitmap file format, although the developers used the .SYS system file extension rather than the standard bitmap file extension (.BMP) in the names of these files. The files are called LO.SYS (Windows startup logo screen), LOGOW.SYS ("Windows is shutting down your system" message) and LOGOS.SYS ("It's now safe to turn off your computer" message). You'll find the startup screen LO.SYS in the root directory (C:\) and the two exit screens under the Windows sub-directory (C:\Windows).

Before you perform the following steps, create your own screens using an image editor of your choice or Windows 98's own Paint applet (under Start|Programs|Accessories). Remember, these screens are visible for only a few seconds, so you should create screens with high impact and few words (see Figure 1.1.1).

If you're into digital photography, this might be a good place to use some of your images. You can also personalize the screens for yourself of your children—"John's PC" or "Kids Keep Out!" Or, you can declare ownership—"Property of the XYZ corporation"—to discourage theft or misuse.

> **WARNING**   The bitmap files you end up with need to be in a particular format or the operating system will reject them. The image size required is 320 pixels by 400 pixels at 256 color depth. Set these parameters in your image editor and the resulting file size will be 127K—the same size as the Microsoft screens.

> **NOTE**   Just to confuse you, Microsoft made replacing the startup screen work a little differently than replacing the shutdown screens. For the shutdown screens, you'll need to rename the existing files—LOGOW.SYS and LOGOS.SYS—and replace them with your own (see steps below). For the startup screen, you can just leave LO.SYS where it is in the root directory. Name your new startup file LOGO.SYS, and place it in the root directory as well. Windows 98 will load yours instead of LO.SYS, if it's the correct size.

Figure 1.1.1

Use Windows's Paint applet or your own image editor to create your new screens.

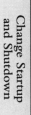

The steps below help you create static or unanimated bitmaps. For animated bitmaps that show moving images, see hint 1.1.2.

Follow these steps to replace the Windows startup and shutdown screens with your own screens:

1. Launch the Windows Explorer (under Start|Programs). From the menus, choose Tools|Find|Files and Folders. Enter **logo*.sys** in the Search For dialog box and press Find. Windows will display a list of the files that match that pattern. Again, the filenames you're looking for are LOGOW.SYS and LOGOS.SYS in the C:\Windows directory. You can leave LO.SYS in the root alone. Don't be fooled if you find these files in some other location on your hard disk. These could be backup files from your old Windows 95 setup.

2. Rename the two exit files by changing their file extensions. You might want to replace these files at a later date, so just rename them, don't delete them. Right-click on the entries in the Find results windows. Change the filenames from LOGOS.SYS to LOGOS.SAV, for example. Or use your initials—LOGOW.JPD for John Patrick Doe.

> **NOTE** Here's how to save an image with 256 colors. In Windows's Paint applet, choose File|Save As from the menus. Then, in the Save As Type drop-down box, select 256 Color Bitmap.

3. Using Windows Explorer, move your newly created exit screen files into the Windows directory. Then move your new startup screen into the root

directory. Then, make sure they have the correct names—LOGO.SYS for the startup screen, LOGOS.SYS and LOGOW.SYS for the exit screens.

The next time you startup and shutdown the operating system, Windows will display your files.

1.1.2 Animate Your Startup Screens

If you want to go further with the last hint, you can animate your new startup and shutdown screens. Look closely and you'll see that the startup screen for Windows 98 uses animation. A blue bar sweeps across the bottom of the static Windows logo during the boot process. It's not exactly Disney-level animation, but what did you expect from Microsoft?

With a little effort, you can design your own animation. If you have any text in your screens, you can now set it in motion. Or, you can just create shifting color patterns.

Windows 98 uses a technique called *palette animation* to give bitmaps motion. In palette animation, there's no real movement or relocation of an image. It's actually just the palette (color) table numeric reference that changes, causing an optical illusion of motion. Manually creating animated bitmaps is a rather complicated process. Fortunately, you don't have to do this manually.

You can download a handy software utility, called LogoMania, that will do all this hard work for you (see Figure 1.1.2). LogoMania was written by Neil Rubenking, and it's available on ZDNet's Software Library online (www.zdnet.com). Rubenking originally wrote this tool for Windows 95, but Windows 98 uses the same startup and shutdown file format, so this tool also works under the new operating system.

To get started with startup and shutdown screen animation, follow these steps:

1. Download the LogoMania utility from the Web. The specific URL is: http://www.zdnet.com/pcmag/pctech/content/16/06/ ut1016.001.html.

2. *PC Magazine* uses the ZIP file compression format, so you'll have to "unzip" it with a decompression tool after you've completed the download process. If you don't have such a tool, try PKWare's PKZip for Windows utility (you can find this at www.pkware.com).

3. To install the program, simply move the three main files—LOGOMANI. EXE, LOGOMANI.HLP, and LOGOMANI.CNT—into a directory of your choice.

4. Launch LOGOMANI.EXE by selecting it in the Windows Explorer. You'll find both a help file and a tutorial. Follow the examples and

instructions in these files to learn the animation process. LogoMania will make sure that both the color depth and size of your animation will work under Windows 98.

Figure 1.1.2
*Download
LogoMania for
ZDNet's
Software Library.*

5. Then follow the steps in hint 1.1.1 to replace Windows 98's original startup and shutdown screens with your new animated files.

Of course, you must reboot before you see these changes.

1.1.3 Remove the Login Screen

If you're the sole user of a PC and you're unconcerned with password protection, the Windows Login screen just adds hassle to the boot-up process. You might also be sharing your PC with colleagues or your family members, but still not require this level of login security. There are several ways to tell Windows to skip this troublesome startup step. Pick one of the following methods:

■ If you've just completed the Windows 98 installation, do not enter any password in the login dialog box. During your next startup, Windows will assume you have no password and it won't display the login screen.

■ Change your Windows password to a null password. Select Passwords in the Control Panel (under Start | Settings | Control Panel). Choose the Change Passwords tab of the Passwords Properties Sheet. Click the

Change Windows Passwords button. Then type your old password in the first box and nothing at all in the two other boxes. Click OK. Then, choose the User Profiles tab and mark the radio button that states, "All users of this computer use the same preferences and desktop settings." Click OK.

■ Use TweakUI (read the Introduction section on how to install the TweakUI utility from the Windows 98 installation disk, if you haven't already). Choose TweakUI in the Control Panel (Start | Settings | Control Panel). Select the Network tab. Put a check next to the option Log on Automatically at System Startup, then enter a username and password in the fields below the sentence. As the text underneath this box reads, you should also make sure that the Clear Last User at Logon line of TweakUI's Paranoia tab is unchecked. Note that this method leaves the password you entered unencrypted—anyone who edits the Registry can find and read this password.

■ Finally, if you want to hack the Registry (make sure you read the introductory section on Registry hacking and its dangers), you can manually set the same key values that TweakUI does in the last method. Launch the Registry Editor (Start | Run and then enter **Regedit**). Navigate to the following Registry key: HKEY_LOCAL_MACHINE\SOFTWARE\Microsoft\Windows\CurrentVersion\Winlogon, then add the following new strings and their respective values, or modify the values if the strings already exist, under this key:

```
DontDisplayLastUserName="0"
DefaultUserName="anyname"
DefaultPassword="anypassword"
AutoAdminLogon="1"
```

> **NOTE** To add a new string to the Registry, right-click on the Registry key and choose New | String Value from the pop-up list. Type in the name of the string and then press **Enter** to set it. To set the value of a string, select the string name. In the Edit String dialog box, enter the string's name and then click the OK button.

Just as in the TweakUI method, your password remains unencrypted in the Registry.

1.1.4 Boot with Different Operating Systems

Here's the trick for configuring your Windows 98 PC for booting different operating systems such as Windows 3.x or MS-DOS: decide on a multi-boot setup *before* you install Windows 98. During the installation process, Windows 98 will configure itself to maintain your Win3.x or MS-DOS options, provided you tell it what to do.

If you didn't plan ahead and have already installed Windows 98, there's still hope for you. (I'll get to that toward the end of this section.)

To make multi-boot work, your PC must have MS-DOS version 5.0 or higher and your hard disk must be formatted with the older FAT16 file system.

> **NOTE** You cannot upgrade your hard drive to Windows 98's new, more efficient FAT32 file system if you plan to maintain a multi-boot configuration. Why? The older MS-DOS and Windows operating systems just don't read this new disk format.

To install Windows 98 for multi-boot configuration, follow these steps:

1. Run through the normal Windows 98 installation, but choose a new directory for the Win98 files, *not* the directory that contains your Win3.x files (usually the Win3.x directory is C:\Windows). Windows 98 will preserve all your Win3.x and MS-DOS files, as well as your AUTOEXEC.BAT and CONFIG.SYS configuration files.

2. Double-check to make sure that your MSDOS.SYS file (in the root C:\ directory) contains the line BootMulti=1. This enables you to boot to your previous version of MS-DOS by pressing **F8** during the startup process and selecting the appropriate option from the Windows 98 Startup menu. To run Win3.x, you would then change to the C:\Windows directory prompt and type **Win**.

> **NOTE** If for some reason MSDOS.SYS has BootMulti=0, you can edit this file and change the line to BootMulti=1. However, you need to uncheck the Read-Only and Hidden file attributes before you make these changes. To do this, access the file's Property Sheet (right-click the file under Windows Explorer, and then choose Properties). Then, uncheck the Read-Only and Hidden file attributes. Make sure to reset these attributes after you've finished editing.

If you've already installed Windows 98 in the regular C:\Windows directory, you won't be able to access your old Win3.x operating system. Sorry! Windows 98 has already removed many of the system files. You can, however, still access your previous version of MS-DOS.

Follow these steps to set up a multiple boot configuration, if you've already installed Windows 98 into the C:\Windows directory:

1. Create a bootable DOS diskette. You must have MS-DOS version 5.0 or higher.

> **NOTE**   Here's how to create a bootable diskette. Select My Computer. Right-click on the A: drive icon and choose Format from the pop-up list. If your disk is already formatted, pick Copy System File Only in the Format Type box. If it's not formatted, pick either Quick or Full in Format Type, and then put a check next to Copy System Files in the Other Options box.

2. Rename the following files on your diskette. *You will probably first have to change the file attributes (to non-Read-Only, non-Hidden) using the DOS ATTRIB command.* For full ATTRIB syntax, type `Attrib /?` at the MS-DOS Prompt. Here, however, is an example showing how to make IO.SYS non-Read-Only and non-Hidden: `Atrrib -r -h io.sys`.

Old Name	New Name
IO.SYS	IO.DOS
MSDOS.SYS	MSDOS.DOS
COMMAND.COM	COMMAND.DOS

3. Copy these new files to the root directory of your Windows 98 PC.

4. Edit the AUTOEXEC.BAT and CONFIG.SYS files in the root directory of your Windows 98 system to load your old MS-DOS configuration. You can do this under Windows by entering **sysedit** at the Start|Run prompt.

5. Make sure that your PC's MSDOS.SYS file contains the line `BootMulti=1` as in step 2 of the last procedure above.

After this procedure, you will be able to boot to your previous version of MS-DOS by pressing F8 during the boot-up process.

1.1.5 Stop Windows from Saving Your Window Locations When You Shut Down

Without any modification, Windows "remembers" which operating system applet windows (such as Windows Explorer, Control Panel, and so on) you had open when you last shut down your computer. And it will restore these windows to the same locations the next time you boot up. This is convenient if you were planning to continue the same type of work, but annoying if you want to work on something else.

> **NOTE**   Disabling this feature also stops Windows from saving new icon locations. If you move icons around on the desktop during a session, they will be back in their original locations the next time you power up.

Use these following steps to disable Windows's save settings function:

1. Launch the Policy Editor (under Start|Programs|Accessories|System Tools—read the introduction section on installing the Policy Editor if you don't find it here).

2. Choose File|Open Registry from the menu.

3. Select Local User.

4. Expand the Registry keys following this path: Local User|Windows 98 System|Shell|Restrictions.

5. Check the line reading, "Don't save settings on exit."

6. Click OK.

7. Select File|Save from the Policy Editor's menus.

8. Close the Policy Editor.

You can also use the TweakUI utility to make this change. Read the introduction section on how to install the Windows 98 Sample Resource Kit tools, if you haven't already done so.

1. Launch TweakUI from the Control Panel (see the introduction for instructions on installing TweakUI if it's not available under the Control Panel).

2. Select the Explorer tab.

3. Remove the check, if one exists, from the line reading, "Save Explorer window settings."

4. Click OK to close TweakUI.

1.1.6 Modify MSDOS.SYS for a Different Look and Feel During Boot

Windows 98 checks several configuration files during boot-up to determine exactly how to launch. One of these is MSDOS.SYS, a file that contains several command options that you can modify. Don't be concerned if you only see a few lines in your system's MSDOS.SYS file. Windows 98 uses default settings when a command line isn't present.

MSDOS.SYS is normally a read-only, hidden, system file. So, to save your changes you need to first adjust the file attributes. Under Windows Explorer, use the Find

Change Startup and Shutdown

tool to search for MSDOS.SYS in the root directory (C:\Windows). When you see the file listed, right-click your mouse with the cursor hovering over the file. From the pop-up menu, choose Properties to bring up MSDOS.SYS's Properties sheet. Uncheck the Read-Only and Hidden attributes before you edit the file.

> **NOTE** It's a good idea to back up MSDOS.SYS by saving it under another name before you alter it. That way, you can quickly go back to your original settings if you run into trouble.

Below is a list of commands and their respective values that Windows 98 uses during startup. If you don't see one of the commands you want to use, simply add it to the file.

Command	Value	Meaning
BootMulti=	0	Starts Windows 98 (default)
BootMulti=	1	Enables booting to previous version of DOS or Win3.1 when the user presses F4 or F8
BootWin=	0	Boots automatically to the previous version of DOS
BootWin=	1	Boots automatically to Windows 98 (default)

> **NOTE** Pressing **F4** during boot changes the result of the BootWin instruction. If BootWin=0 and you press **F4**, then the system boots to Windows 98. With BootWin=1, pressing **F4** forces the PC to boot to the previous version of DOS.

Command	Value	Meaning
BootMenu=	0	Disables the Windows 98 Startup menu unless the user presses F8 (default)
BootMenu=	1	Displays the Windows Startup menu automatically
Logo=	0	Disables the Windows 98 startup logo screen during boot
Logo=	1	Displays the Windows 98 startup logo screen during boot (default)

After you've finished with your changes, make sure you go back and reset the MSDOS.SYS file attributes to Read-Only and Hidden. This will protect the file against unwanted modification.

1.1.7 Force Windows to Display a Hardware Configuration Menu

Are you stuck without a Plug and Play BIOS? If so, Windows won't automatically detect the hardware you add to your desktop computer or know when you attach or detach your notebook to and from a docking station.

The best solution for this problem: Call your computer manufacturer and ask for an upgrade to your PC's BIOS. If the computer manufacturer can't help, you can force Windows to display a hardware configuration menu during boot-up that will let you choose from different hardware setups that you commonly use. The trick is to set up multiple hardware profiles under the Windows Control Panel

Follow these steps to set up additional hardware profiles:

1. Select the Control Panel (under Start | Settings), then choose the System icon.

2. Pick the Hardware Profiles tab of the System Properties sheet. Then highlight your hardware profile, which should be called "Original Configuration," if you haven't modified it (see Figure 1.1.3).

Figure 1.1.3

Set up a new hardware profile in the System Properties sheet of the Control Panel.

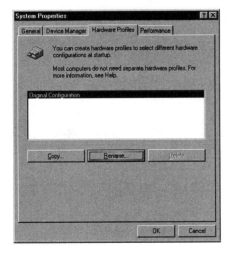

3. Click the Rename... button and type in a new name that describes your most common hardware setup, something like **Docked**. Click OK to save this hardware profile.

4. Now, highlight your new profile and click the Copy button. Enter a new name in the Copy Profile dialog box that describes your alternative hardware setup, something like **Undocked**. Click OK to save this profile.

5. At this point, you can pick and choose the hardware devices that Windows should include within each profile. Highlight a profile that you want to configure. Then select the Device Manager tab of the System Properties sheet. Double-click on a hardware category, such as "Modems," and then double-click on your particular modem's entry. To remove the modem from your current hardware profile, put a check next to the line that reads: Disable in this Hardware Profile. You'll find this line in the Device Usage box under the General tab for this device.

6. Continue removing devices in this manner until each profile is properly configured.

7. The next time you boot up, Windows 98 will automatically display a Hardware Configure menu because you now have more than one to choose from. The menu will read something along the order of:

```
Windows cannot determine which configuration your computer is in.
Select one of the following:

1. Docked

2. Undocked

3. None of the above

Enter your choice:
```

Now, you'll be able to select your hardware configuration manually during the boot process.

> **WARNING**   Avoid choosing 3: None of the Above in the hardware configuration menu. This might alter your system settings. Windows 98 will attempt to patch together its own hardware profile.

Chapter

1.2

Shortcut
Savvy

Almost everyone uses Windows 98 shortcuts for quick access to programs. But, you'll find very little information on how to customize these icons in the Windows 98 documentation. In this chapter you'll find out how to make shortcuts icons look and act the way you want them to.

1.2.1 Set Application Shortcuts to Run in Full-Screen Mode

Most of us run all our applications in full-screen mode or maximized. It's much easier to see what you're doing that way. When an application launches in a regular window, you have to click the Maximize button in the upper-right-hand corner to open the window to full-screen. This extra step is unnecessary. You can set any application to run full-screen upon launch.

The standard property sheet for a Windows 98 application does not have a setting for screen size, but shortcut property sheets do. Every item in the Start menu is a shortcut to an application, so they can all be modified for full-screen mode. For applications not listed in the Start menu, create a shortcut on your desktop or taskbar, and then set this property.

To set up full-screen mode, open the application's property sheet by right-clicking on the shortcut's icon and selecting Properties. Then choose Maximized from the Run drop-down box (see Figure 1.2.1). Click OK. The next time you launch the application, it will run maximized.

Figure 1.2.1

Select Maximized from the Run drop-down box to set a shortcut application to run in full-screen mode.

1.2.2 Make Shortcuts Look Like Standard Icons

Shortcuts don't look like regular icons. Shortcuts have a curled white arrow overlaying the application icon (intuitive, huh?) and the titles always start with the words, "Shortcut to." Although these differences make shortcuts easy to identify, they quickly become annoying. You don't need to be told which icons are shortcuts—you created them, you already know this!

When your desktop only contains one or two shortcuts, this problem is no big deal. But, when you have over 25 shortcuts, you desktop starts to look pretty ugly.

You could get rid of the "Shortcut to…" text by manually renaming each icon. But, with many icons, this gets tedious. And, whenever you create new icons you'd have to go through this process all over again. Moreover, this procedure does nothing to remove the curled arrows.

The best way to makeover your shortcuts is to use TweakUI (see the discussion about TweakUI in the introduction). Launch TweakUI from the Control Panel and then select the Explorer tab. Under the Settings box, remove the check next to Prefix "Shortcut to" on new shortcuts. This solves the text problem.

To remove the curled arrow, look in the Shortcut overlay box on the same sheet (see Figure 1.2.2). You can select None to remove the arrow on new shortcuts. Or, you can change the overlay to a lighter-colored arrow by choosing Light Arrow. You can even overlay another icon of your choosing by selecting Custom. A test area shows what your resulting icon will look like.

Shortcut Savvy

Figure 1.2.2

Remove a shortcut's curled white arrow via the Shortcut Overlay box of TweakUI.

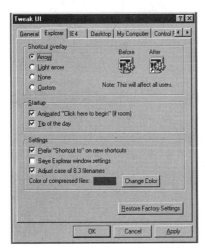

1.2.3 Make Your Shortcuts Open Applications and Documents

Like most people, you probably work with certain files on an ongoing basis—a monthly status Excel spreadsheet or a weekly Word document report, for example. Here's a tip that's useful in these situations. Create special shortcuts that open both your application and a particular document simultaneously. This way, you'll save the extra step required to open your file.

Use the following steps to make your shortcut open an application and a document:

1. Create your application shortcut. You can do this by right-clicking on the application entry in the Start menu and then choosing Send To | Desktop As Shortcut from the pop-up menu. Or, you can simply right-click on the desktop and select New | Shortcut from the pop-up menu. This will launch the Shortcut Wizard (see Figure 1.2.3) which will step you through the process.

Figure 1.2.3

Use the Shortcut Wizard to create a new shortcut.

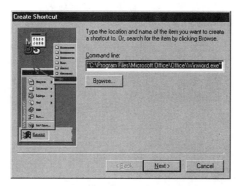

2. After you've created the shortcut, you can proceed with the modification. Right-click on your new shortcut. Then choose Properties from the pop-up menu.

3. Select the Shortcut tab.

4. In the Target field, place your text cursor after the entry for the application's executable file. The target will likely be surrounded by quotation marks. If so, put the cursor after the last quotation marks.

5. Here, enter the full path and filename of the file you want to open with this shortcut. To account for long filenames, put quotation marks around the path and filename. Here's an example of a target you'll end up with. With this example, you'll open the PLANA.DOC file in Microsoft Word:

"C:\Program Files\Microsoft Office\Office\WINWORD.EXE"
"C:\Projects\PLANA.DOC"

6. Click the OK button to save and close the shortcut's Properties sheet.

You don't need to reboot for this change. Now, selecting the shortcut will launch the desired application and immediately open your file.

Shortcut Savvy

Chapter

1.3

Customizing the Start Menu and Taskbar

Windows 98 lets you customize the Start menu and Taskbar much more than you could in Windows 95. Some of these customizations—such as reorganizing items on the Start menu and adding Toolbars to the Taskbar—are easy to learn and are well documented in the Windows Help system. In this chapter, however, I describe lesser-known modifications for these basic Windows elements.

1.3.1 Store More on the Start Menu

You probably know about the ability to drag and drop shortcuts onto the Windows 98 Start menu: You can quickly add a program to the top level of the Start menu, so that you can access it directly rather than wade through the potentially huge Programs list. But it takes a special trick to access the branching feature of the Start menu—a solid black triangle pointing to the right on Start menu items, such as Settings, that brings up sub-menus when you highlight them.

If you try the normal shortcut process to get, say, the Control Panel listed as a branching entry off the Start menu, it won't work. Don't believe me? Give it a try. Right-click the Control Panel entry in the Windows Explorer and then select Create shortcut. Windows will ask you if you want to store the shortcut on the desktop. Choose Yes. Now, drag your new Control Panel shortcut over the Start button. If you hesitate over the Start button, the menu will open up and you can drop the shortcut anywhere you like on the menu. Unfortunately, you'll now notice that the Control Panel item has no black triangle. How can you fix this? You need to delete this shortcut and start over with TweakUI.

Follow these steps to create a branching Control Panel entry on the Start menu.

1. Launch TweakUI from the Control Panel. (Read the introduction section on installing TweakUI if you haven't already.)

2. Select the Desktop tab.

3. Choose the Control Panel entry from the list of Special Desktop Icons. You can either put a check in the box next to the entry and then click the Create as File button at the bottom of the Window, or you can right-click the Control Panel entry and choose Create as File from the list.

4. Save the file to any folder on your hard drive.

5. From Windows Explorer, drag the your new Control Panel file over and drop it on the Start button. Now, your Start menu will have a branching triangle that will get you directly to the Control Panel sub-elements (such as System, Passwords, and so on).

You can use this same procedure to create branching Start menu entries for Dial-Up Networking or for Printers. It's a handy method for gaining quick access to parts of your operating system that you frequently modify.

> **WARNING** When you select Create as File for the Control Panel or any of the
> other special desktop icons, these files will not be updated when you
> install or delete items from their respective folders.
>
> For example, if you were to install a new item into the Control Panel, say, Microsoft
> Desktop Themes, your Control Panel branch off the Start menu would not show this
> new icon. You can, however, still access the updated Control Panel via
> Start | Settings | Control Panel on the Start menu.
>
> If you want to maintain an updated Control Panel branch off the Start menu, you need
> to run through these steps again after a change to the Control Panel.

1.3.2 Remove Animated "Click here to begin" from the Taskbar

Only the most innocent of novices needs the bouncing `Look here, Stupid!`
message that guides you to Windows 98's Start button. Windows 98 will stop
posting the `Click here` message after you've loaded programs into the Startup
folder. I guess at that point Windows figures you know where the Start button is
and what it does. But, if you want to disable this message from the get-go, you
can do with it with either TweakUI or a Registry hack.

To disable the `Click here` message with TweakUI, follow these steps:

1. Launch the TweakUI utility from the Control Panel (see the introduction
   if you haven't installed TweakUI).

2. Select the Explorer tab.

3. In the Startup box, remove the check next to the line: Animated "Click
   Here to Begin."

4. Click OK to exit TweakUI.

Registry hackers can use the following steps to modify the same value in the
Windows Registry:

1. Type Regedit in the Start | Run dialog box to launch the Registry Editor.

2. Navigate to the following key: HKEY_CURRENT_USER\Software\
   Microsoft\Windows\CurrentVersion\Policies\Explorer.

3. Check for the Binary Value `NoStartBanner`. If the entry doesn't exist,
   create it by right-clicking in the right-hand pane of Regedit and selecting
   New | Binary Value. When the value appears in the right pane of Regedit,
   type in the name **NoStartBanner** without quotation marks and then
   press **Enter** to set it.

Customizing the Start Menu and Taskbar

> **TIP** Here's how to quickly get to a Binary Value, DWORD Value, or String in the Registry Editor. After you've drilled down to the Registry Key you want to modify, move your cursor over and click somewhere in the right pane of Regedit. Then, press the first letter of the Value or String you're looking for, in this case, **N** for NoStartBanner. Regedit will highlight the first entry it finds with that letter under the current key. And, guess what? This same trick also works with files in Windows Explorer.

4. Change, or if it didn't exist, create the following Value for NoStartBanner: 01 00 00 00. To do this, select the value for NoStartBanner. This action displays a dialog box called Edit Binary Value. The text cursor will flash in front of the first set of two digits; there will be four sets total. To change these first two digits, move your mouse cursor over the digits and double-click to select them. Then enter the new values, in this example, 01. You can change the other three sets of two in the same way if you need to modify them. To save the new value and close the Edit Binary Value dialog box, click the OK button.

The next time you power up, you won't see the pesky message.

1.3.3 Remove the Favorites Item from the Start Menu

How many quick-reference resources does one person need? The new Favorites entry on the Start menu seems ridiculously redundant. We already have access to multiple taskbars, shortcuts on the desktop, and a recent documents list.

> **NOTE** Microsoft structured the Start Menu to enable access to the Active Desktop's Channels through the Favorites item. If you remove the Favorites entry, you need to access the Channels through the Channel Bar in the Quick Launch Tray.

If this redundancy irks you, remove the Favorites item from the Start menu using either TweakUI or a Registry hack. As always, TweakUI is the preferred choice for novices.

Perform these tasks to remove Favorites from the Start menu using TweakUI:

1. Launch TweakUI (under Start | Settings | Control Panel). If you haven't installed the sample Resource Kit utilities, check the introduction to this book for instructions.

2. Select the IE4 tab.

3. Scroll down the Settings list until you see the entry for Show Favorites on Start menu. Remove the check next to this entry.

4. Click OK to exit TweakUI.

You'll need to reboot before the change takes effect.

Follow these steps to remove "Favorites" from the Start menu with a Registry hack:

1. Launch the Registry Editor by choosing Start | Run and then entering **Regedit**.

2. Navigate to the following Registry key: HKEY_CURRENT_USER\ Software\Microsoft\Windows\CurrentVersion\Policies\Explorer.

> **TIP**   In the Registry Editor, you'll find a new item on the right-click menu called Expand. While navigating through Registry branches, you can right-click and select Expand to open up a Registry key.

3. Locate the DWORD value `NoFavoritesMenu`. If that value doesn't exist, you must create it. Right-click in the right-hand pane of Regedit and then select New | DWORD Value and then press **Enter**. Enter the name **NoFavoritesMenu** when the value appears in the right-hand pane of Regedit.

4. Change (or create it if it didn't previously exist) the value of NoFavoritesMenu to 1.

5. Click OK and exit Regedit.

Upon your next boot, you'll see that this change has taken effect.

1.3.4 Remove the Log Off Option from the Start Menu

Just as with the login screen (see hint 1.1.3), not all users need the `Log Off` *username* entry on the Start menu. If you're the sole user of your PC, or if all users have the same rights and privileges on a system, there's no need whatsoever to distinguish between one user and another.

In corporate environments, the login/logout process is sometimes used for employee time-tracking. Although I'm not personally in favor of this "Big Brother" technique, you might not want to disable Log Off on office PCs.

The general rule is, if you don't need to log in, you also don't need to log off, and you should delete this space wasting entry from your already crowded Start menu.

Customizing the Start Menu and Taskbar

To delete the Log Off entry from the Start menu, use the following steps:

1. Launch the TweakUI utility under Start | Settings | Control Panel. (Read the introduction about TweakUI if you haven't yet installed the Sample Resource Kit tools from the Windows 98 CD.)

2. Select the IE4 tab.

3. Remove the check next to the Allow Logoff entry (see Figure 1.3.1). It should be the fourth item from the top of the list.

Figure 1.3.1

Remove Logoff from the Start menu via the TweakUI utility.

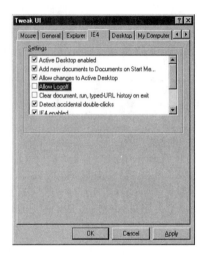

5. Click OK to close TweakUI.

The next time you power up, this change will have taken effect.

1.3.5 Create Windows Commands that You Launch from the Start Menu

Windows 98 is a very mouse-oriented operating system. Unless you know all the keyboard equivalents, you have to point and click your way around to get anything done. Anyone who's suffered a repetitive stress injury knows the wrist pain involved in the constant movement of a mouse device.

Some people still prefer the old feel of DOS, where you could launch a home-made batch file just by typing in its name. For those people, there's good news. You can still create custom batch files and launch them from Start menu's Run option.

Here's how it works:

1. Launch either the Notepad or Wordpad applet. If you use Wordpad, make sure to save your file as a Text file.

2. Type in your batch commands. The following example opens Windows Explorer and displays the contents of a CD-ROM drive that's been assigned drive letter E.

   explorer E:

3. Save the file by any name you prefer. Remember, you'll invoke the command by this name, so it should be both short and meaningful. In this example, perhaps "mycd.bat." Again, if you've used Wordpad, make sure that you save the file as Text. Always put the .bat file extension on these command files.

4. Using Windows Explorer, move this file into your C:\Windows\Command directory. Windows will quickly find and launch batch files stored here.

5. Also in Explorer, right-click on your newly created batch file. Select Properties. Choose the Program tab from the properties sheet and place a check next to: Close on Exit. Click OK to close the Properties sheet.

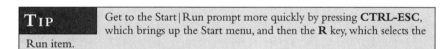

| **TIP** | Get to the Start | Run prompt more quickly by pressing **CTRL-ESC**, which brings up the Start menu, and then the **R** key, which selects the Run item. |

From here, you can activate your batch file by selecting Start | Run and then entering the name of your batch file. The batch file will do its job and then disappear, so that you can get on with your work.

Customizing the Start Menu and Taskbar

Chapter

1.4

Desktop Hints

During most computer sessions, you'll spend a lot of time staring at the Windows 98 desktop. It's the launching pad for every task you undertake. You can use these hints to alter how the desktop appears and how it acts.

1.4.1 **Rename System Objects**

Microsoft chose cute, even politically correct, names for their system objects—Inbox, Network Neighborhood, and, of course, the Recycle Bin. These names get old very quickly, and, after a while longer, they make you feel like just another cog in the big Microsoft machine.

Unfortunately, as part of the operating system, you can't change the names of these objects by the normal means—right-clicking on the folder and selecting Rename. You can, however, use the trusty TweakUI utility or a Registry hack. But, Novices should stick with TweakUI. Renaming system objects through the Registry can get ugly.

Follow these steps to rename the Recycle Bin using TweakUI:

1. Launch TweakUI by accessing Start | Settings | Control Panel. Read the introduction if you haven't installed the Sample Resource Kit utilities.

2. Select the Desktop tab. You'll see a list of all the system icons. You can check or uncheck the boxes next to these items to remove them from the desktop, but see hint 1.4.2 for special conditions.

3. By right-clicking on any of these entries, you'll bring up a pop-up list that includes Rename. Select Rename to display the dialog box in which you can enter any name you like. For the Recycle Bin, try **Black Hole**, **U.S. Dept. of Justice files**, or any other name of your choosing.

4. Click OK to exit TweakUI.

In the following text we'll walk through the steps for renaming the Recycle Bin through a Registry hack. Use a similar approach for changing the name of the Inbox, Network Neighborhood, and other system objects.

> **WARNING**   Always make sure you only change *string* values, not Registry *keys* with the Recycle Bin name. You can introduce serious system errors by changing Registry key names.

Follow these steps to rename the Recycle Bin using a Registry hack.

1. Launch the Registry Editor by entering **Regedit** at the Start | Run prompt.

2. Open the Registry branch titled: HKEY_CLASSES_ROOT.

3. From here, use the search function to find the phrase "Recycle Bin." Do this by opening the Edit menu and selecting Find. Then enter **Recycle Bin** in the dialog box.

4. Depending on the software applications and shareware you have loaded on your system, you might hit several references to the Recycle Bin during your search. On my system, the first hit was the "Recycle Bin Cleaner." This is not the value I wanted. If this is the case with you also, press F3 to continue searching, or select Find Next from the Edit menu. Stop when you see only the words, "Recycle Bin." The exact location is: HKEY_CLASSES_ROOT\CLSID\{645FF040-5081-101B-9F08-00AA002F954E} (see Figure 1.4.1), but to save the trouble of finding this long, cryptic key you can use the search function. Double-click on the "default" string and enter your new name for the Recycle Bin.

Figure 1.4.1
The Recycle Bin's Class ID entry in the Registry.

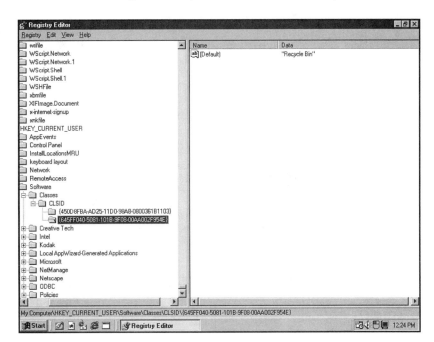

5. Exit the Registry Editor. You'll need to restart your PC to see this change take effect.

Desktop Hints

1.4.2 Remove the Network Neighborhood and Other System Objects from the Desktop

If you want to remove some or all of the system objects—such as Inbox, Microsoft Network, and so forth—from your desktop, execute the steps laid out in the following numbered list. This list focuses on Network Neighborhood because it's a special case, but the same steps apply to the other system objects.

The Network Neighborhood icon illustrates another of Microsoft's assumptions—that your PC is connected to a LAN (Local Area Network) or WAN (Wide Area Network), even if you've just installed Dial-Up networking to connect to the Internet via an Internet Service Provider. Microsoft could, of course, have built Windows so that this icon was displayed only on truly networked systems, but instead, they made the Network Neighborhood a default for any connected PC setup.

In the following procedures, you do not actually *remove* the Network Neighborhood, you *hide* it. To remove it completely, you need to remove all the network components of Windows 98, including Dial-Up networking, through Add/Remove Programs under the Control Panel. This isn't an option for most users.

> **WARNING** Do not hide the Network Neighborhood if you are using any network resources such as shared directories or printers. After the Network Neighborhood is hidden, you will not have access to these resources unless you have mapped them to a drive letter (see Windows Help for information on this). If you hide the Network Neighborhood, Windows stops using Universal Naming Conventions (UNC) that grant access to remote resources.
>
> Hiding the Network Neighborhood object also affects the Direct Cable Connection (DCC) feature of Windows 98, which you can use to quickly connect and share files between two PCs. DCC no longer lists the files available on the host computer, but it will otherwise function normally if the Network Neighborhood is hidden.

Overall, if your PC stands alone, the Network Neighborhood icon just takes up real estate on your desktop. Click on it and you'll see that there's no information inside of any value for non-networked systems. Once again, though, you can't simply delete it as you would another icon or shortcut. You'll need to use either TweakUI or the System Policy Editor.

To remove the Network Neighborhood using TweakUI, perform the following steps:

1. Launch the TweakUI utility via the Control Panel.

2. Select the Desktop tab.

3. Scroll down the list of Special Desktop Icons until you find the Network Neighborhood.

4. Remove the check next to Network Neighborhood.

5. Click OK. Windows will then warn you about the effects of hiding this special icon. I've listed these warnings in the note above. Click Yes if you want to see the warning from Microsoft's Help system, otherwise click No.

You need to restart the computer before the change takes effect.

To hide the Network Neighborhood via the System Policy Editor, perform the following steps:

1. Launch the System Policy Editor under Start | Programs | Accessories | System Tools. If you have not installed the Policy Editor from the Windows 98 disc, read the introduction.

2. Select Open Registry from the File menu.

3. Choose the Local User icon.

4. Drill down the branches following this path: Local_User\Windows 98 System\Shell\Restrictions.

5. Put a check next to the Hide Network Neighborhood entry.

6. Click OK.

7. Choose Save from the File menu, then close the System Policy Editor.

You'll need to restart your PC before this change takes effect.

1.4.3 Change Desktop Icons

One way to add some personality to Windows 98 is to change some of the desktop icons.

Switching from one icon to another on your desktop is a pretty easy process. To do this, access the Folder Options, under Start | Settings. Then, click on the File Types tab. Here, you'll see a list of all the file types on your system. The list includes everything from application document types (such as Word and Excel, if you have them installed) to system file types (such as briefcase files, file folders, and Outlook Express Mail Messages).

Desktop Hints

> **NOTE**   Icons can be stored in many different file types including: .EXE
> (executable), .DLL (Dynamic Link Library), .BMP (Bitmap), and
> .ICO (icon) files.
>
> To extract and edit icons from these files, you'll need a special icon editor tool. You can
> download some shareware programs from the Internet. Two such utilities are: Hagen
> Wieshofer's IconEdit Pro and Pascal Tremblay's TurboIcon. Both are available from
> CNET's Download.com Web site (www.download.com).
>
> To create your own brand new icons, work your magic in Windows 98's Paint applet
> (under Start | Programs | Accessories) and save your files as bitmaps (.BMP file
> extension).

Either double-click on an entry or highlight an entry and click the Edit button to
bring up the Edit File Type dialog box. At the top of this dialog box, you'll see the
icon used by this file type and a button that says Change Icon. By clicking this
button you can pick another icon that's included in that reference file (they are
visible on the same screen) or pick another icon file by clicking the Browse
button from the list.

Windows 98 maintains special control over some of the desktop icons and you
won't find them under Folder Options. For system objects such as the Recycle
Bin or the Network Neighborhood, you'll need to edit the Registry key that
references their icon files.

Follow these steps to change the icon file for a Windows 98 desktop object:

1. Launch the Registry Editor by entering **Regedit** at the Start | Run
   prompt.

2. Navigate to the following key: HKEY_CLASSES_ROOT\CSLID\

3. Pick one of the following keys, below the
   HKEY_CLASSES_ROOT\CSLID\ key, that references a system desktop
   object and select it:

Briefcase	{85BBD920-42A0-1069-A2E4-08002B30309D}
Inbox	{00020D75-0000-0000-C000-0000000000046}
Internet Explorer	{FBF23B42-E3F0-101B-8488-00AA003E56F8}
Microsoft Network	{00028B00-0000-0000-C000-0000000000046}
Network Neighborhood	{208D2C60-3AEA-1069-A2D7-08002B30309D}
Recycle Bin	{645FF040-5081-101B-9F08-00AA002F954E}

4. Beneath these keys, you'll find a DefaultIcon key. Select it.

5. In the Default string below this key, you'll find the path and filename that holds the system object's icon. Double-click on Default to change this reference to an icon file of your choice. Be sure to include the full path to your file.

1.4.4 Squeeze More Icons onto the Desktop

Have you run out of space for new icons yet? Be careful. Icons breed like rabbits. And, Microsoft starts you off with seven when you install Windows 98 onto a fresh hard drive. Add shortcuts to your favorite programs, printers, Web sites, and DOS, and your screen starts to look like the wall of an Egyptian tomb.

You might even start to wonder how you could use that extra space *between* the icons. It's just sitting there, right?

Yes, you can reduce the amount of space between icons by adjusting the horizontal and vertical icon spacing parameters. This way you'll be able to pack icons closer together.

Follow these steps to adjust the icon spacing settings:

1. Right-click on the desktop. Select Properties from the pop-up list.

2. Select the Appearance tab of the Display Properties sheet.

3. In the Item drop-down box, select Icon Spacing (Horizontal). Then, in the Size (which is measured in pixels) box, reduce the current number by 10 or 20. So, for example, you would reduce 50 pixels to 30 pixels (see Figure 1.4.2).

4. Perform the same reduction for vertical spacing by selecting Icon Spacing (Vertical) from the Item drop-down box and then adjusting the size parameters.

| **WARNING** | Reduce the spacing too much and you won't be able to read your icon names. Microsoft truncates the name of an icon and adds an ellipsis if there isn't enough room to display the full text. |

Similarly, increase the spacing by too much, and your icons will overlap one another on your desktop, making them difficult to select.

Trial and error is your best approach. Experiment with the size parameters by clicking the Apply button on the Display Properties sheet.

Desktop Hints

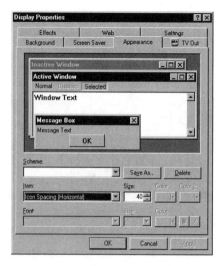

Figure 1.4.2
*Reduce the Icon
Spacing via the
Display
Properties
Appearance tab.*

1.4.5 Configure My Computer to Launch Explorer

The My Computer object is a strange one. It grants access to specific elements of your system—such as your files, data, Control Panel, Printers, and Dial-Up networking settings. And, of course, it lets you format floppies and such. But, you can already get to these system elements via the Explorer and the Start menu. Moreover, the format of My Computer, even with the new Web Page option, isn't as efficient as the Explorer interface for quickly digging down into subfolders.

If you find My Computer to be redundant, you can convert it into an Explorer shortcut with a Registry hack.

Follow these steps to transform My Computer into an Explorer shortcut:

1. Launch the Registry Editor by entering **Regedit** at the Start | Run prompt.

2. Navigate to the following key: HKEY_CLASSES_ROOT\CSLID\{20D04FE0-3AEA-1069-A2D8-08002B30309D}. This is the operating system's Class ID for My Computer. Searching the Registry for "My Computer" won't really help you here. On most Windows 98 systems, there'll be no value for "My Computer" under this key.

3. Right-click on the Shell key beneath this Class ID. Then, choose New | Key. And enter the name **Open**.

4. Now, right-click on the Open key and choose New | Key again. This time enter the name **Command**.

5. Finally, under the Command key, double-click on the default value and enter **explorer.exe** into the dialog box.

6. Exit the Registry Editor.

7. In this case, you don't need to restart your computer. Just click on an empty desktop space and press the F5 key. This will refresh the desktop.

Selecting My Computer will now bring up the functional Explorer interface. To go back to the standard My Computer interface, remove the Registry keys that you added during this procedure.

1.4.6 Modify the New Menu

The New menu, which you can access under the Windows Explorer's File menu or by right-clicking a blank space on your desktop, is a powerful tool. With one mouse click you can generate a new file of any type you specify.

Windows 98 preloads certain file types into the New menu during installation and more get added when you load applications. You can, however, modify the New menu so that it includes only file types you designate.

Removing existing entries from the New menu is easy, and we'll discuss that in the following text. For adding new entries, you first need to create a file association for your new file type, if one doesn't already exist.

Windows 98 stores the file associations under Start | Settings | Folder Options (you can also access this dialog via the Explorer's View menu). Click on the File Types tab of Folder Options to bring up the list of currently registered file types.

If you want to add a new type, press the New button on this dialog box and follow the instructions. If you want to select one of the existing file types to add to the New menu, double-click on its entry in this dialog box and make a note of its Default Extension for Content Type item. It'll be a .*XXX* listing where the *XXX* is some three-character combination of letters and numbers.

To modify the New menu, bring up TweakUI (under Start | Settings | Control Panel). Then select TweakUI's New tab. At this point, you can remove any item you want from the New menu by removing the X next to its entry.

To add a new type, move the mouse to a blank space on the desktop. Right-click and select the New menu item. You'll see a list of file types, the same list represented in TweakUI. From here, select any file type. It doesn't matter which one, because you'll change it in the next step.

When you've selected a file type, Windows will post a new file on the desktop. The file's name will be highlighted, ready for you to change. Now, type in any name that includes a .*XXX* at the end that matches the file type you want to add into the New menu. For example, .EML is the file type for an Outlook Express Mail Message. So, if I wanted to add that type to my New menu, I would change the file name to: MYMAIL.EML.

Finally, drag this file over to TweakUI and drop it anywhere on the New tab. Windows 98 will automatically add it to the list with the correct file type listing, in my case, it adds Outlook Express Mail Message. Put an X next to your new entry. Then, choose OK to exit TweakUI.

At this point, whenever you bring up the New menu, you'll see your customized list.

1.4.7 Transform the Feel of Your Mouse

With the default settings of Windows 98, you end up clicking your mouse much too often. You click to highlight files and icons, double-click to launch programs, and right-click to bring up property sheets and other settings parameters. You even need to click on a window to activate and bring it to the foreground. Clickity, clickity, click. It's enough to drive you crazy.

You guessed it! There are ways to change this click-happy behavior so that your mouse feels more like a tool and less like a burden.

First, change the system settings so that *activation follows the mouse*. These means you can bring the "focus" to a window just by passing your mouse over it. You don't need to click on anything.

Set Activation Follows Mouse by performing these tasks:

1. Launch TweakUI from the Control Panel (under Start | Settings | Control Panel).

2. Select the Mouse tab.

3. At the bottom of the dialog box, put a check next to Activation Follows Mouse (X-mouse). The will give a window the focus when you pass your mouse over it.

4. Wait! You're not done. Select the General tab of TweakUI. Then scroll down in the Effects box until you find X-Mouse AutoRaise. Put a check in the box next to this entry. This brings the window to the foreground when you pass your mouse over it.

Spend a few minutes just getting comfortable with your new mouse. You'll be amazed at the difference these settings make. At first, you might be slightly annoyed with how quickly windows shoot forward as you move your mouse around the desktop. But give it a chance. With clicking, less is better!

Finally, set your mouse to single-click mode to reduce your click rate even more. To do this, follow these steps.

1. Open Windows Explorer (under Start | Programs).

2. Choose Folder Options from the View menu.

3. In the General tab, select the Custom button.

4. Click the Settings button (it activates after you select Custom) to bring up the Custom Settings screen.

5. In the Click Items as Follows box, choose Single-Click to Open an Item. Then choose either one of the underlined options below this entry.

6. Choose OK, then select Close to exit the Folder Options.

These changes take effect immediately.

1.4.8 Bring Back the Program Manager Interface from Windows 3.1

Believe it or don't, Windows 3.1 users still number in the millions. Many of these people will probably upgrade directly to Windows 98 via an upgrade disc or simply by buying a new computer with Windows 98 pre-installed.

If you're one these of leap-froggers, you might just be a little intimidated by the Windows 98 interface. It's quite a bit different than the old Program Manager of Windows 3.1. Take heart, though, the Program Manager is still around. And so are some of Windows 3.1's helpful tools, such as the File Manager, Calculator, and Paint.

Microsoft provides no direct access to the Program Manager from the Windows 98 desktop, so you must create your own. The executable file is Progman.exe under the C:\Windows directory.

To create a Program Manager shortcut on the desktop, run through these steps.

1. Right-click on the desktop and select New | Shortcut.

2. On the first Create Shortcut dialog box, enter the following command line: **C:\Windows\progman.exe**. You can also click the Browse... button and navigate to that file on your hard disk. Click Next to move on.

Desktop Hints

3. The next screen asks you to select the name. Try **Program Manager**, **The Return of Windows 3.1**, or a name of your own choosing. Click Finish.

4. If you haven't upgraded your PC from Windows 3.1, the Program Manager will initially be empty. If so, you'll have to manually enter Program Groups and Program Items. Use the New option from the File menu of the Program Manager to do this.

If you want a real blast from the past (and an interesting trick to stupefy your friends), you can make the Program Manager launch full-screen at startup. Here's how:

- Set the Program Manager shortcut to full-screen by accessing its property sheet and selecting Maximized from the Run drop-down box.

- Drag the shortcut over the Start button. Hesitating will cause the Start menu to open up. Follow the path and drop the shortcut into the Programs | Startup folder.

- Then, for full effect, right-click your Taskbar, Select Properties, and place a check next to Auto Hide on the Taskbar Options sheet.

The next time you power up, Windows 98 will look like Windows 3.1.

Chapter

1.5

Backgrounds

In Windows 98, you can use your background for information as well as jokes or just pretty pictures.

1.5.1 Make Your Background an HTML File

Kudos to the Microsoft developers for enabling HTML (Hyper Text Markup Language) files as backgrounds for the desktop! They often receive harsh criticism (sometimes justly deserved), but in this case, they've delivered a very powerful feature that you can use to greatly enhance the look and feel of your computer.

With an HTML background, your desktop can display a to-do list, a table of business contacts, or a spreadsheet of your current project schedule. And, this file can hyperlink to files on the Web or your desktop for updates.

> **NOTE**   You must enable the Active Desktop for this hint to work. To enable the Active Desktop, right-click a blank space on the desktop and choose Active Desktop | View As Web Page from the pop-up list.

Changing your background from useless wallpaper into a very functional HTML file is simple. It's creating a good HTML file to use that's a little tougher. We'll discuss the creation later.

To make your background an HTML file, follow these steps:

1. Right-click a blank space on the desktop and select Properties from the pop-up list.

2. Click the Background tab of the Display Properties sheet.

3. Click the Browse button and navigate to the HTML file on your hard disk that you want to use as wallpaper.

4. Choose OK to exit the Display Properties and post the HTML file as wallpaper.

If you're a novice at HTML, don't worry. Microsoft has included a basic HTML editor called Frontpage Express with Windows 98. You'll find it under Start | Programs | Internet Explorer.

With Frontpage Express you can quickly create basic HTML files that combine text, graphics, tables, and so on. You could figure out how to create a basic to-do list in about half an hour, even if you never worked with HTML files before.

After you get comfortable, try a couple more sophisticated tricks. You can insert hyperlinks to files on the Internet, besides your Channel Bar choices. Or, you can hyperlink to files on your hard drive. Another advanced option is to use other applications, such as Microsoft Word or Excel, to provide information and data for your HTML background. Both Word 97 and Excel 97 have Save As HTML options under the File menu. These options invoke wizards that guide you through the translation from a document or spreadsheet into an HTML file.

1.5.2 Get Wallpaper from the Web or the Windows 98 CD

Are you tired of trying to make your own creative wallpaper? Let someone else do the work for you. Plenty of mad artists post Windows 98 wallpaper up on the Web and make it available for free, or a small fee, to anyone who wants to download it.

Check out JokeWallpaper.com (`www.jokewallpaper.com`) for some free current events humor. These folks continually crank out new wallpaper poking fun at the latest political scandal or big-budget Hollywood movie. They've even set up the site to help people whose corporate IS managers monitor employee "Net activity." In stealth mode, you can access JokeWallpaper.com through a Corporate-Excellence domain name (`www.corporate-excellence.com`)

Second Nature Software (`www.secondnature.com`) posts wallpaper in several categories, including: Pop Art, Nature, Space, Fine Art, Comics, and Sports. They charge a small fee for their images.

With a little Web surfing, you'll find 50 or more personal Web pages that offer wallpaper for Windows. In your favorite search engine, enter the keywords "Windows wallpaper" and browse through the returned hits. In just a few minutes you'll find wallpaper involving rock bands, religion, TV shows, cartoons, and more.

As a teaser for their Plus! software, Microsoft includes some Desktop Themes on the Windows 98 installation disc (see Figure 1.5.1). The Desktop Themes provide wallpaper, icons, sound files, and mouse pointers all relating to a single theme such as baseball, the jungle, space, and so on.

To install the Desktop Themes from the Windows 98 installation disc, follow these steps:

1. Launch the Control Panel under Start | Settings.

2. Select Add/Remove Programs.

3. Choose the Windows Setup tab.

4. Scroll down the list of Components and place a check next to Desktop Themes. Click OK. Windows will ask you to insert the Windows 98 CD

into your CD-ROM drive. Then it will copy the files to your hard drive and add a Desktop Theme object to your Control Panel.

Figure 1.5.1
*Digitizing the
rain forest:
Microsoft
Desktop Themes.*

To use a desktop theme, follow these steps:

1. Choose Start | Settings | Control Panel from the Start menu.

2. Select the Desktop Themes object.

3. Preview the 15 different themes by pressing the Theme drop-down arrow and selecting on of the entries (Sports, Mystery, The 60's USA, etc…) from the list. In the preview window, you'll see the background, system object icons, window, and message box scheme that your chosen theme will evoke.

4. Preview the Screen Saver used by your theme by clicking the Screen Saver button in the Previews box. You can also check the pointers and sounds by pressing the Pointers, Sounds, Etc… button.

5. Remove any individual theme elements by removing the checks in the Settings box.

6. To enable the theme, press the Apply button. Then click the OK button to exit.

These changes take effect immediately.

1.5.3 Add Free Utilities to Your Active Desktop

Your Active Desktop can do much more than subscribe to Web sites for updated content. With Java and Visual Basic script capabilities, your desktop can interact with programs on the Web to deliver specific answers and information on both personal and business topics.

To start taking advantage of these features, browse Microsoft's Active Desktop Gallery online (`www.microsoft.com/ie/ie40/gallery`) (see Figure 1.5.2). You'll find utilities that: map out addresses for you (Address Finder), deliver a continually updated weather map (MSNBC Weather Map), and help you search for jobs (JobNet) among other things. All the tools come with instructions for installation and use.

Figure 1.5.2
Microsoft's Active Desktop Gallery provides interactive tools for your system.

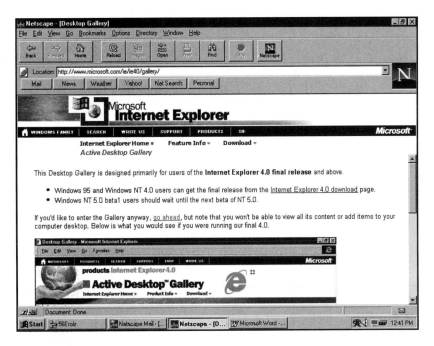

> | **TIP** | Microsoft included direct access to the Desktop Gallery in Windows 98. First, right-click a blank space on the desktop and make sure that the View as Web Page option is checked. This sets up the Active Desktop. Next, select Customize My Desktop from the right-click pop-up menu. Windows 98 displays a dialog box that asks if you want to go to the Active Desktop Gallery. Click the Yes button and Internet Explorer will take you directly there. |

Because Microsoft plans to update this site on a regular basis, you should check back every few weeks for additional tools.

1.5.4 Store Multiple Images on Your Desktop

Windows 98's Active Desktop lets you create a digital photo album as your background. You can add new images at any time and place them where you like. This is a new feature. Windows 95 restricted you to one centered image for the background.

Follow these steps to add images to your Active desktop:

1. Right-click a blank space on the desktop where you want to post a new image. Make sure the View as Web Page listing is checked.

2. Choose Customize My Desktop.

3. Select the Web tab.

4. Click the New button. Then, select No when you're asked whether or not you want to go to the Active Desktop Gallery.

5. In the New Active Desktop Item dialog box, enter the name of the image location. The address can be a Web URL (Unique Resource Locator) or a file on your hard drive. For faster selection, you can also click the Browse button and navigate there.

These changes will take effect immediately.

Chapter

1.6

Command Line Coolness

If you already use the MS-DOS prompt, you know about its convenience and flexibility. If you don't use MS-DOS, give it a try. Either way, read this chapter for information on changing the MS-DOS prompt's fonts, prompts, and command set.

1.6.1 Change the Font of the MS-DOS Window

Depending on your display resolution setting, your DOS window might become difficult to read. Windows 98 uses a small font when your DOS box runs in Auto font mode. Fortunately, it's easy to change this system setting to a larger and more readable font size and type.

> **TIP**   For quick access to DOS parameters make sure that you display a toolbar over the top of your DOS window. To do this, right-click on your MS-DOS shortcut, or simply right-click on the MS-DOS window title bar after you launch it via Start | Programs | MS-DOS Prompt. Then choose Properties from the pop-up list. This displays the MS-DOS Prompt Properties sheet. Select the Screen tab and, under the Window box, place a check next to the line Display Toolbar.
>
> With the toolbar active you can quickly choose a new font by selecting an entry in the font drop-down box or by pressing the font button (which looks like a capital A). Remember, though, the toolbar won't be displayed while MS-DOS is running in full-screen mode.

To change the font used in the MS-DOS window, follow these steps:

1. Display the MS-DOS Prompt Properties sheet by right-clicking on your MS-DOS Prompt shortcut or the title bar of the MS-DOS window after you've launched it. Then select Properties from the pop-up menu.

> **NOTE**   Altering the MS-DOS font only affects the DOS window. If you set your MS-DOS window to run in full-screen mode, you'll be back to using the standard font.
>
> Also, if your DOS program is running in graphics mode, as opposed to text mode, you might not notice any change when you switch to a TrueType versus a Bitmap font. For graphics mode DOS programs, Microsoft recommends using Bitmapped fonts.

2. Select the Font tab.

3. For flexibility, select the Both Font Types radio button item beneath the Available Types box. This way, you can choose either Bitmap or TrueType fonts for your MS-DOS window.

4. In the Font Size box, select the font you want to use in your MS-DOS window (see Figure 1.6.1). You'll see a preview of the font you choose in the Font Preview box below.

Figure 1.6.1

Select the MS-DOS font from the MS-DOS Prompt Properties sheet.

1.6.2 Modify the MS-DOS Prompt

Altering MS-DOS system parameters is a little like a lost art. In olden days, many people knew the ins-and-outs of DOS, but times and operating systems have changed. Most of the old tricks have been forgotten.

The DOS prompt, for example, is extremely customizable. The default setting, which most Windows users never change, is `Prompt=$p$g`, which means set the prompt to the current directory path (`$p`) and place a right-arrow symbol (`$g`)at the end.

You can get a full listing of the MS-DOS Prompt command settings by entering **prompt** /? in the command line of your DOS session. This instruction will display the help text of the `prompt` command. Here are some of the special codes:

Special codes for the MS-DOS prompt.

Code	Meaning
$T	Current Time
$D	Current Date
$P	Current Drive Letter and Directory Path
$V	Windows Version Number

continues

Command Line Coolness

Special codes for the MS-DOS prompt

Code	Meaning
$N	Current Drive Letter
$_	Carriage Return and Linefeed
$G	Greater–Than Sign
$L	Less–Than Sign

Follow these steps to change your MS-DOS command prompt:

1. At the Run prompt under the Start menu, enter **Sysedit** and press **Return**. This will display the System Configuration Editor.

2. Select the AUTOEXEC.BAT Window. Then insert a line for your new MS-DOS command prompt which uses the following format: **Set Prompt=*text_and_or_special_codes***. For example, to create a prompt that displays the Windows version number on one line then the current date and time on the next line use: **Set Prompt=v_$d tg**. The prompt for this example look like the following:

    ```
    Windows 98 [Version 4.10.1998]

    Sun 11-01-98 12:16:21.46>
    ```

> **TIP**   Windows 98 has two separate MS-DOS modes. One is the MS-DOS that launches before Windows, during the boot process; and the second is the MS-DOS prompt box that you can activate from the control panel. If you like you can set up a different prompt for each. In AUTOEXEC.BAT, use **Set Prompt=*text_and_or_special_codes*** for the initial DOS session and **Set Winpmt=*text_and_or_special_codes*** for the DOS box under Windows. If it is not defined, Winpmt just uses your Prompt setting.

3. Save your new AUTOEXEC.BAT by selecting File | Save from the System Configuration Editor menu.

4. Exit the System Configuration Editor by choosing File | Exit from the menu.

You can also change the DOS prompt anytime during a session by entering the set prompt command at the DOS prompt. Your changes will take effect immediately.

1.6.3 Add UNIX Commands to MS-DOS

UNIX is the grandfather of command-line operating systems. It's been around longer than DOS and, in many respects, UNIX is much more sophisticated than DOS. In UNIX you can search binary files for text strings, search any file for pattern matches, quickly display segments of a file, sort files, compare them, and a whole host of other things.

Now, you can use UNIX commands in your MS-DOS environment. A company called Professional Software Solutions offers a shareware program called The UnixDos Toolkit which adds 65 Unix commands like grep, fgrep, sort, split, sed, and more to your command line. UnixDos also includes 28 new utilities that aren't part of the UNIX operating system.

This shareware program is free to download and use in an evaluation capacity. If you plan to continue using it, Professional Software Solutions (`www.profsoftware.com`) asks that you send them $54.50 for a license.

Whether you've come from a UNIX computing environment or you'd like to learn more about UNIX but don't have access to a UNIX system, these tools will help make MS-DOS more like UNIX.

Follow these steps to download and install The UnixDos Toolkit:

1. Launch Internet Explorer by choosing Start | Programs | Internet Explorer | Internet Explorer. Or, launch your alternative Web browser.

2. Enter the following URL into the address bar: `www.profsoftware.com`.

3. Click on the UnixDos Toolkit hyperlink.

4. Click on the Download hyperlink.

5. Select the Windows 95/NT UnixDos Toolkit. This 32-bit version also works under Windows 98.

6. Save the file to a directory on your hard drive. The file is 3.6 megabytes in size and might take several minutes to download, depending on the speed of your Internet connection. It's compressed with the zip format, so you'll need a decompression tool such as PKWare's PKZip for Windows (`www.pkware.com`) to extract the setup files from this downloadable file.

7. Extract the files with an unzip utility.

8. Select the SETUP.EXE program in Windows Explorer.

9. On the Welcome screen, click the Next button.

10. On the License Agreement screen, click the Accept button.

Command Line Coolness

11. This next screen asks if you want the program files installed into the C:\Unixdos directory. Unless you have a very good reason not to, click the Next button.

12. The next screen sets up a Unixdos program group. Click the Next button.

13. The next screen tells you that your free trial period expires after 30 days. Click the OK button.

14. The next screen says the installation is complete. Click the OK button.

15. To make the UnixDos commands work from any directory, you must add C:\Unixdos to the path statement in your AUTOEXEC.BAT file. From the Start menu, choose Start | Run. Enter **sysedit** into the Run prompt to launch the System Configuration Editor. Find the line beginning with the word "**Path**" in your AUTOEXEC.BAT file and add **C:\Unixdos** into that line. Choose File | Save from the System Configuration Editor menus in order to save your changes. Then choose File | Exit to close the application.

Now, whenever you run in MS-DOS, you can invoke UnixDos commands.

For detailed online documentation on the UnixDos commands, launch the Windows Explorer and select the file UNIXDOS.HLP in the C:\Unixdos directory.

Enhancing Explorer

You'll probably use Windows Explorer more than any other tool in Windows 98. Even in its default mode, it displays valuable information about files and folders. With a little tweaking, it becomes even more valuable.

1.7.1 Changing the Color of Compressed Files in Explorer

It's important to track which areas of your hard drive contain compressed files. Certain Windows applications and programs, such as Windows 98's FAT32 Disk Converter for example, cannot operate on compressed files. So, if you use DriveSpace 3, DoubleSpace, or any other disk compression utility, you'll want to be able to quickly identify such files.

> **NOTE**   DriveSpace, DoubleSpace, and the like are disk compression tools that use a designated area on your hard drive to store compressed files. File compression tools, such as WinZip, work differently. File compression tools only compress individual files and folders, but you can store them anywhere. Under Explorer, "zipped" files will not show up as color-coded compressed files.

The Windows Explorer will highlight compressed files on your disk with the color of your choice. To modify this setting, use the TweakUI Sample Resource Kit utility.

Follow these steps to modify the color of compressed files in the Windows Explorer:

1. Launch TweakUI under Start | Settings | Control Panel. (Read the section in the Introduction about installing TweakUI if you haven't already installed it.)

2. Select the Explorer tab.

3. Under the Settings box, click the Change Color button. Choose a Basic color or click the Define Custom Color button for a wider selection (see Figure 1.7.1).

4. Click OK to close the Color dialog box.

5. Click OK to close TweakUI.

This change will take effect immediately.

Figure 1.7.1

Choosing Define Custom Color gives you a wider range of color choices.

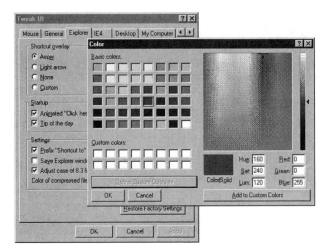

1.7.2 Tell Explorer Where To Go

Without modification, Windows Explorer opens with a view of your C: drive's root directory. But, you might prefer that Explorer opened with a view of the folder you most frequently access, such as a Projects or Documents folder.

Telling the Explorer where to go is as simple as changing the program's parameters in its Properties sheet.

Follow these steps to change the initial view for Windows Explorer:

1. If you haven't already done so, create a shortcut for the Windows Explorer. Right-click on the Windows Explorer entry under Start | Programs. Then select Copy. Now, right-click an empty space on the Windows desktop and select Paste Shortcut.

2. To access your Explorer shortcut's Property sheet, right-click on the shortcut and choose Properties.

3. Place your cursor at the end of the text field labeled Target, and press the left mouse button to enter text edit mode. The target line should initially read: `C:\WINDOWS\EXPLORER.EXE /n,/e,C:\`.

4. Change the "C:\" at the end of this entry to the drive and directory of your choice. Entering "C:\Projects," for example, will force Explorer to launch with a view of the Projects directory

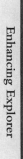

Enhancing Explorer

| **WARNING** | If you enter a target drive/path combination that does not exist, Windows Explorer displays an error message and will not launch properly. |

> **TIP** Place a "/root" option in this target entry if you want Explorer to open with your new folder as the root. Example:
> C:\WINDOWS\EXPLORER.EXE /n,/e,/root, "C:\Blah" makes C:\Blah the root directory in this Explorer view. Specifying a "root" folder limits your ability to access parent folders or navigate upward in a directory structure.

5. Click OK to close the Property sheet.

This change will take effect immediately. For more flexibility, create additional Explorer shortcuts that point to other folders you frequently use. Don't forget to rename the shortcuts with descriptive titles.

1.7.3 Add Hyperlinks to Explorer

Windows 98's Active Desktop capability lets you add a new dimension to the Windows Explorer—Web links. By customizing the Active Desktop, you can embed Web hyperlinks within individual folders. When you view these customized folders, you'll see both the files residing on your hard drive and the link to the Web sites you've included. If you select the Web link, the Internet Explorer immediately connects to the Web and displays the site.

This feature is particularly useful for software applications or utilities. It's easy to check in with a company about the latest news or product updates if the company's Web site is listed right next to their program's files on your hard disk.

Follow these steps to embed a Web link in a folder under Windows Explorer:

1. Open Windows Explorer by selecting it under the Start | Programs item on the Start menu.

2. Browse the folder you want to customize. This example uses C:\Program Files\SnadBoy Software\Revelation. This folder stores Snadboy Software's Revelation utility (which is described in the Administration section of this book).

3. From Windows Explorer's menus, choose View | Customize This Folder. Windows 98 will launch the Customize This Folder wizard (see Figure 1.7.2).

4. Mark the entry labeled Create or Edit an HTML Document. This is the default choice, so it will probably be marked already. Click the Next button.

5. Click the instructions on editing a HyperText Template and then click the Next button again.

6. Windows 98 will launch the Notepad editor and automatically open a file called FOLDER.HTT. Click the Maximize tool (the square in the upper

right-hand corner between the X and _), so that you'll have a better view
of the template.

Figure 1.7.2

*Use the
Customization
wizard to embed
a hyperlink in a
folder.*

7. Scroll down to the bottom of the template. Near the bottom of the file
    you'll see a comment reading: HERE'S A GOOD PLACE TO ADD A FEW
    LINKS OF YOUR OWN.

> **TIP** To quickly get to a particular line in Notepad, use the Search|Find
> choice from the Edit menu.

8. Beneath this line, you'll see a line reading: <!-- (examples commented
    out). You want to use these lines following this one so you must close the
    comment brackets here. To do this, add the characters -- >. Your line
    should then read:

    `<!-- (examples commented out) -- >`

9. Find the entry, three lines down, reading: <a href="http://
    www.mylink1.com/">Custom Link 1</a>. This is the line in which you
    will add your Web link. Remove the mylink1 characters and replace them
    with the URL of the Web site to which you want to link. Then remove
    the link title Custom Link 1 and replace it with the title of your choice.
    In my Snadboy example, the line becomes:

    `<a href="http://www.snadboy.com/">SnadBoy Software</a>`

10. If you want to add a second Web link, then modify the line reading "<a
    href="http://www.mylink2.com/">Custom Link 2</a>" in the same
    manner as in Step 9. If you do not want to add another link, you must
    comment out this second hyperlink by surrounding the line with the
    comment brackets. Here's how the line would look when it is com-
    mented out:

```
<!-- <a href="http://www.mylink2.com/">Custom Link 2</a> -- >
```

11. When you've finished modifying this secton of the template, choose File|Save from the menus. This saves the template.

12. Select File|Exit from the menus to close the Notepad editor.

13. Click the Finish button on the last screen of the Customize This Folder wizard. The Snadboy Software example will look like the screen in Figure 1.7.3.

Figure 1.7.3

In one screen you can browse a program's files or jump to the software developer's Web page.

The Windows Explorer will immediately update its screen and show this change.

Chapter

1.8

Miscellaneous

Some hints can't easily be categorized, but are incredibly useful nonetheless. This chapter describes how to erase Windows 98's tracking features, convert to the metric system, enhance the controls of the ActiveMovie Player, and more.

1.8.1 Make Yourself a Ghost

Do you share a PC with colleagues or members of your family? If you do, you've probably already stumbled across the imprints of other users on your system. Windows 98 retains all kinds of information about each PC session. It tracks the Web sites you browse, the documents you open, the files for which you search, and even the entries you make in the Run item of Start menu. And, although this is a convenience for sole users of a PC, this residual information can lead to frustration on shared systems.

The easiest way to delete most of the evidence of your PC session is through the TweakUI utility. Follow these steps to "cover your tracks" during PC use:

1. Launch TweakUI under Start | Settings | Control Panel. (Read the section in the Introduction about TweakUI if you don't find this item on your Start menu.)

2. Select the Paranoia tab. You might have to use the left-right scroll arrows at the top of the dialog box to find the Paranoia tab. It should be the farthest tab to the right (see Figure 1.8.1).

Figure 1.8.1

Use the Paranoia tab of the TweakUI utility to delete evidence of your last PC session.

3. Scroll through the list in the aptly named Covering Your Tracks text box. You'll probably want to place a check next to each of the eight items in the list. Checking these entries forces Windows 98 to clear session

information at the next user logon. To erase the evidence immediately, click the Clear Selected Items Now button.

4. Click OK to close TweakUI.

For an additional "ghosting" procedure, check hint 1.5.1.

1.8.2 Convert to Metric

Better software applications access Windows 98's Regional Settings before they display information such as dates, times, monetary values, and so on. This way, an application can personalize data with the correct format and symbols for your country.

Here's a quick trick to help you learn the metric measuring system that is used throughout most of world, excluding, of course, the United States.

Access the Regional Settings Property sheet. You'll find it under Start | Settings | Control Panel. Select the Number tab. The second-to-the-last item is Measurement System. Use the drop-down menu to select Metric instead of U.S. (see Figure 1.8.2).

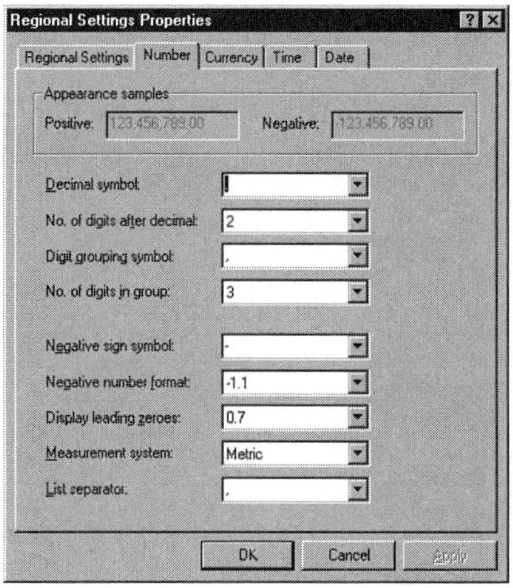

Figure 1.8.2

Change to the metric measuring system in the Regional Settings Property sheet.

Keep in mind that software that doesn't access Windows 98's regional settings will not display metric measurements even after you make this change.

1.8.3 Control your Video

In the old days, when you selected a video clip via the Windows Explorer, you launched the Media Player utility. Now, with the advent of Microsoft's

Miscellaneous

ActiveMovie technology, this action will most likely launch the ActiveMovie
Control utility (but this depends on how your file associations are set up).

The default settings for the ActiveMovie Control are the most basic—just the
Start, Stop, and Pause buttons and a slider bar that enables you to scroll forward or
backward in the movie. You can, however, access a more extensive set of controls.
Among other things, the expanded controls let you mark segments of video with
time stamps so that you can quickly set up a clip for recording. The full set of
movie controls is most useful for video editing.

Follow these steps to configure the ActiveMovie Control for the advanced video
controls:

1. Launch the ActiveMovie Control by selecting a video clip from the
   Windows Explorer or by choosing the ActiveMovie Control under
   Start | Programs | Accessories. If you launch the utility from the Start menu,
   you'll have to immediately open a video clip file.

> **TIP**   Looking for some sample video clip files? Browse the
> Cdsample\videos\ directory of the Windows 98 installation disc. You'll
> find over 30 MPEG and AVI files, most of which advertise Microsoft software.

2. Right-click on the ActiveMovie Control window. Then select Properties
   from the pop-up menu.

3. Choose the Controls tab from the Properties sheet. Then place a check
   next to the Control Panel item and, for the full set of controls, check each
   of the three sub-items within the Control Panel box: Position Controls,
   Selection Controls, and Trackbar.

> **TIP**   Playing a video as an "endless loop" turns your PC into an informa-
> tion kiosk—or a truly annoying distraction, depending on what you
> play back. To set a video to play repeatedly, choose the Auto Repeat radio button on
> the Playback tab of the ActiveMovie Control Properties sheet.

4. Click OK to close the ActiveMovie Control Property sheet.

The new controls will immediately appear on your ActiveMovie Control
window.

1.8.4 Change Your Desktop with Every Boot

Change is constant, so why not go with the flow and switch your display's properties every time you start up your computer? There's no way to set this up within Windows 98 itself, but you can download a shareware utility called Media Changer Deluxe that will do this switch for you.

Media Changer Deluxe installs itself into your Windows Startup folder. Then each time you power up, it switches your background wallpaper or your entire desktop theme, if you've installed the sample desktop themes available on the Windows 98 CD.

The utility also loads its icon into the System Tray for convenience. You can quickly alter the settings or cancel Media Changer's modifications by right-clicking on the icon.

As with all shareware, Media Changer Deluxe is free to try, but Swoosie Software (the creators) ask that you pay an $18 fee when you register the program.

Follow these steps to download and install Media Changer Deluxe:

1. Point your Web browser to PC World's FileWorld site (`www.fileworld.com`). You can either use the Search FileWorld tool to look for Media Changer, or just enter the URL in your browser. The location for Media Changer Deluxe is: `http://www.pcworld.com/fileworld/file_description/frameset/0,1458,1367,00.html`.

2. Click the mcdeluxe.zip hyperlink to display the download page.

3. Select Download File Now! to begin the download process. Save the file as MCDELUXE.ZIP to a temporary folder on your hard drive. It's about 1MB, so the download might take a few minutes on slower computers.

4. This file has been compressed with the Zip format, so you'll need a Zip decompression utility such as PKWare's PKZip for Windows (`www.pkware.com`) to unzip it prior to installation.

> **TIP** Media Changer Deluxe switches the entire desktop theme, not just the background wallpaper. But you must have some themes installed for this to work. The Windows 98 CD includes several sample desktop themes. To install them, run through the following steps. Select Start | Settings | Control Panel from the Start menu. Choose Add/Remove Programs. Pick the Windows Setup tab in the Add/Remove Programs Properties sheet. In the Components list, put a check next to the Desktop Themes item. Insert your Windows 98 CD into your CD-ROM drive, then click the OK button. Windows will install the themes from the CD.

Miscellaneous

5. After you've decompressed the file into a temporary directory, choose the utility's SETUP.EXE executable file from within Windows Explorer. This program will install Media Changer Deluxe and load the program into the Startup folder and into the System Tray.

To alter Media Changer's settings, right-click on the System Tray icon and choose Configure Media Changer Deluxe from the pop-up list (see Figure 1.8.3).

Figure 1.8.3

Configure Media Changer Deluxe to alter the background every few minutes or just once during startup.

1.8.5 Make Your Keyboard Sound Off

I don't know about you, but I believe the Caps Lock key is in the wrong place on the keyboard. Why? Because I press it accidentally several times daily when I reach for the left Shift key. SUDDENLY, I FIND MYSELF TYPING WITH ALL CAPS.

Oh, this happens to you too, does it? Actually, it happens to most people (at least, to most touch typists), because they're not looking at the keyboard.

Wouldn't it be nice if Windows warned you when you pressed the Caps Lock key? Ask and you shall receive.

Follow these steps to make Windows sound off when you press the Caps Lock key:

1. From the Start menu, choose Start | Settings | Control Panel.

2. Select the Accessibility Options item.

3. Pick the Keyboard tab in the Accessibility Properties sheet.

4. In the ToggleKeys box, put a check next to Use ToggleKeys.

> **TIP** Would you like the Caps Lock warning even if you don't have your PC speakers turned on? Run through the steps in this hint, then add the following steps. In the Accessibility Properties sheet, select the Sound tab. Put a check next to Use SoundSentry, then click the Settings button. In the Warning For Windowed Programs drop-down box, select Flash Desktop. Now, Windows will flash the display, as well as beep, when you press the Caps Lock key.

5. Click the OK button.

You don't need to restart the PC to hear this change.

Miscellaneous

Chapter

1.9

Altering the Active Desktop

The Active Desktop creates a seamless link between your computer and the Internet. Unfortunately, the Windows 98 documentation does a very poor job of describing how you can customize this new interface.

In this chapter, you'll learn how to turn your computer into an information kiosk, clean up the overloaded Channel Bar, and perform other neat tricks.

1.9.1 Change Your Web Search Engine

Windows 98 enables you to begin a search of the World Wide Web directly from the Start menu. Choosing Start | Find | On the Internet brings up the Internet Explorer browser and your default Web search site.

But this convenience quickly becomes a hassle when you decide you want to change search engines. Internet Explorer makes it easy to modify your Home page setting through its View | Internet Options menu item, but you won't find a search engine listing here. You need to edit the Registry to make this change.

To modify your Web search page, use the following steps:

1. Launch the Registry Editor by entering **regedit** at the Start | Run prompt.

2. Navigate to the following key: HKEY_CURRENT_USERS\Software\ Microsoft\Internet Explorer\Main.

3. Select the Search Page String Value, then enter your new search engine's

TIP	You can also quickly search the Internet by entering **?** *keywords* on Internet Explorer's Address Bar.

URL in the Value Data field of the Edit String dialog box.

4. Click OK to close the dialog box and the exit the Registry editor.

Read Appendix A, "Useful Web Sites," for interesting Web search engine alternatives.

1.9.2 Display Active Channel Content in a Screen Saver

Let's face it, most screen savers are either pretty pictures or some mediocre attempt at humor. Without much difficulty, though, you can transform your monitor into a useful information kiosk during screen saver down time.

The key: Windows 98's Active Desktop. Before you walk through this hint you should subscribe to some Active Channel sites. Your Channels will be the information sources for this tip. If you need instructions on adding Active Channels to your desktop, launch Windows Help (under Start | Help), and search the help system with the keyword "channels."

> **NOTE** The phrase "screen saver" has become a misnomer. It's been passed down since the early PC days when monitors could actually be damaged by, and "burn in," an unchanging display. Modern monitors no longer have this problem.
>
> You don't need to use a screen saver to avoid monitor damage. Only use one for fun or for a password protection mode against intruders.

Here's how to turn your desktop into an information terminal when it goes into screen saver mode.

1. Right-click a blank space on the desktop. Then select Properties from the pop-up menu to bring up the Display Properties sheet.

2. Choose the Screen Saver tab.

3. In the Screen Saver box, click the drop-down box arrow and scroll through the list of screen savers until you find Channel Screen Saver. Select this item.

> **TIP** Press **C** to jump down the list to the first screen saver that starts with the letter C.

4. Now, click the Settings button to display a list of your Channel subscriptions. Select the subscriptions you want to run in a slide-show during Windows screen saver mode. Also in this dialog box, choose the number of seconds you want each "slide" to be visible and whether or not you want to hear audio.

5. Click OK to close the Screen Saver Properties sheet. Then click OK to exit the Display Properties sheet.

1.9.3 Clean Up the Channel Bar

You can't help but wonder about the negotiations that decided the layout of the Windows 98 Channel Bar. How did Disney gain a top slot instead of a listing underneath the Entertainment heading? Who decided which sites would be listed beneath the Business category and what criteria did they use? Did money change hands in these discussions? Hmmm.

Don't let Microsoft set the layout of your Channel Bar. It's very unlikely you'll subscribe to all the Web sites in the default list. In fact, you might want to delete entire categories even after viewing the multimedia ads included with Windows 98.

Your best bet is to pick a few interesting sites and place them on the top of the Channel Bar then delete the remaining links.

Follow these steps to move sites to the top of the Channel Bar:

1. Using the Channel Bar, navigate to the site you want to move. For example, for Companies Online, select the Business category. Your first click on the Channel Bar launches Internet Explorer.

2. Right-click on the icon you want to move. Then select Cut from the pop-up menu.

3. Close Internet Explorer.

4. Right-click a blank space on the desktop. Then select Paste from the pop-up menu. This will post the site's link onto your desktop. And the link will be removed from the Channel Bar sub-menu where you first found it.

5. Now, drag the link onto the Channel Bar. By moving the mouse up and down the Channel Bar, you can drop the icon into any position you like.

These changes will take effect immediately.

To delete any unwanted Channel Bar items, navigate to a link or a category. Right-click on the entry and then select Delete from the pop-up menu.

For the finishing touch, increase or decrease the size of the Channel Bar (by dragging the window edges in or out) to fit your new icon layout.

1.9.4 Use New Fonts with Internet Explorer

It's easy to change the font settings for a single Internet Explorer session. From IE's View menu, you can select fonts and pick the size and international alphabet type from the pop-up list. However, these font choices all revert back to the default settings when you exit the application.

For permanent Internet Explorer font settings, follow these steps:

1. Launch Internet Explorer under Start | Programs | Internet Explorer.

2. Select View | Internet Options from the menu bar, then choose the General tab of the Internet Options sheet.

3. Click the Fonts button at the bottom of the General tab to display the Fonts sheet (see Figure 1.9.1).

Figure 1.9.1

Use Internet Explorer's Font sheet to make your font changes permanent.

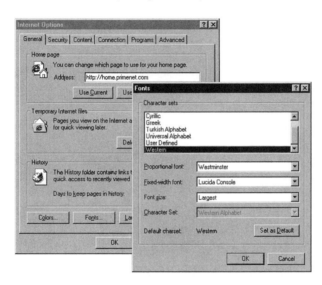

4. On the Fonts sheet, choose your Character Set (Western for U.S. users) from the scrolling list. Then select your Proportional Font, Fixed Width Font, and Font Size from the drop-down lists.

5. Internet Explorer retains these new font settings even after you exit the application, but to make them even more permanent, you can select the Set as Default button on the Font sheet. This will replace IE's default font settings with yours.

6. Click OK to exit the Fonts sheet, then click OK to exit IE's Internet Options.

This change will take effect immediately.

Altering the Active Desktop

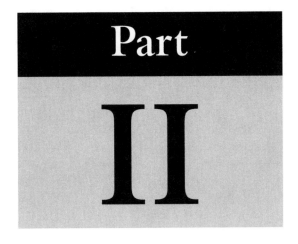

Part

II

Productivity

Even nerds need an occasional break from the computer. Wouldn't it be great if you could do a week's worth of work in two and a half days? Well, I can't promise that level of efficiency, but if you implement all of the tips in this section, I guarantee you could work smarter and faster than you do now. Besides, saved seconds add up to minutes, and saved minutes add up to hours.

The flexibility of Windows 98 is astounding. You can perform almost every task in more than one way. In this section, I'll show you the fastest and most effective way to perform these tasks. Like we did in Part I, "Look and Feel," we'll cover tips for the Taskbar and Start menu, the Active Desktop, Internet Explorer 4, the command line, and more. You'll also find ways to cut down troubleshooting time.

Analyze the tasks you do and determine which chapters would benefit you most. Or go ahead and read the entire section. Then plan your vacation for the second half of this week!

Chapter

2.1

Right-Click Fun

Windows's right-click context menu provides fast access to tools and tasks. This chapter describes how to customize the right-click menu, enhance the Quick View utility, and add encryption capability.

2.1.1 Modify the Send To Pop-Up Menu

One of the most effective productivity tools within Windows 98 is the Send To right-click menu item. Within Windows Explorer, My Computer, or for objects on the desktop, Send To lets you quickly transport a file to a new location.

To make this feature even more effective, you should customize the Send To list to suit your work. You can easily add your printer, fax, modem, or other device to the list. Or you can set up project folders and forego the regular file move and copy procedures.

Follow these steps to modify the Windows 98 Send To list:

1. Bring up the Run dialog box by selecting the Run item from the Start menu.

2. Enter **sendto** into the Run dialog box. This displays the SendTo folder and its list of current objects. You can also access this folder via the Windows Explorer. You will find the folder listed as the C:\Windows\SendTo subdirectory.

3. To delete an object from the SendTo list, right-click on it and choose Delete from the pop-up menu.

4. To add objects to the SendTo list, drag and drop them into the SendTo folder. You can select items from the Windows Explorer, the desktop, or any other location.

5. Close the folder by selecting the X (close) button in the upper right-hand corner of the window, or by choosing File | Close from the menu items.

Your changes to the SendTo list take effect immediately.

2.1.2 Enhance Quick View

Windows 98 includes a viewer utility called Quick View. It enables you to look into files without the time-consuming procedure of launching the related software application. For example, you can browse a Word document without launching Microsoft's Word application.

The Quick View utility is much smaller in size than any software application, and therefore it loads more quickly into memory. For this reason, it's a great tool for quickly scanning files, spreadsheets, and image files.

> **NOTE** Microsoft preloads over 30 Quick View templates for different types of files in Windows 98. Each template targets a particular file extension type such as .DOC (Word document), .BMP (bitmap), .TXT (text file), and so forth. The list includes templates for word processing documents, spreadsheets, image files, and system files.
>
> You won't find any reference to this template list in the Windows Help system, but you can find it in the Registry. To view the complete list, launch the Registry editor (Regedit) and navigate to this key: My Computer\HKEY_CLASSES_ROOT\ QuickView. Below this key, the Registry stores all the Quick View templates referenced by the associated file extensions (such as .INF, .BMP, and so on). Double-click these subkeys to display a text description for each template in the Regedit's right-hand pane.

To launch the tool, simply right-click on a file (under Windows Explorer, My Computer, or on the desktop) and choose Quick View from the pop-up menu. Unfortunately, only Quick View-enabled file types will display the Quick View choice on the pop-up menu.

You can activate the Quick View option for any registered file type by following these steps:

1. From the Start menu, choose Settings | Folder Options.

2. Select the File Types tab of the Folder Options sheet.

3. Highlight an entry in the Registered File Types list (GIF image, for example), then click the Edit button.

4. On the Edit File Type sheet, put a check next to the Enable Quick View item (see Figure 2.1.1).

If, however, your Windows 98 system does not contain a template for this new file type, Quick View will use its default template, which might display the file as a mess of unreadable characters. New applications might load new Quick View templates during the installation process, but this isn't always the case. To get a large set of new templates you can buy Quick View Plus from Inso (www.inso.com), the creators of the Quick View tool.

Right-Click Fun

Figure 2.1.1

Place a check next to Enable Quick View to activate the Quick View option on a new file type.

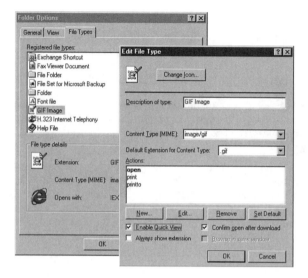

> **TIP** At some point you'll encounter text files that don't use the standard .TXT extension. People often save configuration files, for example, using their initials for the three characters of the file extension.
>
> Here's a trick that will let you view any unregistered file type through Quick View's default viewer. Using the Registry Editor (Regedit), navigate to the following key: My Computer\HKEY_CLASSES_ROOT*\. Create a new key beneath this key and call it QuickView. Then exit the Registry.
>
> After you perform this Registry hack, right-clicking on any file type will show the Quick View option.

2.1.3 Encrypt Your Files

Almost every PC contains files that need protection against intruders, whether it's personal financial information on home systems or corporate confidential data on business systems. The problem is that most encryption software is a hassle to use. The extra time involved in securing files often slows down workflow.

The Austrian company FIM has solved this convenience problem for Windows 98 PCs. You can download their CodedDrag shareware and install it for a free trial. CodedDrag loads itself into Windows Explorer's right-click context menu, so that you can encrypt files with just a couple of mouse clicks.

Better still, CodedDrag is flexible with its encryption schemes. You can create your own encryption keys and you can shift from a good 56-bit encryption algorithm to a very secure 448-bit encryption scheme.

Follow these steps to download and install CodedDrag:

1. Launch the Internet Explorer by choosing Start | Programs | Internet Explorer | Internet Explorer. Or, start your alternative Web browser.

2. Enter the following URL into the Address bar: **http://www.pcworld.com/fileworld/filedescription/frameset/0,1458,4895,00.html**.

> **TIP** You don't need to type in this long Web address. You can also just browse PC World's FileWorld site at **www.fileworld.com** and use the Search FileWorld utility to find "CodedDrag."

3. Select the hyperlink for the file CD2100EE.EXE. You'll find it in the Download box near the top of the Web page.

4. Choose the Download File Now! hyperlink to begin the download. Save the file CD2100EE.EXE to a folder on your hard drive.

5. This download is a self-extracting Zip file, so you don't need a decompression utility. Just select the file CD2100EE.EXE in Windows Explorer and the program will extract the data files to its current folder.

6. Select the SETUP.EXE program from the list of files under Windows Explorer. Follow the instructions to complete the easy installation routine.

CodedDrag installs itself into the right-click context menu of Windows Explorer. After the installation, right-clicking any file or folder presents you with two new options—Encrypt and Decrypt (see Figure 2.1.2).

Right-Click Fun

Figure 2.1.2
CodedDrag stores its Encrypt and Decrypt choices conveniently on the right-click menu.

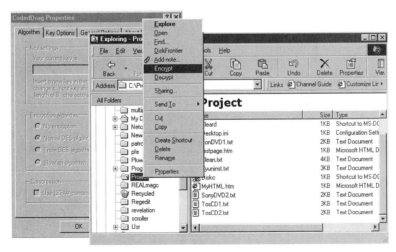

When you choose the Encrypt option CodedDrag will ask you to input your *key*. It should be at least eight characters and a combination of letters, numbers, and punctuation marks.

To modify the program's setting, select the CodedDrag shortcut (which looks like a padlock) that the setup program installed onto your desktop. This action displays the CodedDrag Properties sheet (see Figure 2.1.3). On the Algorithm tab you can switch to the more secure Blowfish encryption scheme. The Key Options tab lets you set whether or not the program should remember your encryption keys for you.

Figure 2.1.3

The CodedDrag Properties sheet lets you modify the encryption settings.

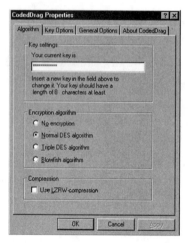

FIM asks that you send them $29 if you plan to use the program past a 30-day evaluation period. You'll find their address listed in the ORDER.TXT file in the program's folder.

Chapter 2.2

Mega Mouse

Depending on your setup, your mouse could be your best friend or simply a desktop pest. Here you'll find out how to tame the mouse, or just do without it altogether.

2.2.1 Move Your Cursor Without Your Mouse

Many computer tasks involve both keyboard and mouse input. But switching back and forth between the two often slows you down. Most people need to take their eyes off of the screen as they find where they last left the mouse and then again when they go to reposition their fingers in the "home" position on the keyboard. Wouldn't it be easier if your keyboard alone were adequate for these tasks?

Windows 98's MouseKeys feature lets you control your mouse pointer through the numeric keypad of your keyboard (that's the adding machine-like key layout to the far right on most standard 101-key desktop keyboards).

You'll need the Accessibility Options installed on your Windows 98 system to access MouseKeys. If you don't have them installed, use the Windows Setup tab under the Add/Remove Programs icon in the Control Panel to add this component to your PC.

To activate MouseKeys, use the follow procedure:

1. Choose Accessibility Options from the Control Panel (at Start|Settings|Control Panel).

2. Select the Mouse tab of the Accessibility Properties sheet.

3. Put a check next to the Use MouseKeys entry in the MouseKeys box. Now, when the NumLock key on your keyboard is on (a light shines above the key indicating when your NumLock key is activated), your keypad moves your mouse pointer up (8), down (2), left (4) and right (6). The Plus (+) key becomes the left mouse button. You can even drag items by pressing the 5 key. The status of your MouseKeys is displayed in the small mouse icon in the System Tray on the right-hand side of the taskbar.

4. Wait! You're not done. You need to adjust the default settings to make this feature really useful. To modify the defaults, click the Settings button on this page.

5. On the Settings for MouseKeys sheet (see figure 2.2.1), in the Pointer Speed box, slide both the Top Speed and Acceleration sliders to the far right. Then put a check next to the entry that reads: Hold Down Ctrl to Speed Up and Shift to Slow Down. This will make the pointer move

more quickly across the desktop. To cover large distances quickly, hold down the Ctrl key while you move the mouse; for fine pointer control, hold down the Shift key while you move it.

Figure 2.2.1
Modify the Settings for the MouseKeys to increase the speed of your new keyboard mouse.

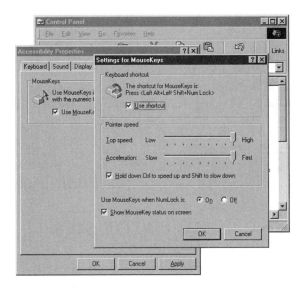

> **NOTE** For a look under the covers, browse the following Registry key using the Registry Editor (regedit): My Computer\HKEY_CURRENT_USER\Control Panel\Accessibility\MouseKeys. Here you'll find all the numeric values for the MouseKey settings. However, it's best to modify these values within the Control Panel.

2.2.2 Maximize Your Mouse's Scroll Wheel

Several new mouse devices feature a small scroll wheel embedded between the left and right mouse buttons. While browsing documents, spreadsheets, or even within Windows Explorer, you can use this wheel to scroll up and down instead of using the scroll bar and buttons provided on the application window.

By default, the wheel scrolls by only three lines at a time with each ratcheted turn of the wheel. You can, however, modify this setting, so that the wheel scrolls more quickly through pages.

To increase the scroll rate of your embedded mouse wheel, use the following steps:

1. Select the mouse icon from the Control Panel (under Start | Settings | Control Panel).

Mega Mouse

2. Choose the Wheel tab of the Mouse Properties sheet.

3. If there is no check next to Turn On the Wheel inside the Wheel box, place one there now. Then click the Settings button.

4. Inside the Scrolling box, either choose the Scroll *X* Lines at a Time radio button or the Scroll one screen at a Time radio button. If you choose Scroll *X* Lines at a Time, enter a number between 1 and 24.

> **NOTE**   Windows 98 will set the number of scroll lines to a maximum of 24 (a page's worth) even if you enter a larger number in the Settings for Wheel sheet.

> **TIP**   You can also adjust these same Mouse Wheel settings via the TweakUI utility.

2.2.3 Increase Your Mouse's Sensitivity

No, your mouse device doesn't have any emotions, thankfully. But, Windows does use sensitivity settings for the mouse so that it can correctly interpret when you double-click and drag objects.

By default, Windows mouse settings are fairly unforgiving. For example: If you move your mouse more than two pixels (a tiny distance) on the screen between the first and second click of a double-click, Windows assumes you didn't really intend to double-click anything and it won't respond.

If you find Windows ignoring your double-clicks, you need to adjust these mouse sensitivity settings. And, for that, we'll use the TweakUI utility.

Follow these steps to adjust your mouse sensitivity settings:

1. Launch the TweakUI utility under Start | Settings | Control Panel. Read the introduction for instructions on installing TweakUI if you haven't already done so.

2. Click the Mouse tab of TweakUI (see Figure 2.2.2).

3. Find the Double-Click entry field in the Mouse Sensitivity box. Use the up scroll arrow to increase the Double-Click setting. Start with a setting of "5" or "6." You can increase it again in a moment if those settings aren't high enough.

4. Test the setting by double-clicking the Test Icon to the right of the Mouse Sensitivity box. Move your mouse slightly, as you normally would when

working quickly, between the first and second clicks. The gears pictured will shift positions if Windows recognizes your double-click. If you'd like to increase the setting even more, go back to step 3 and crank the Double-Click setting to "9" or "10."

Figure 2.2.2

Use TweakUI to increase the pixel area for mouse double-clicks.

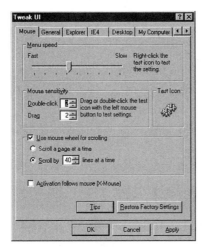

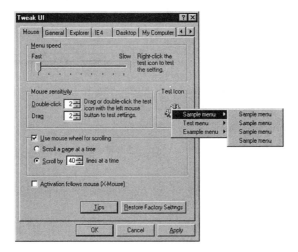

TIP   While you're viewing the Mouse sheet of TweakUI, you might want to make another helpful productivity adjustment. In the Menu Speed box, drag the slider bar to the far left (under Fast). This setting increases the speed at which Windows will display submenus on the Start menu and right-click menus. Test the setting by right-clicking on the Test Icon. Windows will bring up sample menus at your new speedy rate (see Figure 2.2.3)

Figure 2.2.3

Give your menus a pick-me-up by adjusting the Menu Speed slider bar.

Mega Mouse

5. Click the OK button to save your new mouse settings to the Registry.

These changes happen immediately. There's no need to restart your system.

2.2.4 Make Your Mouse Left-Handed

Most lefties just suffer with ill-suited computer input devices. Standard keyboards and mouse devices are designed for right-handers; a keyboard's numeric keyboard usually lies to the right of the QWERTY keys and most mouse devices curve at the tail to fit a right-hander's palm.

If you're left-handed, consider investing in specially designed input devices (see tip). But, without spending any money, you can customize your mouse under Windows for use with your left hand.

> **TIP**   For left-handed computer input devices, check with the New Zealand mail-order company The Left Center. You'll find their Web site at `http://www.lefty.co.nz/`.

Follow these steps to make your mouse function with your left hand:

1. Choose Start | Settings | Control Panel from the Start menu. Then select the Mouse object from the list on the Control Panel.

2. Pick the Basics tab.

3. Find the Button Selection box. If you use a two-button mouse and you want to switch the buttons for left-handed use, select the Right radio button. This switches the function of the left and right mouse buttons for lefties. If you use a three-button mouse, select the Other radio button. Then click the More Buttons button. Follow the instructions that have you select which buttons do what on a three-button mouse.

4. Wait! You're not done. You should set the orientation of your mouse because you will switch it from the right to the left of your keyboard. Pick the Productivity tab of the Mouse Properties sheet.

5. In the Orientation box, click the Set Orientation button.

6. Windows displays an initial instruction screen. Hold your mouse in a comfortable working position (in its new location to the left of your keyboard). Then click the Next button.

7. Windows shows you a little motor-skills game (see Figure 2.2.4). Drag the racing car through the checkered flags to set your mouse orientation. Click the Next button.

Figure 2.2.4

Baby, you can drive my car: Set your new left-handed mouse orientation.

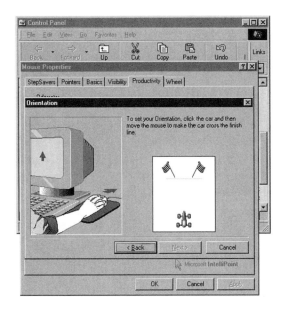

8. Move your mouse pointer around the screen. If you like its response, click the Finish button. If not, click the Back button and play the car game again.

9. To save your new left-handed settings, click the OK button of the Mouse Properties sheet.

These changes happen immediately. There's no need to restart Windows.

Mega Mouse

Chapter

2.3

More Effective Use of the Taskbar and Start Menu

Most of your Windows 98 tasks begin with the Start menu and Taskbar. Here are some tips that will make these fundamental elements more productive for you.

2.3.1 Restart Your Taskbar Without Restarting Windows

New software installation procedures often request that you restart Windows before you begin using an application. Additionally, simply altering settings in the Windows 98 Control Panel might require a restart before changes take effect. You'll even find Registry hacks in this book where an operating system restart is needed.

Windows 98 is faster than Windows 95 with startups and restarts. But even a short time spent waiting for your system to recycle is time wasted.

There is a way to restart only your Windows Taskbar and the desktop without recycling the entire operating system. This procedure is equivalent to a full restart for many system changes.

Use the following procedure to restart Windows 98's Taskbar and desktop:

1. Simultaneously press the **CTRL**, **ALT**, and **DELETE** keys on your keyboard. This action displays the Close Program dialog box.

2. Choose the Explorer (the Windows desktop shell program) item from the list of active programs on your system. Then press the End Task button at the bottom of the dialog box.

> **TIP**   To quickly refresh the look of the Windows desktop, right-click a blank space on the desktop and choose Refresh from the pop-up menu. However, this action simply updates your desktop object icons, their titles, and their positioning. It does not update your system configuration in the way that most system changes require.

3. The Shut Down Windows dialog box now appears. Click the Cancel button here. You do not want to shut down your operating system.

4. Even though you've pressed Cancel, the operating system will still try to terminate the Explorer shell as you requested in step 2. Therefore, after a few seconds, you'll see an Explorer dialog box appear that states that the program is not responding (because it's busy running your desktop). On this screen, click the End Task button. Now, your Taskbar and icons will disappear momentarily as the Explorer shell restarts.

> | NOTE | Be aware that restarting the Explorer shell can affect your Internet-connected Active Desktop. After Explorer restarts you might see a message titled: Active Desktop Recovery. Within the text of this message you'll see an underlined choice called Restore My Active Desktop. Select this option to restart your Active Desktop. |
> | --- | --- |
>
> On some systems, this Active Desktop restoration process unloads programs from your system tray. If this happens to your system, you might be better off simply restarting your system normally, when necessary, rather than use this shortcut approach.

2.3.2 Manage the System Tray

The System Tray takes up prime real estate on the Windows 98 Taskbar. In a default setup, the System Tray resides in the right-hand bottom corner of your desktop screen. It's the box with the tiny icons and, depending on your configuration, a small clock.

You cannot drag and drop objects onto the System Tray, like you can with the Taskbar. This resource is a reserved "parking space," where software applications can load small programs during installation routines.

These System Tray programs perform a variety of tasks. You might, for example, have a special display driver program (such as Matrox Graphics' DeskNav) in your System Tray that lets you introduce special video effects. Or you might also have an uninstallation routine (like Symantec's Norton Uninstall Deluxe) that constantly monitors new software installations so that they can be removed completely at a later time.

The good news: Windows 98 includes a special tool, called Quick Tray, that lets you quickly add or remove your own items to and from the System Tray. Quick Tray (see Figure 2.3.1) comes with the Sample Resource Kit utilities. So, read the introduction if you haven't already installed these special tools.

Figure 2.3.1

Quick Tray lets you add and remove programs from the Windows 98 System Tray.

You can launch Quick Tray by simply entering **quick tray** at the Start|Run prompt. Or you can access Quick Tray via the Microsoft Management Console (under Start|Programs).

After it has been launched, simply click Quick Tray's Add and Remove buttons to create your own System Tray menu. You can either enter the path to an application or click the Browse button to search through your directories.

> **NOTE** Quick Tray doesn't enable you to unload items already placed on the System Tray by the Windows Registry. To remove items loaded on the System Tray during startup, use the System Configuration Utility.

Another useful aspect of Quick Tray is its portability. Read Part 4, "Administration," to find out how to quickly customize several PCs with the same Quick Tray menu.

2.3.3 Store Text and URLs on Your System Tray

The super-organized have a place for everything and put everything in its place. Then there's the rest of us. Often during a computing session, you'll stumble across a passage of text, either in a desktop file or on the Web, that you want to save. Or you'll encounter a Web URL that you think you might want to pass along to someone else or record in a document. The problem is that you need a temporary repository in which to store all this information while you ponder exactly where it belongs.

That's where the ClipTray tool comes in handy. Microsoft includes ClipTray with the Sample Resource Kit tools stored on the Windows 98 installation disc. Read the introduction if you haven't already installed these tools.

ClipTray loads into the System Tray and lets you store text and URLs in a concise and organized way while you decide what to do with them. It uses the Windows clipboard for storage, but unlike normal cutting and pasting procedures that utilize the Windows clipboard, ClipTray enables you to name entries with memory-jogging words and phrases. You can even modify entries whenever you like or reorder the positions of items already stored there.

Launch ClipTray by entering **cliptray** at the Start | Run prompt. Or select the Microsoft Management Console (from Start | Programs) and choose it from the Windows 98 Resource Kit Sampler console. ClipTray loads directly into the Windows System Tray (in the right-hand corner of the Taskbar in default setups).

After it is loaded, double-click on the ClipTray icon, which looks like a small clipboard, to display the Add New ClipTray Entry dialog box (see Figure 2.3.2). Here you can label your text and URL entries with relevant titles.

To access the other features of ClipTray, right-click on the ClipTray icon and select either Options (for editing existing items) or More (to reorganize the list of current entries) from the pop-up menu (see Figure 2.3.3). You can also select Help in the pop-up menu to display detailed help screens.

Figure 2.3.2

ClipTray lets you label text and URL entries with memory-jogging words or phrases.

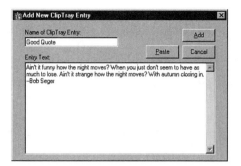

Figure 2.3.3

You can reorganize and edit ClipTray entries at any time.

2.3.4 Speed up the Start Menu

Beginners usually don't mind all that much when computer software runs slowly—it's easier for them to follow along that way. Perhaps this is why the default setting for the Start bar's cascading menus is Medium.

Experienced users never enjoy waiting on software. So, to increase your productivity under Windows 98, you'll want to modify the Start menu speed setting.

Use the following procedure to speed up Windows 98's cascading menus:

1. Launch TweakUI under Start | Settings | Control Panel. If you don't find TweakUI listed here, read the introduction to find out how to install the Sample Resource Kit utilities.

2. Select the Mouse tab.

3. In the Menu Speed box, drag the slider bar all the way to the left to maximize menu speed (see Figure 2.3.4).

2.3.5 Reach Out and Touch the Start Menu

Why force your mouse to scurry around the Start menu when a few quick clicks of the keyboard will get you to your destination faster? Without any modification, you can activate a Start menu item by pressing the keyboard key that matches the underlined character on the menu item ("P" for Programs, for example). But, there's an even better way to organize your Start menu for fast access.

More Effective Use of the Taskbar and Start Menu

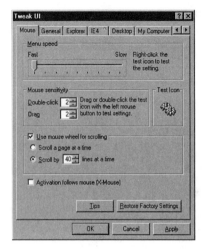

Figure 2.3.4

Drag the TweakUI's Menu Speed slider bar all the way to the left to make the Start menu fly.

Did you know that Windows 98 automatically alphabetizes and/or numerically sorts Start menu items? Well, now you do.

To organize your Start menu for fast keystroke selection, just rename the text descriptions so that they begin with "a,b,c,…" or "1,2,3,…."

Your most frequently used programs should rank near the top of your list ("a" or "1") and your infrequently accessed tools can reside down near the bottom ("i" or "9").

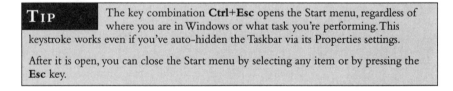

TIP The key combination **Ctrl+Esc** opens the Start menu, regardless of where you are in Windows or what task you're performing. This keystroke works even if you've auto-hidden the Taskbar via its Properties settings.

After it is open, you can close the Start menu by selecting any item or by pressing the **Esc** key.

Use the following steps to reorganize the items on your Start menu:

1. Right-click a blank space on the Taskbar. Then choose Properties from the pop-up menu.

2. Select the Start Menu Programs tab from the Taskbar Properties sheet.

3. Click the Advanced button in the Customize Start Menu box. This action will display a Windows Explorer view of the Start menu items.

4. Right-click an entry in the list and choose Rename from the pop-up list. Now you can preface the entry's name with the characters "A." or "1."

5. Continue renaming other items until you've assembled an alphabetic or numeric list. You do not need to order these items in this Explorer view. Windows will rank them correctly when it loads the Start Menu.

6. Choose File | Close from the menus to exit the Explorer view.

7. Click the OK button on the TaskBar Properties sheet.

These changes will take effect immediately.

More Effective Use of the
Taskbar and Start Menu

Chapter 2.4

Smart Shortcuts

Shortcuts help you quickly launch Windows programs and utilities. But Microsoft doesn't offer much advice for creating useful ones. They leave you to figure it out on your own. Here are some shortcut hints to make you more productive.

2.4.1 Edit Images Quickly

With the boom of Web development going on, image viewing and editing has become a regular activity even for those not in desktop publishing and production roles. The QuickView utility makes viewing images easy, but QuickView offers no zoom in capability. And, you still need to launch an image processing application if you want to make any changes.

Windows 98 users often overlook the drag-and-drop features of the operating system. But, when used with shortcuts on the desktop, drag-and-drop functionality can really speed up your workflow. For this reason, shortcuts remain your best bet for fast image editing tasks. Place a shortcut to Paint (under Start | Programs | Accessories | Paint), Imaging for Windows (in the same location), or your own image application onto your desktop. Then drag and drop images onto that shortcut. The application will launch immediately and you'll be up and editing in seconds.

2.4.2 Use a Shortcut to Clear the Documents Menu

One way to increase your productivity is to decrease the time you spend on maintenance and cleanup tasks.

For example, many people periodically clean out the Recent Documents folder that Windows uses to track your active files. But it takes at least four mouse clicks and a few seconds to purge the Documents folder through the Taskbar Properties sheet—and that's if you know what you're doing.

What is your best bet? Create a shortcut to a DOS batch file that you can use anytime. The batch file will have the following two instructions:

```
@echo off
deltree /Y C:\Windows\Recent\*.*
```

Call the batch file CLEARD.BAT or some other descriptive name. Make sure you set this batch file to Close on Exit. Do this by right-clicking on the batch file's shortcut. Select Properties from the pop-up menu. Choose the Program tab and put a check next to Close on Exit near the bottom of the Program page. Click OK to exit the Properties sheet.

If you place this batch file on your desktop, you can clear out your Documents folder at any time just by double-clicking this object.

Or, if you prefer to let Windows do the work for you, you can set up a regular schedule for this event via the Scheduled Tasks feature of Windows 98. To do this, open the Scheduled Tasks applet (under Start | Programs | Accessories | System Tools), then select Add Scheduled Task from the list and follow the instructions to insert a task for your document-clearing batch file.

> **TIP** With the TweakUI utility you can clear out the Documents list each time you exit Windows. To do this, launch TweakUI (under Start | Settings | Control Panel), select the IE4 tab of TweakUI. Then put a check next to Clear Document, Run, Typed URL History on Exit in the Settings list. Click OK to exit TweakUI.

Keep track of the other regular tasks you perform on your system, then create batch files and schedule tasks similar to this Documents example that will ease your maintenance burden.

2.4.3 Shut Down Windows with One Click of the Mouse

Have you ever needed to rush for the door? It's amazing how long the Windows Shutdown procedure feels when you're in a hurry. First you have to open the Start menu, then choose Shutdown, then pick among the exit choices (Shut down, Restart, Restart in MS-DOS mode), then click OK to really begin the procedure.

With the help of a batch file, you can shorten this wait to just one click of the mouse. Use the follow procedure to create a one-click exit for Windows 98:

1. Start an MS-DOS session by selecting Start | Programs | MS-DOS Prompt.

2. Edit a batch file by typing **edit *myfilename*.bat** at the command prompt. Use a descriptive name such as CloseWin.bat.

3. Enter the line **C:\WINDOWS\RUNDLL32.EXE user.exe,ExitWindows** into your batch file. This is the only line required.

4. Save and exit this batch file.

5. Exit your MS-DOS session.

6. Using Windows Explorer, right-click on your batch file. Then select Properties from the pop-up list.

7. Choose the Program tab of the Properties sheet. Then put a check next to the line Close on Exit. Click OK to exit the Property sheet.

8. Using the Windows Explorer again, right-click on the batch file and select Send To from the pop-up list. Then choose Desktop as Shortcut.

9. Drag the batch file shortcut from the desktop onto your Quick Launch toolbar.

Now, for quick escapes, simply choose your batch file from the Quick Launch toolbar. Don't forget to turn your monitor off before you race for the exit.

Chapter

2.5

Clever
Keystrokes

This chapter describes the use of Windows 98 keyboard equivalents and shortcut keys. It also shows you how to add auto-correct capability to any Windows 98 application.

2.5.1 Use the Desktop's Shortcut Keys

In the first transition from text-based MS-DOS to a graphical operating system like Windows, many users complain about being slowed down. For many, typing a few quick keyboard characters and pressing the **Enter** key is a lot faster than hunting for the mouse, moving it, and clicking the mouse buttons.

Windows 98 does offer keystroke equivalents for mouse moves and clicks; they're called shortcut keys. Here's a list of the most useful Windows Explorer and desktop Shortcut Keys:

Windows Explorer and desktop shortcut keys

Key combination	Action
Press **Shift** while inserting CD-ROM	Disable AutoPlay
Press **Ctrl** while dragging a file	Copy file
Shift+Delete	Delete file without moving it to Recycle Bin
Ctrl+Shift while dragging a file	Create Shortcut
F2	Rename an object
F3	Display Find dialog box
F5	Refresh the desktop
Ctrl+A	Select all objects

Also, make sure you're getting all the information you can about application Shortcut Keys. To do this, set your Accessibility Options to Show Extra Keyboard Help. Follow these steps to modify this setting:

1. Choose Accessibility Options under Start | Settings | Control Panel.

2. Select the Keyboard tab.

3. Put a check next to the line: Show Extra Keyboard Help in Programs.

4. Click OK to close the Accessibility Properties sheet.

TIP	Several keyboard designs now feature a special Windows key—a key with the Windows logo on it. This key can be used in combination

with others for Shortcut Key controls. Here's a quick list:

Windows Key Shortcut Keys

Key combination	*Action*
Windows+E	Launch Windows Explorer
Windows+Break	Show the System Properties dialog box
Windows+D	Minimize all windows
Shift+Windows+M	Undo minimize all windows
Windows	Open the Start menu
Windows+R	Show the Start | Run dialog box

Clever Keystrokes

Now, programs that interrogate this setting will deliver additional instructions on Shortcut Keys.

2.5.2 Define Hotkeys for Your Shortcuts

When is the last time someone asked you for your mouse-clicks-per-minute rating? Probably never. A good typist is always faster with a keyboard than with a mouse. Make productive use of this skill by attaching keystroke equivalents, called shortcut keys, to the shortcuts on your desktop. This way, you can launch programs without ever taking your fingers off the keyboard.

Follow these steps to add shortcut keys to your shortcuts:

1. Right-click on the shortcut icon in which you're interested. Then select Properties from the pop-up menu.

TIP	You can also bring up an object's Property sheet by holding down the **Alt** key as you double-click it with the mouse, or by selecting the

icon and then pressing **Alt+Enter**.

2. If the object is a Windows program, you'll see a Shortcut tab on the Properties sheet. Choose it. If the object is an MS-DOS program or batch file, you'll see a Program tab on the Properties sheet. Select it.

3. If your object has no current Shortcut Key, the corresponding line in the Property sheet will read: None. Place your cursor in the text box by clicking once over the field. Your insert-text cursor will flash just behind the word None. From here, simply press the key combination you want to use to activate this shortcut. Something such as **Ctrl+Alt+X** (where *X* is any letter) is most common. Do not use a key combination that already invokes some other application. Don't worry, you'll find out if this is the case. If you press an already-assigned key combination, the application that uses that combination will launch immediately.

2.5.3 Use Internet Explorer's Shortcut Keys

The World Wide Web has become the world's largest mousetrap. Most Web designers force you to use your mouse to navigate through their site. Stop the madness and use IE4's shortcut keys while you browse the Web. You might be surprised at the controls the keyboard offers.

Here's a list of Internet Explorer 4's most useful Shortcut Keys:

Internet Explorer Shortcut Keys

Key Combination	Action
Alt+Right Arrow	Next page
Alt+Left Arrow	Previous page
Shift+F10	Show a link's right-click pop-up menu
Ctrl+Tab	Move to the next frame
Shift+Ctrl+Tab	Move to the last frame
F5	Refresh the current page
Esc	End the current page download
Ctrl+N	Open a new browser window
Ctrl+S	Save the current page

If you're a real keyboard fan, check into the latest keyboard designs. Some, such as IBM's $109 TrackPoint Keyboard, incorporate a pointing device and mouse buttons right into the keyboard itself. So there's no need to switch back and forth between keyboard and mouse.

2.5.4 Use Shorthand on Your Keyboard

The latest word processors, such as Microsoft's Word, come with an auto-correction feature that corrects your typos on-the-fly. For example, in Word, your misspelled "responsability" gets replaced by the correct "responsibility" automatically during your typing session. Unfortunately, Windows 98 does not provide this auto-correct feature within the operating system itself. You can, however, download a utility that adds this capability to your system.

The Aimsoft Development Corporation has a shareware tool called AIM Keys that will auto-correct in any application. AIM Keys also lets you record and playback keyboard macros that repeat keyboard and mouse steps automatically.

Follow these steps to download and install AIM keys:

1. Launch the Internet Explorer by choosing Start | Programs | Internet Explorer from the Start menu. Or, start your alternative Web browser.

2. Enter the following URL into the Address bar: **http://www.pcworld.com/fileworld/file_description/frameset/0,1458,3196,00.html**. Or, point your browser to PC World's FileWorld site (**www.fileworld.com**) and use the Search FileWorld tool to find "AIM Keys."

3. Select the hyperlink called AK125EV.EXE to jump to the download page.

4. Choose the Download File Now! hyperlink. Save the file AK125EV.EXE to a folder on your hard drive.

5. The download file is a self-extracting Zip file, so you don't need a decompression utility. Select AK125EV.EXE in the Windows Explorer. This launches the installation program.

6. Follow the installation program's instructions to install AIM Keys into your system.

7. You can run AIM Keys through the menu item that it places on your Start menu—Start | Programs | AIM Keys 1.2 | AIM Keys 1.2 (see Figure 2.5.1).

Read the AIM Keys help files for information on creating your own shorthand phrases and keyboard macros.

Aimsoft asks that you send in $30 if you plan to use AIM Keys beyond the 30-day trial period.

Clever Keystrokes

Figure 2.5.1

The AIM Keys utility provides "shorthand" capabilities in any Windows application.

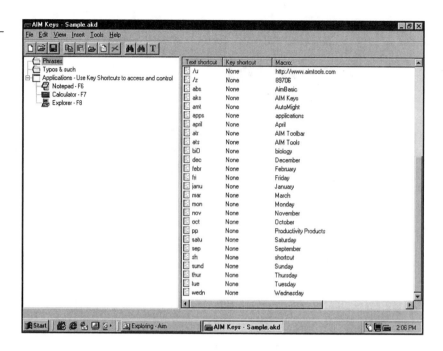

Chapter

2.6

Efficient File and Disk Management

Managing your hard drive and files takes up a significant portion of almost every computing session. In this chapter, you'll learn some of the productivity tips and tricks that Windows experts use to keep this time to a minimum.

2.6.1 Create a Diskcopy Shortcut

Due to their limited storage capability, floppy disks will soon be replaced by the floppy-replacement category of removable storage drives such as Sony's HiFD, Caleb's UHD144, Iomega's Jaz or Zip, Imation's SuperDisk, or one of the other contenders. At this point, though, it's anyone's guess which drives will succeed in the marketplace. Until there's a clear winner, we still have to make use of those trusty ol' 1.44MB floppies.

Speed up your floppy disk copy procedures through the use of a batch file. Follow these steps to create a diskcopy shortcut on your desktop:

1. Launch an MS-DOS session by choosing the MS-DOS Prompt item from the Start | Programs menu.

2. Create a temporary directory off the root directory to store this and other batch files by entering **md** *dirname* (for Make Directory) at the DOS prompt. Use a descriptive directory name such as Batch.

3. To change directories to your new directory, enter **CD** *dirname* at the DOS prompt.

4. Create a new batch file by typing **edit** *newbatch***.BAT** at the DOS prompt. Use a descriptive name such as DISKC.BAT.

5. Enter the following line in your new batch file: **diskcopy a: a:**

6. Save and exit the Editor program. Then type **Exit** to end this DOS session.

7. Launch the Windows Explorer (under Start | Programs). Navigate to your new batch file directory. Then right-click on your DISKC.BAT batch file and choose SEND TO. Then choose Desktop as Shortcut from the pop-up menu.

8. Right-click on the DISKC object on your desktop and choose Properties from the pop-up menu.

9. Select the Program tab of the Properties sheet. Put a check next to the line: Close on Exit. This will ensure that Windows doesn't leave a DOS session open after the disk copy procedure completes.

Now, whenever you need to make a quick copy of a floppy, simply double-click this shortcut. The program will instruct you as to when to insert the source and destination disks into your floppy drive.

2.6.2 Store More on Your Floppies

Through the use of compression technology you can store much more than 1.44 megabytes on a single floppy disk. Many people use third-party compression utilities such as the popular PKZip from PKWARE Inc. (www.pkware.com), but you really don't need to look anywhere other than your own Windows 98 system to find a handy disk compression tool.

Windows 98 includes both the DriveSpace 3 disk compression program and a Compression Agent utility. DriveSpace 3 initially compacts a drive. Then you can use the Compression Agent to increase the compression ratio of this compressed volume.

NOTE	Hard drives using the FAT32 file system cannot be compressed with DriveSpace 3.

TIP	Compression slows access to files because they must be decompressed before they can be used by applications. Only use compression on files that don't require quick access.

I personally don't recommend using DriveSpace 3 or any other compression utility on a hard drive. I've heard too many disaster stories from friends and associates. In my experience, compressed hard drives crash far more often than uncompressed drives. And the data stored on compressed drives is often unrecoverable. One friend lost a draft of a novel when his compressed hard drive crashed.

Compressing a floppy drive, however, is another matter entirely. Usually, files stored on floppy disk are temporary copies that you transport from one location to another. Even if your compressed floppy becomes unreadable, you most likely have a backup on a hard drive. So feel free to use Windows 98's disk compression tools on a disk. You'll be amazed how much extra space you can squeeze out. You can often double or triple the amount of storage space on a disk.

Follow these steps to compress a floppy disk with DriveSpace 3 and the Compression Agent:

1. Insert a formatted floppy into your PC's A: drive. It doesn't matter whether or not you already have files stored on the disk. You can compress the disk's volume and add files later if you want.

2. Launch the DriveSpace utility (under Start | Programs | Accessories | System Tools). You'll see a drive list that includes your floppy drive and all of your hard drive's disk partitions.

Efficient File and Disk Management

3. Select Drive A: (the floppy drive), then choose Compress from the Drive menu. This will display the Compress a Drive dialog box (see Figure 2.6.1).

Figure 2.6.1

Use Windows 98's DriveSpace tool to compress your floppy's volume.

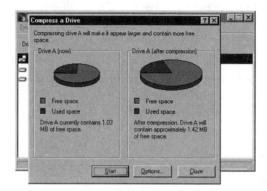

4. Click the Start button and follow the instructions to compress the floppy's volume. Click the Close button to exit DriveSpace.

5. After you've finished the compression, copy the files you want onto the disk using the Windows Explorer.

6. Now, launch the Compression Agent (under Start | Programs | Accessories | System Tools). There are 3 levels of compression used by this tool: Normal, HiPack, and UltraPack. UltraPack, the highest level, makes disk access slow because the decompression takes a little longer. By default, the Compression Agent uses UltraPack on files older than 30 days and HiPack for the rest of the files. I recommend going with the default. For maximum compression (and slightly slower performance) you can set the Compression Agent to UltraPack all your files. Do this by clicking the Settings button and choosing your new settings.

7. Click Start to re-compress your files with the Compression Agent.

> **WARNING** Floppies compressed with Drive Space 3 can only be read by Windows 98 systems! Windows 95 systems do not have the ability to decompress this data. If you load a compressed diskette into the A: drive of a Win95 system, you'll only see a readme text file warning when you open the disk under Windows Explorer.

You can now share this compressed disk with any Win98 system.

2.6.3 Rename Multiple Files Simultaneously

DOS aficionados fondly remember the ability to rename several files simultaneously. At the command line, simply entering Rename ★.BAT ★.TXT quickly changes files with the batch file extension into files with a text file extension.

Microsoft never figured out how to pull off this trick in the graphical Windows environment. Or if they did, they never implemented it.

Fortunately, you can download a free utility, called MultiRen, from PC Magazine Online's Software Library that rejuvenates this long lost magic.

Follow these steps to download and install the MultiRen utility.

1. Launch your Web browser and type in the following URL: **www.pcmag.com**. This will open the homepage for PC Magazine Online.

2. Select Downloads on the left side of the main screen.

3. Choose Software Library from the Downloads screen. Then enter **MultiRen** into the Search box at the bottom of the Software Library page. The search results should list: PC Magazine's MultRen v1.0. Click on the hyperlink to bring you to the download page.

4. On the MultiRen page click Download Now to start the download process. Save the file to a temporary directory on your hard drive. The file extension and type is .ZIP, the ZIP compression format.

5. You'll need a Zip decompression utility such as PKUNZIP from PKWARE Inc. (**www.pkware.com**) to extract the data from the download file. Create a separate directory, such as MultiRen, to store the application.

6. After you've extracted the files, run MultiRen's setup program, MRSETUP.EXE. This will install MultiRen into the Windows Explorer on your Windows 98 system.

How do you use MultiRen? Anytime you select multiple files under Windows Explorer, you can right-click on the group and select the new Multiple Rename option from the pop-up menu. This will bring up the Rename Multiple Files dialog box (see Figure 2.6.2), which you can use to rename all the files simultaneously. Use the help feature to learn the basics of the program.

Keep in mind, the Multiple Rename option will not appear on your right-click context menu unless you have more than one file highlighted.

Efficient File and Disk Management

Figure 2.6.2

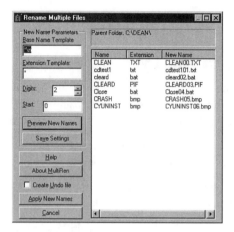

*MultiRen's
dialog box
enables you to
rename several
files simulta-
neously.*

2.6.4 Remove Explorer's Web View Warning

In most cases, Windows 98 helps you get work done more quickly. Sometimes, however, it just gets in the way.

For example: Windows posts an irritating warning message when you browse the Windows folder in the Windows Explorer's Web View mode (Activate this mode by choosing View | As a Web Page from the Explorer's menus). It says, `Warning, modifying the contents of this folder may cause your programs to stop working correctly.` Then, to continue on, you must click the Show Files hyperlink.

Unfortunately, most of us browse the Windows folder quite often—there's a lot of important stuff in there! After about the fifth time you hit this same message, you'll never want to see it again.

> **WARNING** The following steps are somewhat complicated. They involve modifying the HyperText template used for the Explorer Web View. Only intermediate and advanced users should attempt them.

Follow these steps to remove the Windows folder warning from the Windows Explorer's Web View:

1. Launch the Windows Explorer (under Start | Programs). In the left pane, select the C:\Windows folder. If Web View is active, the warning message will appear. If not, activate it by selecting As Web Page from the View menu.

2. Choose Customize this Folder from the View menu. This displays the Customize this Folder dialog box (see Figure 2.6.3).

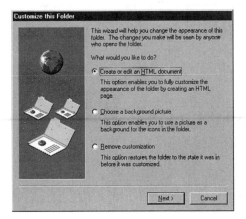

3. Select Create or Edit an HTML Document. Then click the Next button.

4. Click Next again after reading the instructions for editing a HyperText Template. This displays the template file FOLDER.HTT from the C:\Windows folder in the Notepad editor. Windows uses this template to map out the Web View.

5. Make sure your flashing text insert cursor is flashing at the top of this file. Open the Search menu and choose Find. Then, enter **prompt1** in the Find What box. Click Find Next.

6. The first instance of the string prompt1 is a variable definition; the line begins with "var." Do nothing on this line. Click Find Next again.

7. The next instance begins with "document.all.Brand.innerHTML =..." Comment out this line by inserting two forward slash characters // at the beginning of the line. Immediately after this line, insert a new line that reads **ShowFiles();**.

8. Click Find Next again. The last instance of "prompt1" begins with "Info.innerHTML=..." Just as in step 7, comment out the line by preceding it with // characters. Then, immediately following the line, insert a new line reading **ShowFiles();**.

9. Click Cancel to close the Find dialog box. Then choose File | Save and then File | Close from Notepad's menus to save and close the template.

10. Click the Finish button on the Customize this Folder dialog box.

Efficient File and Disk Management

> **NOTE** To remove this customization, repeat steps 1 through 3 of the above procedure but, in step 3, choose Remove Customization in the Customize this Folder dialog box.

The change will take effect immediately. In Web View you'll still see the warning message when you browse the Windows folder, but you'll no longer have to select the Show Files hyperlink to continue. Explorer will automatically display the files.

2.6.5 Stop Phantom Disk Drive Access

Is there a ghost in your machine? You might think so if you've ever suddenly heard the whirring of your floppy drive and you weren't anywhere near it...Yikes!

What's going on? It's a fairly common problem called phantom drive access. And it can slow down your productivity by displaying pesky error messages—stating that your floppy drive is inaccessible—during your computing sessions.

The culprit: Some program on your system has an unneeded reference to your A: drive. This used to happen all the time in Windows version 3.1. People would accidentally leave open a File Manager window that browsed the A: drive. Whenever they launched Windows, the floppy drive would start spinning. Unfortunately, similar problems sometimes occur in Windows 98.

The two most likely suspects are your anti-virus software, which might be set to check for viruses on floppies, and Microsoft's Find Fast indexing applet, which might be indexing the A: drive.

You'll have to investigate your anti-virus package on your own, but you can follow these steps to check Find Fast:

1. Launch Find Fast (under Start | Settings | Control Panel). You'll see a list of drives that it is set to index (see Figure 2.6.4).

Figure 2.6.4

Find Fast might be the culprit that's mysteriously accessing your A: drive.

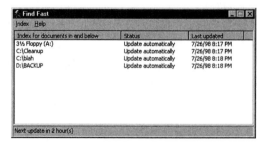

2. If you do see a reference to the A: drive in the list, highlight it, then choose Delete Index from the Index menu.

3. Choose Close from the Index menu to exit Find Fast.

Another possible cause would be a recent document shortcut to your A: drive. To check this browse your recent document list (under Start | Documents). Then right-click on any A: drive reference and choose Delete from the pop-up menu.

Finally, look into the Close Programs dialog box by pressing **Ctrl-Alt-Delete**. This will bring up a list of all your active programs. Check each program in the list for references to your A: drive, and remove these references.

Efficient File and Disk Management

Chapter

2.7

Command Line Productivity

With these hints, you can weave MS-DOS and Windows more tightly together. Learn how to launch Windows programs from the MS-DOS prompt, cut and paste from Windows to DOS, and more.

2.7.1 Cut and Paste From a DOS Window

By now, you're probably familiar with Windows's cut and paste capability. You can quickly copy or move text, graphics, and other objects from one Windows application to another using the Windows Clipboard behind the scenes.

Did you know that this trick also works between Windows applications and a DOS session? Say you want to print out a list of files. One easy way is to create the list using DOS's DIR command. Then copy and paste the list from DOS to a printer-friendly Windows application like Notepad or Word.

You can also paste from Windows into DOS. The next time a product's README.TXT file gives you a DOS command for use in troubleshooting or configuration, just cut and paste the instruction directly into a DOS session Window. There's no need to retype DOS commands.

Modify two settings to get this DOS copy and paste working. You must set your MS-DOS session to run in a Window rather than Full-Screen mode. And you should also set MS-DOS's properties to display the DOS toolbar.

Follow these steps to set your MS-DOS session for cut and paste functionality:

1. On the Start menu, select Start | Programs, and then just highlight MS-DOS Prompt. Don't select MS-DOS Prompt, just highlight it. Then right-click on MS-DOS Prompt and choose Properties from the pop-up menu. This displays the MS-DOS Prompt Properties sheet.

2. Choose the Screen tab.

3. In the Usage box, select Window. In the Window box, select Display Toolbar.

4. Click OK to save these setting and exit the Properties sheet.

> **NOTE**   Why do you need the toolbar for the DOS session? Because the right-click mouse feature of Windows doesn't work in DOS. You need the toolbar's cut and paste buttons to perform these actions in a DOS window.

These changes will take place immediately.

2.7.2 Super-Charge Your MS-DOS Prompt

The `DOSKEY` command ranks high on the list of great DOS features. `DOSKEY` lets you quickly edit your command line, recall previous commands, and create macros for other DOS commands. If you've ever retyped a DOS command that you entered just a few minutes before, you'll save yourself some time by loading this command into every DOS session.

Perhaps the most powerful aspect of `DOSKEY` is its command line edit and recall capability. Here's a list of its instructions and the keys that activate them:

DOSKEY Edit Controls

Keys	Action
Up Arrow	Display last DOS command in the history list
Down Arrow	Display next DOS command in the history list
F7	Displays command history list by number
F9	Chooses a previous DOS command by number
Alt+F7	Clears command history list
[*characters*] **F8**	Searches for previous commands beginning with *characters*
Esc	Clears current command line

For macros, `DOSKEY` lets you quickly customize other DOS commands with extra parameters. For example, the following `DOSKEY` instructions set a macro for the DOS `DIR` (directory) command so that `DIR` displays with page pauses (`/p`) and verbose mode (`/v`):

```
DOSKEY DIR=DIR /p /v
```

You can set up several DOSKEY macros and display the list with the command `DOSKEY /MACROS`.

If you want to set up DOSKEY macros for use with every session, insert the macro lines in your AUTOEXEC.BAT file.

If, on the other hand, you're mainly interested in DOSKEY's command line editing features, use the following steps to load DOSKEY into your DOS sessions:

Command Line Productivity

1. Right-click on your MS-DOS Prompt shortcut on your desktop or in the Start menu (under Start | Programs). Choose Properties from the pop-up list.

2. Select the Program tab of the MS-DOS Prompt Properties sheet. In the Batch File entry box, enter the word **DOSKEY**.

3. Choose OK to save and exit the MS-DOS Prompt Properties sheet.

Now, you'll be able to use DOSKEY's editing command in every DOS session. For a full list of DOSKEY's features type in **DOSKEY /?** at your DOS prompt.

2.7.3 Launch Windows Programs From DOS

The start command lets you quickly activate Windows programs directly from the DOS command line. You don't need to waste time opening the Start menu or switching back to the desktop. You can load Windows applications, open documents, or browse folders, all with short DOS commands.

The start command uses the following options:

start Command Options

Options	Action
/m	Run the program minimized in the background
/max	Run the program maximized in the foreground
/r	Restore the already launched program to the foreground
/w	Wait until the launched program returns before returning control to the DOS session

For launching programs, use the following syntax:

```
Start [options] program_name [program_parameters]
```

Here are some real-world examples:

```
Start /max winword.exe C:\myfolder\mydoc.doc
```

This instruction launches Microsoft Word, maximized, and opens the file MYDOC.DOC.

```
Start calc.exe
```

This instruction launches Windows's Calculator applet.

```
Start /r explorer.exe
```

This instruction restores the already-loaded Windows Explorer to the foreground.

Just as in Windows, the **start** command is aware of your file type associations. Simply entering a document's name will open a file in its corresponding application. Here are some examples:

```
Start C:\Projects\PlanB.doc
```

This opens PLANB.DOC in Microsoft Word.

```
Start C:\spreadsheets\mortgage.xls
```

This opens MORTGAGE.XLS in Microsoft Excel.

```
Start C:\notes\test.txt
```

This opens TEST.TXT in Notepad.

And, finally, just enter:

```
Start .
```

This launches Windows Explorer with a view of your current DOS directory.

2.7.4 Send Deleted DOS Files to the Recycle Bin

Don't get too comfortable with that Recycle Bin safety net for deleted files. It doesn't work in a DOS session. If you (or your kids) accidentally delete a file, image, or program from a DOS session—it's gone. Adios! You might salvage the lost file with some heavy-duty utility suite, such as Norton Utilities, but who needs that much hassle?

Fortunately, a free utility posted on PC Magazine's Software Library can give you a second chance with these files. BigBin, written by Rick Knoblaugh for the Ziff-Davis Publishing Company, reroutes deleted DOS files into Windows 98's Recycle Bin. If needed, you can restore accidentally deleted files before they go away forever.

Follow these steps to download and install the free BigBin utility from the Web:

1. Launch your Web browser and type in the following URL:
   www.pcmag.com. This will open the homepage for PC Magazine Online.

2. Select Downloads to the left on the main screen.

3. Choose Software Library from the Downloads screen. Then enter **BigBin** in the Search box at the bottom of the Software Library page. The search results will list: PC Magazine's BigBin v1.2. Click on the hyperlink to bring you to the download page.

4. On the BigBin page, click Download Now to start the download process. Save the file to a temporary directory on your hard drive. The file extension and type is .ZIP, the ZIP compression format.

5. You'll need a Zip decompression utility such as PKUNZIP from PKWARE Inc. (www.pkware.com) to extract the data from the download file. Create a separate directory, such as BigBin, to store the application.

6. After you've extracted the files, run BigBin's installation program, BIGBIN.EXE. This will install BigBin into the System Tray of your Windows 98 system.

By default, BigBin does not display the "Are you sure you want to send this file to the Recycle Bin" message that Windows 98 does. However, you can tell BigBin to do this by launching it with a /R option.

To remove BigBin from your System Tray, simply right-click the icon and select Exit Program from the pop-up menu.

If you want this utility constantly watching over your DOS sessions, put BIGBIN.EXE in your Startup folder (under Start | Programs) where it will load every time you boot Windows 98.

2.7.5 Use Command Line Wildcards to Launch Windows Applications

Wildcarding ranks high on the list of cool DOS features that got lost during the development of Windows. Luckily, you can add this feature to your Windows 98 system with the help of a freeware download.

Wildcards are two special characters, "*" and "?," that enable you to work with multiple files at the same time *and* let you guess when you're not sure of a particular file's name. In wildcarding, the asterisk (*) means any number of characters of any type, and the question mark (?) means any single character of any type.

Here are some examples. Win*.* specifies any file that begins with the characters "win." This would include Winmax.exe, Windowsthings.ini, win.bat, and so on. Bac?.exe specifies any executable file that begins with the characters "bac" followed by any single character. This would include Back.exe, Baca.exe, Bacx.exe and so forth.

PC Magazine's Software Library offers a set of four MS-DOS Whiz Utilities that add wildcard capabilities to Windows applications, such as Notepad, that normally don't work with these special characters. Faisal Nasim, also known as The Whiz Kid, wrote the programs.

Follow this instructions to download and install Whiz Utilities from PC Magazine's Software Library:

1. Launch Internet Explorer by choosing Start | Programs | Internet Explorer from the Start menu. Or, start your alternative Web browser.

2. In the Address bar, enter the URL for PC Magazine's Software Library— **www.hotfiles.com**.

3. In the Search field near the top of the Web page, enter **Whiz Utilities**. Then click on the Search button.

4. On the search results Web page, click on the hyperlink for Whiz Utilities v2.0.

5. On the Whiz Utilities Web page, click on the Download Now button. Save the file to a new folder on your hard drive. Use a descriptive folder name, like WhizUtil. The download file is compressed with a zip compression algorithm, so you'll need a decompression tool, such as PKWare's PKZip for Windows (www.pkware.com) to extract the data files from the download file.

6. Decompress the download file WHIZUTIL.ZIP using your unzip program. Extract the files to the directory you created in step 5.

7. You're done with the installation! Start an MS-DOS session by choosing Start | Programs | MS-DOS Prompt from the Start menu.

8. Use the Change Directory CD command to move to the WhizUtil folder on your hard drive (i.e. CD C:\WhizUtil).

9. For information on the four new utilities, enter **readme** at the MS-DOS prompt.

Each of the four utilities—Super Starter (WKSTART.EXE), Whiz Launcher (EXEC.EXE), Case Changer (CASE.EXE), and Windows Customizer (CUSTOM.EXE)—comes with its own instructions. Just enter the utility's name, with no parameters, at the MS-DOS prompt for syntax and usage help.

Command Line Productivity

Here's an example of the power of just one of the new tools. By entering **WKSTART C:\Projects*.txt** on the command line, you'll automatically launch a Notepad session for every text file in the Projects folder.

You don't need to register or send any money for the Whiz Utilities.

Chapter

2.8

Wrangling the Desktop

Make your desktop more productive for viewing multimedia elements by upgrading your Media Player utility and customizing the Windows Explorer. This chapter tells you how to stop the Recycle Bin from talking back and how to obtain a useful editor.

2.8.1 Preview All Your Multimedia Files in Windows Explorer

If you've read any computer magazine write-ups on Windows 98, you've probably learned about Windows Explorer's Thumbnail View. It lets you configure individual folders to display image and HTML files in small sketches while you browse in the Explorer (see Figure 2.8.1). Unfortunately, in terms of productivity, Thumbnail View sucks!

Figure 2.8.1

Windows Explorer's limited, resource-hogging Thumbnail View.

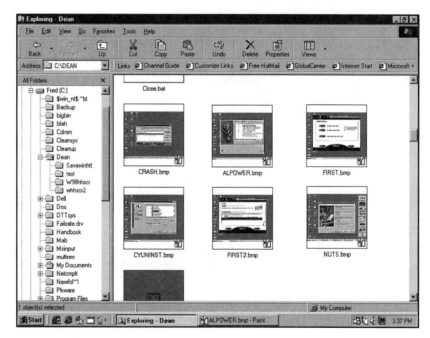

Thumbnail View doesn't work on sound and video files. It only displays useless icons for these file types. Additionally, Thumbnail View drains computing resources. If your folder is filled with image and HTML files, Explorer must chug away to create thumbnail sketches of each and every file.

With a quick hack, you can configure Explorer to display multimedia files, of all types, in a much more efficient and effective way. With this tip, Explorer previews only one file at a time. You can quickly scan an entire folder by simply moving your mouse up and down a list of files (see Figure 2.8.2).

Figure 2.8.2

Windows Explorer's efficient and effective "multimedia preview" mode

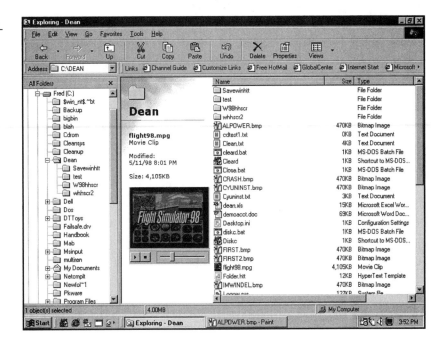

To configure Windows Explorer for "multimedia preview" mode, follow these steps:

1. Launch the Windows Explorer (under Start | Programs).

2. Select the folder in which you want to configure "multimedia preview" mode. Just as with the Thumbnail View, you must enable preview mode on one folder at a time.

3. Open the View menu and choose Customize This Folder.

4. In the Customize This Folder dialog box, select Create or Edit an HTML Document. This selection should be the default. Click the Next button.

5. Read the instructions regarding HyperText Templates. Then click the Next button again. This opens a FOLDER.HTT hypertext template in Notepad.

6. Open Notepad's Search menu and select Find. In the Find dialog box, enter **wantMedia**. Then click the Find Next button.

7. The first instance found should read `var wantMedia=False`. Highlight the word `False` and change it to `True`.

8. Click Cancel on the Find dialog box to close it.

9. Open the Notepad's File menu and select Save. Then choose File | Exit to close Notepad.

10. Click the Finish button on the Customize This Folder dialog box.

This change takes effect immediately. Run your mouse up and down your list of files to experiment with the preview capabilities.

2.8.2 End the Recycle Bin Warning

Recycle Bin warnings continually interrupt your work flow. Whenever you delete a file, Windows displays the Confirm File Delete message box and forces you to click Yes before sending the file to the Recycle Bin. The question: How often do you delete files by accident? Intermediate and advanced PC users almost never make this mistake. And, even if they do, they know the files reside safely in the Bin, waiting to be rescued in case of emergency.

Skip this unnecessary step in your daily tasks by telling the Recycle Bin to stop displaying this message. Follow these steps to do so:

1. Right-click on the desktop's Recycle Bin icon. Choose Properties from the pop-up menu.

2. Select the Global tab.

3. Remove the check next to Display delete confirmation dialog box.

4. Click OK to save and exit the Recycle Bin's Properties sheet.

As implied by the "Global" tab, this setting encompasses all of your logical and physical hard drives. Even if you have more than one Recycle Bin repository, Windows will never display the warning message again.

2.8.3 Download a Real Editor

Windows 98 abounds in software development capabilities. Right out of the box, you can create programs in Vbscript, JavaScript, and HTML and run them on your Win98 system. With a little effort, you can create your own tools and utilities, Web sites, and small-scale applications.

So what's the problem? Unless you spend some extra money on a software development kit (SDK), you're extremely limited in your choice of editors in which to create your programs. Win98's FrontPage Express works all right for simple HTML pages, but for anything else, you'd have to go with Notepad and Wordpad—neither of which is the most powerful editor on the planet.

For developing software, you need an editor designed for programming, not word processing. Programming editors provide special indent capabilities, templates, macro recorders, and many other features that you won't find in word processing software.

Luckily, The Web can help. Here are some Web sites from which you can download free editors:

- Programmer's File Editor (`www.lancs.ac.uk/people/cpaap/pfe/`): A powerful yet free editor that includes many of the features a software developer needs, including custom indenting and quick access to Windows system files.

- PageMill 3.0 Tryout (`www.fileworld.com`): PC World Online offers a 15-day only free trial of Adobe's latest version of PageMill Web site development package. Work fast and create a Web site.

- Simtel.net Windows Collection (`http://www.simtel.com/simtel.net/win95/editor-pre.html`): A wide assortment of shareware and freeware editors.

2.8.4 Download the New Media Player

Surprise! Microsoft has enhanced the Media Player utility since they shipped Windows 98. The new Media Player plays many more types of multimedia files than the version that shipped with Win98, including QuickTime and RealVideo movies, and RealAudio music and sound files.

In addition to files stored on your hard drive, Media Player now also plays multimedia "streams" from the Internet or intranet. With this capability, you can tune into live concerts, online classes, events, and more. The utility even downloads new Codecs (compression-decompression programs) if it can't play the file you've loaded.

But wait there's more! You can also create *playlists* that combine several multimedia files into one show and run the whole thing in an endless loop. Use this feature to create your own multimedia information kiosk or standalone presentation.

Follow these steps to download the new Media Player:

1. Launch the Internet Explorer by choosing Start | Programs | Internet Explorer | Internet Explorer from the Start menu. Or, start your alternative Web browser.

2. Enter the following URL into the Address bar: **http://
   www.microsoft.com/Windows/MediaPlayer/**. This address brings you to
   Microsoft's Media Player Web page.

3. Select the Download Now hyperlink on the far right.

4. In the drop-down box labeled Step 1 of 3, choose the download file you
   want. If you use Internet Explorer as a Web browser, pick the version
   optimized for IE4 (see Figure 2.8.3).

Figure 2.8.3

*Choose a version
of the Media
Player from
Microsoft's Web
site.*

5. On this screen, choose the download server location that resides closest to
   you. Click the Next button in that row.

6. Save the 4-megabyte download file (MPFULL.EXE) to a folder on your
   hard drive.

7. When the download process completes, run the .EXE file from within
   Windows Explorer. This setup program will install the new Media Player
   into your Windows 98 system.

Access the new Media Player by choosing Start | Programs | Accessories |
Entertainment | Media Player on the Start menu. The Media Player also launches
automatically when you select a file type associated with it under Folder Options
(Start | Settings | Folder Options).

Chapter

2.9

Smart Trouble-shooting

Was your Windows 98 upgrade worth the money? Some people would answer "No!" Read this chapter for tips on fixing what Windows 98 broke, restoring previous versions of your Registry, and tracking bad software, as well as hints for preventive maintenance.

2.9.1 Create Your Own System Tools Folder

Troubleshooting normally requires many different tools. But in Windows 98, these tools are scattered throughout the operating system. You'll find a lot of useful utilities under Start | Programs | Accessories | System Tools; but others are not so easily selected off the Start menu and lie hidden in folders on your hard drive.

To reduce the time you spend finding troubleshooting tools, create your own System Tools folder and place a shortcut to it on your desktop. If you have tools that you've purchased separately, feel free to include these in your new folder. Here is a list of the most useful troubleshooting tools that Windows 98 offers along with their filenames, locations, and brief descriptions:

> Name: System Information Utility
> Filename: Msinfo32.exe
> Location: C:\Program Files\common files\microsoft shared\msinfo

SIU lists your hardware resources, your Windows version, your running tasks, and much, much more. You can also use it to launch other utilities (pick them off SIU's Tools menu) such as System File Checker, Registry Checker, and Scandisk.

> Name: Automatic Skip Driver Agent
> Filename: Asd.exe
> Location: C:\Windows

The Automatic Skip Driver Agent determines which devices and drivers are preventing Windows from loading properly.

> Name: Registry Checker
> Filename: Scanregw.exe
> Location: C:\Windows

The Registry Checker scans the Windows Registry for errors and also backs up the Registry files. It runs every time Windows starts, but if you hack the Registry you will run it occasionally during your computing sessions.

> Name: Dr. Watson
> Filename: Drwatson.exe
> Location: C:\Windows

Use Dr. Watson to diagnose software errors. When loaded, Dr. Watson inserts its icon into the System Tray. Launching it from the System Tray takes a "snapshot" of your system including information about running tasks, kernel drivers, user drivers, and more. For the most information, choose the Advanced mode by right-clicking the icon in the System Tray and selecting Options from the pop-up list.

> Name: System File Checker
> Filename: Sfc.exe
> Location: C:\Windows\System

The System File Checker is aptly named. It checks all the Windows system files to ensure none are damaged or corrupt. If needed, it can extract new copies of system files from your Windows 98 installation CD.

> Name: System Editor
> Filename: Sysedit.exe
> Location: C:\Windows\System

The trusty old System Editor is still around (from previous Windows versions) and is still useful. For quick modifications to AUTOEXEC.BAT, CONFIG.SYS, WIN.INI, and SYSTEM.INI, nothing beats this tool. New Windows applications no longer use these configuration files—they use the Windows Registry instead—but many of us still own older Windows programs that need periodic tweaking.

Smart Troubleshooting

2.9.2 Find the Missing Link—and Kill It

It's okay to be a little anal-retentive regarding your computer. Carefully organizing files will help keep your system running smoothly and help you stay on top of your work.

Even the obsessively clean, though, can't keep track of all of their computer's files. Normal use, which includes occasionally deleting files and applications, often leaves shortcuts and links that point to nowhere sitting around your desktop. That's where Windows Link Check Wizard comes in handy.

The Link Check Wizard (Checklinks.exe) resides within the Sample Resource Kit utilities that Microsoft included on the Windows 98 installation disc. Read the introduction if you haven't already installed the Resource Kit tools.

Link Check scans your computer and finds all the unresolved shortcuts and links. And it helps you delete them in a careful and safe manner. Follow these instructions to use the Link Check Wizard:

1. Launch the Link Check Wizard via the Microsoft Management Console. Choose Start | Programs[hr. Windows 98 Resource Kit | Tools Management Console. If you do not see this Start menu item then you did not install the Sample Resource Kit. Read the introduction for instructions.

2. Open the Tools A to Z folder within the Resource Kit folder. Then open the A to C folder. Select Checklinks from the list of tools.

> **TIP** You can also launch the Link Check Wizard by entering **Checklinks** at the Start | Run prompt.

3. Read the Link Check Wizard introduction page then click the Next button to start the session.

4. If you've never run this tool before, it will probably display a long list of "dead" links (see Figure 2.9.1). To remove individual links, put a check next to the item's entry. To remove all the unresolved links, just click the Select All button. To find out more about an individual item, right-click on its entry. The Link Check Wizard will display additional information about why it appears in the list (see Figure 2.9.2).

Figure 2.9.1

You might be surprised by the number of "dead" links the Link Check Wizard finds on its first run.

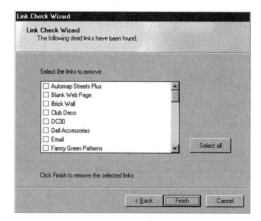

5. Click the Finish button to remove the links you've requested. The Link Check Wizard will close automatically after it completes the operation.

Figure 2.9.2

Afraid to delete a lost link? Check the entry's properties by right-clicking on it.

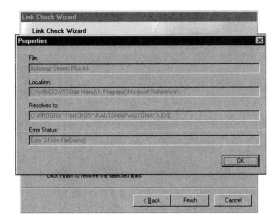

2.9.3 Track Bad Applications

As you probably already know, software developers sometimes release applications that include bugs. Shocking, huh? Even Microsoft has been guilty of this consumer crime. Luckily, Windows 98 includes some tools to help you quickly spot troublesome software.

If you're experiencing mysterious error messages, system crashes, or just bizarre behavior during a computing session, turn on the fault log under TweakUI. This will help you quickly isolate the offending software so that you either fix or remove the associated application.

Follow these steps to turn on Windows 98's fault log:

1. Launch the TweakUI utility under Start | Settings | Control Panel. Read the introduction if you haven't yet installed the Sample Resource Kit utilities from the Windows 98 installation CD.

2. Select the Paranoia tab. This tab is the farthest right of all the tabs. You might have to use the right scroll arrow to find it.

3. In the Illegal Operations box, put a check next to the line reading `Log Application Errors to FAULTLOG.TXT` (see Figure 2.9.3).

4. Choose the OK button to close TweakUI.

Now, when errors occur, you can track them by browsing the FAULTLOG.TXT file. Search for the file under Windows Explorer.

> **TIP** When an error occurs, supplement your log with a Dr. Watson "snapshot" of your system. Enter **Drwatson** at the Start | Run prompt to load the Dr. Watson utility in the System Tray. Select the icon and choose Dr. Watson from the pop-up menu. After the utility records the state of your PC, save the snapshot to disk by choosing Save from the File menu.

Figure 2.9.3

Use TweakUI to capture application errors in a log file.

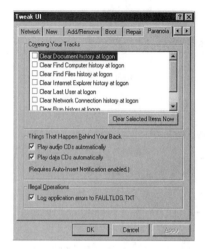

2.9.4 Diagnose Startup Troubles

Wouldn't it be nice to have a Microsoft technical support staffer sitting next to you during startup trouble? Unless you live in Redmond, Washington, this won't happen anytime soon. But, an integrated Windows 98 tool, called the System Configuration Utility, can make you feel like you have a virtual Microsoft employee right inside your PC.

The System Configuration Utility (Msconfig.exe) re-creates the steps that Windows support personnel use to diagnose Windows startup problems. With it, you can interactively load device drivers one by one or you can select and deselect configuration files to process during the boot procedure.

Strangely, Microsoft buries this powerful tool under the System Information utility (which you'll find under Start | Programs | Accessories | System Tools). You can launch the System Configuration utility from the System Information utility's Tools menu. Or you can load it from the Start menu's Run prompt.

Follow these steps to use the System Configuration Utility:

1. Enter **Msconfig** at the Start | Run prompt.

2. Select the General tab.

3. To run a step-by-step Windows startup, choose Diagnostic Startup. This action is similar to pressing the F8 key during the Windows boot process. Windows 98 will ask you whether or not to load each and every line configuration instruction it comes across. This process might take several minutes if your system stores a lot of instructions in the AUTOEXEC.BAT.

If you've narrowed down the problem to a particular configuration file, choose Selective Startup and then place a check next to the configuration files you want to process (see Figure 2.9.4).

Figure 2.9.4

To diagnose startup problems, choose Msconfig's Selective Startup option and then select the configuration files you want to process.

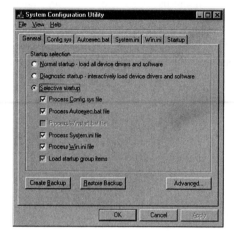

Smart Troubleshooting

4. Use the other tabs to select or remove individual lines from the configuration files for your diagnosis purposes.

5. Click the OK button. Msconfig will then ask if you want to restart your system. Click the Yes button.

When you're finished with the diagnosis, go back and choose Normal Startup from the General tab's list. Otherwise, all your restarts will take place in diagnosis mode.

2.9.5 Fix What the Windows 98 Upgrade Broke

Did the Windows 98 upgrade screw up your PC? Polls on the World Wide Web report that it wreaked havoc for many users. The key problem: Older applications no longer run correctly. Software that used to work perfectly now either produces error messages or doesn't run at all.

How could this happen? Pretty easily. During the upgrade process, Windows 98 secretly replaces many system files with newer versions. And, if you're getting errors, you can be sure the new files are incompatible with your old applications.

Why did Microsoft do this? Because they tried to improve the system overall, and this effort required upgrading code from previous incarnations of Windows. Unfortunately, you can't please everyone, or all software, all the time.

But there's some good news. Windows 98 backs up your old files just in case you need them. The Version Conflict Manager (Vcmui.exe) utility will help you restore needed files and get your system back up and running.

Follow these steps to launch and use the Version Conflict Manager:

1. Enter **Vcmui.exe** at the Start | Run prompt or Launch the System Information utility (under Start | Programs | Accessories | System Tools) and choose Version Conflict Manager from the Tools menu.

2. The Version Conflict Manager's main screen presents a list of replaced files and the version numbers of both the new and old files (see Figure 2.9.5). How do you know which files you need to restore? Your error message will likely report the name of the trouble-causing file. If not, use the Registry Editor to search the Windows Registry on each filename in the VCM's list. The Registry keys will link the file to an application name. When you find a match between your crippled application and a system file in VCM's list, restore the old version.

Figure 2.9.5

The Version Conflict Manager shows you a list of files that it replaced and their backups.

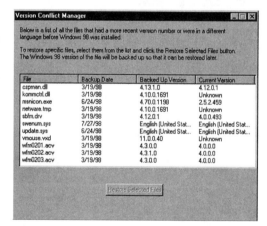

3. Select the files you want to restore. If you want to restore more than one file, hold down the **Ctrl** key while you select files. This action enables you to select a group of files.

4. Click the Restore Selected Files button. If you make a mistake, don't worry. The newer Windows 98 file will be backed up so that you can restore them with VCM later.

> **TIP**   Whatever you do, don't buy off-the-shelf computer software that assists you in removing Windows 98 from your PC. You'll be wasting your money. If you've had enough, and really want to revert back to your previous operating system, just search the Windows Help system with the phrase **Uninstalling Windows 98**. The Help system includes detailed instructions on removing Windows 98 and will even walk you through the process.

2.9.6 Deal With Programs That Don't Handle Long Filenames

The ability to use long descriptive filenames in Windows 98 is a great feature, except when your applications don't recognize them. Problems sometimes result from spaces embedded in the middle of a filename. MY DOCUMENT.DOC and PROJECT X.XLS are examples of potentially troublesome filenames.

You shouldn't encounter any problems with 32-bit applications designed for Windows 98, but older applications might balk at spaces within names. You'll notice the problem when you attempt to open a document directly from the Windows Explorer by double-clicking on it. The error messages will state that the application can't open the file. And the message will contain a clue to the root of the problem. In the above MY DOCUMENT.DOC example, the resulting error message will likely read, `Can't open file 'MY.' Please verify the correct path and filename are given.` The problematic application thinks the filename ends where it sees the space.

Fortunately, you can rectify this situation, with any program, by editing the actions performed on file types. Follow these steps to force an application to recognize long filenames:

1. Choose Start | Settings | Folder Options from the Start menu.

2. Select the File Types tab.

3. Scroll down the list of Registered File Types until you come to the type of file that's causing problems.

4. Highlight the file type and click the Edit button.

5. On the Edit File Type sheet, highlight the Open item in the Actions box. Then click the Edit button.

6. In the box labeled Application Used to Perform Action, find the reference to %1. This is the reference used to process the filename in the Windows Explorer. Replace the %1 with **"%1"** (include the quotation marks). This will instruct the application to use the entire long filename, even if it has embedded spaces.

7. Click the OK button on each of the three open sheets to close them.

The change will take effect immediately.

> **NOTE**   Experts can use the Registry Editor to perform this tip. Use Regedit and search the Registry for all application references to %1. Replace each with "**%1**" (include the quotation marks).

2.9.7 Stop Programs from Running Automatically at Startup

Call this the Case of the Missing Startup Shortcut. You know a particular program launches during the Windows startup process because you can plainly see its icon in the System Tray or the Taskbar. But when you try to remove it from the Windows Startup folder (where it must be referenced, you think), you can't find it.

What's going on? How does the application launch on its own? Are you going crazy? No. For whatever reason, probably a diabolical one, the application has registered itself to start automatically during the Windows boot process.

The only way to thwart this dastardly program is to hack the Registry and, oh yes, you can use Dr. Watson's help as well. The game is afoot!

Use the following steps to stop a program from loading during Windows startup process:

1. Launch the Registry Editor by entering **Regedit** at the Start | Run prompt.

> **TIP**   To see a list of programs that launch automatically at startup, use the Dr. Watson tool. Enter **Drwatson** at the Start | Run prompt. Click on the Dr. Watson icon in the System Tray. Choose Dr. Watson. Then select the Startup tab.

2. Navigate to the following key: My Computer\HKEY_LOCAL_MACHINE\SOFTWARE\Microsoft\Windows\CurrentVersion\.

3. From here, check each of the following subkeys for a reference to the offending application: Run, Run-, RunOnce, RunOnceEx, RunServices, RunServices-, and RunServicesOnce.

4. Double-click on the String Value that holds the name of the application and delete the reference in the box Value Data. Then click OK.

5. Close the Registry Editor by choosing Exit from the Registry menu.

> **NOTE**   You can also use the System Configuration Utility to view hidden startup programs and stop them from launching. Check the Startup tab of SCU for details.

If you can't find a reference to the offending application in the Registry, then you must check the configuration files that load before Windows starts, namely AUTOEXEC.BAT and WIN.INI.

2.9.8 Back Up To Hard Copy

I won't berate you about backing up your computer. I'm sure you already understand the importance of that menial task. And, I'm also certain that you take time out of every day to ensure you have a copy of your computer files safely stored away on tape, CD-R, or other backup medium. *Right???!* (If not, stop reading immediately. Go make a backup. I'll meet you back here.)

Okay, here's a clever way to enhance your backups and cut down on troubleshooting time—make a complete hard copy of your system configuration. No, you don't have to run around cutting and pasting files into a Word document. The System Information utility can round up everything you need in a flash.

Follow these steps to print out a complete system configuration:

1. Choose Start | Programs | Accessories | System Tools and then select System Information to launch the System Information utility.

2. Select File | Export from the menu bar.

3. Choose a filename and folder for the resulting text file. Make the filename descriptive, something like MYCONFIG.TXT.

4. Click the Save button. The utility will collect all your system information and save it to disk.

5. Choose File | Exit from the menu bar to close the System Information utility.

Wasn't that easy? Prepare to be amazed when you browse the resulting file. You'll find information about your computer that you didn't even know. When you do browse the file, you'll find that it's too large for the Notepad editor. Instead, Windows 98 will use Wordpad to open it. Keep this list in a safe place and refer to it whenever you begin a troubleshooting session.

Smart Troubleshooting

2.9.9 Access a Previous Windows Registry to Recover from a Crash

Windows has come a long way with Registry backups. In the past it was a manual process. Now, a utility called the Registry Checker backs up and optimizes your Registry every day, automatically, during the Windows boot process.

The Registry Checker also looks for errors in the Registry. If, however, it inadvertently missed a problem and you're encountering trouble when launching Windows, you can cycle back to a previous functioning version of your Windows Registry.

> **TIP**   Always keep your Windows 98 Emergency Startup disk on hand. Also, make sure it works by booting from the disk periodically. To make a new Emergency Startup disk, choose Start | Settings | Control Panel | Add/Remove Programs. Then select the Startup Disk tab and click the Create button.

Follow these steps to load a previous version of your Windows Registry:

1. Boot your PC with your Emergency Startup Disk.

2. At the command line prompt, enter **SCANREG/RESTORE**.

3. The Registry Checker will load and present a list of the last five Registry backups. Select the most recent one unless you're aware of some problem with that Registry. Then click the Restore button. The Registry Checker will automatically restore that version and your problem should be fixed.

> **TIP**   To increase the number of previous backups that Registry Checker maintains, edit the file SCANREG.INI in the C:\Windows directory. Change the number in the line reading MaxBackupCopies=X. Then save and exit the file.

2.9.10 Run a Customized Version of ScanDisk

The disk fix-it tool called ScanDisk is so good that Microsoft included two different versions in Windows 98, one for DOS and one for Windows. Strangely, the DOS version allows more customization possibilities, through an .INI file, than the Windows program.

For most disk problems, the Windows ScanDisk(SCANDSKW.EXE) tool will perform adequately. But, for a troublesome hard drive, choose the DOS version (SCANDISK.EXE), instead. After customization, the DOS ScanDisk can run more passes on your hard drive, check volume labels, mount unmounted DoubleSpace compressed drives, and more.

Follow these steps to customize the DOS version of ScanDisk:

1. In Notepad, open the file SCANDISK.INI. You'll find the file in the C:\Windows\Command directory.

2. Read the detailed comments within this file to choose your own settings. Here are some of my suggestions:

   ■ Change NumPasses=1 to NumPasses=10

   This will force ScanDisk to check each cluster 10 times for errors and problems. ScanDisk does not always finds and fixes problems with 1 pass.

   ■ Change LabelCheck=off to LabelCheck=on

   This tells ScanDisk to check Volume Labels as well as data clusters for errors.

3. Further down in the file, you can set ScanDisk to always mount un-mounted drives, perform a surface scan, and create an undo disk for its disk fixes.

4. Save the file by choosing File | Save from the menus. Then close it by selecting File | Exit.

This customized version of ScanDisk might take several minutes to run. It might even take an hour or more depending on the number and size of your hard drives. It would be nice if you could use the Task Scheduler to run this program during the middle of the night; unfortunately, you can't run SCANDISK.EXE within Windows. You must either boot to DOS or shutdown to DOS to execute it. Your best bet is to set this program off just as you leave for the day. When you return in the morning, your drive(s) will be thoroughly scanned.

Smart Troubleshooting

Chapter

2.10

Useful Scheduling

For maximum efficiency, your computer should be working even when you're not around. Make your PC work the nightshift with the Task Scheduler. These hints show you how to make a backup, perform maintenance, and even power-up your computer, while you're off having fun.

2.10.1 Schedule an Unattended Backup

Seagate Technology, Inc., the hard drive manufacturer, developed the new Windows 98 backup utility called Microsoft Backup. All in all, it works very well, but close inspection uncovers one key fault: It can't perform an unattended backup. After it's started, the utility will backup your data without further interaction with you, but you must be around to start it.

If you search through Microsoft's online technical support database for help with this problem, you'll find this great advice, "Upgrade to a backup utility that can perform an unattended backup." Gee, thanks!

I have a better idea. With a freeware download, the Windows 98 Task Scheduler, and a little ingenuity, you can turn Microsoft Backup into a better tool. In this tip you'll create two scheduled tasks. One will launch the Microsoft Backup tool and the other will send the keystrokes needed to start the Backup.

Follow these steps to schedule an unattended backup:

1. Browse *PC Magazine*'s Web site at www.pcmag.com. Access their Software Library by selecting Downloads on the homepage and then choosing Software Library from the following page.

> **TIP**   You can also browse PC Mag's Software Library by entering the URL:
> **www.hotfiles.com**.

2. In the Software Library section of the site, search for the words "Send Keystrokes." You'll find the search field at the bottom of the Software Library page. The results should include SendKey Utility v1.03. Click this link and follow the instructions to download J.H.A. van de Weijer's SendKey Utility (see Figure 2.10.1). The download file will be in Zip format, so you'll need an unzip utility, such as those from Pkware, Inc. (www.pkware.com), to decode the file.

3. Unzip the file in any temporary directory, then in Windows Explorer, double-click on SendKey's SETUP.EXE program to install the utility.

Figure 2.10.1

Download the SendKey Utility from PC Magazine's Software Library Online. This tool enables you to start the Backup utility while you're away.

4. Now it's time to set up your backup routine. Choose Start | Programs | Accessories | System Tools | Backup to launch the Microsoft Backup utility. Follow the help files' instructions to create a new backup job either for your whole disk or only for selected files. Make sure you select the location to which you want the files backed up under Where To Back Up.

5. Still in Microsoft Backup, click the Options button, then select the Report tab and put a check next to the line: Perform an Unattended Backup. This will ensure that the backup proceeds without stopping after you start it (see Figure 2.10.2). Click OK to close the Backup Job Options dialog box. Also, make sure you save the backup job. Choose Job | Save from the menus and give it a name. Then click OK.

NOTE   These steps require less effort if you close Microsoft Backup with the job you want to schedule displayed on the main screen. If you have multiple backup jobs saved under Microsoft Backup, you must script your SendKey routine to open the specific job you want run. To avoid confusion I won't list these keystrokes here, but experts can figure it out on their own.

6. Choose Job | Exit from the menus to close Backup. Make sure that the job you want to schedule is the job displayed on the main screen when you exit.

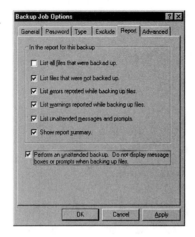

Figure 2.10.2

Specify "unattended backup" within the Backup utility. This ensures that the job will proceed without any interaction from you.

7. Now, create a batch file called STARTB.BAT and save it in the folder of your choice. The file should have only one line, reading: C:\windows\sendkeys.exe "Microsoft Backup", "5", "%S", "Start Backup", "1".

8. After it's saved, right-click on the batch file and choose Properties from the pop-menu. Then select the Program tab and put a check next to the line: Close on Exit.

9. Still with me? Now open the Task Scheduler by choosing Start | Programs | Accessories | System Tools | Scheduled Tasks.

10. Choose Add Scheduled Task to start the Scheduled Task Wizard. Click the Next button. From the application list, select Backup, then click the Next button. Enter a name for the task, such as Backup, and select how often you want to run it by choosing one of the buttons below Perform This Task. Click the Next button. Choose a start date and time. Then click the Next button again. On the following screen, click the Finish button.

11. Finally, add the second task (by clicking Add Scheduled Task again) that runs your STARTB.BAT batch file. It is very important to set the batch file to run 1 or 2 minutes after your Backup task runs. This way, the Backup utility will launch first, then STARTB.BAT will send it an **Alt-S** key combination which starts the backup job. Voilà!

Make sure that you leave a backup tape or disk in your backup drive so that the utility will have someplace to put the data.

2.10.2 Customize the Maintenance Wizard

Windows 98's Maintenance Wizard can increase your productivity in two ways. First, you can schedule its tasks to run during the night while you're away from your computer, thereby freeing your daytime computing hours for work. And second, its maintenance routines tune your system for better performance, making your computing session all the speedier.

Setting up the Maintenance Wizard is easy. Just don't cop out and use the default settings. The Wizard will do a better job if you take a moment or two to customize the settings.

Follow these steps to customize the Maintenance Wizard:

1. Choose Start | Programs | Accessories | System Tools | Maintenance Wizard to launch the Wizard applet.

2. On the initial screen, select Custom. Then click the Next button.

3. On the schedule screen, choose a category appropriate to your work habits. For most people, Nights or Evenings would be the best choice.

4. On the defragmenter screen, select Yes, Defragment My Disk Regularly. Adjust the scheduled time, if desired, by clicking the Reschedule button. Then click the Settings button.

5. In the settings screen, push the drop-down arrow and select All Hard Drives. Then put a check next to Rearrange Program Files So My Programs Start Faster. Click OK. Then click the Next button to move to the following screen.

6. Select Yes, Scan My Hard Drive for Errors Regularly. Adjust the schedule if you like, then click the Settings button.

7. In the ScanDisk screen, select Thorough in the Type of Test box. Click the Options button and make sure the Areas of the Disk to Scan box has System and Data Areas selected. Click OK. Then put a check next to Automatically Fix Errors.

8. Still on the ScanDisk screen, click the Advanced button. Under Lost File Fragments, select Free. Under Cross-Linked Files, select Delete. Click OK to exit this screen. Then click OK to exit ScanDisk Settings.

9. On the Delete Unnecessary Files screen, pick Yes, Delete Unnecessary Files Regularly. Click the Settings button. Put a check next to the entries that suit your needs. Most users should include Temporary Internet Files,

Useful Scheduling

Old ScanDisk Files in Root Folder, and Temporary Files. Click OK to exist Disk Cleanup.

10. Click Next to move to the final Maintenance Wizard screen. Read the list of tasks the Wizard will perform, then click Finish.

2.10.3 Run Scheduled Tasks with Your PC in Standby Mode

Don't leave your computer running all night simply because you want to run scheduled tasks after hours. If your computer's BIOS supports Advanced Power Management (APM) 1.2 or Advanced Configuration and Power Interface (ACPI) you can leave your computer in standby mode and Windows will automatically wake up your system to run a scheduled task.

Read your system's documentation regarding power management to determine if it will support APM or ACPI. If it does, set up a power management profile that will put your computer in standby mode.

Follow these steps to create a power management profile that puts your PC in standby mode.

1. You might need to enable power management in your system's BIOS firmware. Read your PC's documentation on how to do this. Then enable this feature before proceeding.

2. In Windows 98, choose Start | Settings | Control Panel. Then select the Power Management icon.

3. In the Power Schemes box, click Save As. Enter a new descriptive name for your standby mode scheme. Click OK to close the Save As dialog box.

4. In the System Standby box, click the drop-down arrow and choose a time delay. Your system will wait for this period of inactivity before entering standby mode.

5. At this point you can also set the other parameters for this new power scheme. In the Settings For... box, select the time-outs for the devices listed. These should include hard disk and monitor as well as other devices (if your BIOS supports device-level power management).

> **TIP** You can also manually put your PC in standby mode. In the Power Management Properties screen, select the Advanced tab. Under When I Press the Power Button on My Computer, select Standby from the list of options. Then click OK.

6. Click OK to save your power scheme settings.

The Task Scheduler requires no additional modification. With a standby power scheme, Windows 98 automatically wakes up your system to perform a scheduled task.

Useful Scheduling

Chapter

2.11

Proficient Printing

Windows 98 offers advances in both hardware and software for smarter printing. This chapter describes how to use infrared ports, how to print offline, and how to launch the new, improved Print Troubleshooter.

2.11.1 Print Offline

For mobile users, printing can be a hassle. Often, notebook users finish polishing a document or presentation only to find themselves with no printer attached to their system. Many in this situation simply shut down their application and wait until they return to their office, where they can connect to the docking station or LAN and print.

If you encounter this scenario, don't wait! Use Windows 98's offline print capability. With your application launched and document open, you're more than halfway through the printing process. Leverage this readiness by completing the preprocessing that's required for all print jobs.

When you do reconnect to your docking station, LAN, or local printer, Windows 98's print spooler will immediately print out your waiting job.

Follow these steps to print offline:

1. Open My Computer and select Printers.

2. Choose the Printer to which you would normally send the job.

3. From the Printer menu, select Print Offline.

> **NOTE** To use offline printing you must enable Windows 98's print spooling process. To check this setting, click the Spool Settings button on the Detail tab of your printer's Properties sheet (right-click on the printer icon and choose Properties from the pop-up list).

> **NOTE** Desktop systems that use printers over a network and notebook PCs of any configuration will have a Print Offline option under the Printer menu. Other system configurations display a Pause Printer menu option instead. Either command will complete the print preprocessing and hold the job until your system is connected to a printer.

4. Select Printer | Close from the menus to exit.

5. Activate the Print command from your application.

2.11.2 Print Through Your Infrared Port

Many notebook computers now feature infrared (IR) communication ports, the same technology used for TV remote controls. Similarly, many printer manufacturers include this technology in their products or offer IR add-on ports as options. Until the release of Windows 98, however, getting these ports to work properly was a tedious and complicated task.

But Windows 98 provides native support for these ports and will install the needed software through the internal Plug and Play process. If both your computer and your printer have IR ports, use them! You'll no longer need to fuss with docking stations, LAN connections, or printer cables when printing.

Follow these steps to set up and use IR ports for printing:

1. During the installation process, Windows 98 will search for IR ports and set up the required software. If, however, you add an IR port after you've installed Windows 98, you'll need to use the Add New Hardware icon (under Start | Settings | Control Panel) to set up your IR port. The New Hardware Wizard will walk you through the process.

2. After you've configured your IR port, you need to assign a printer to it. Choose Start | Settings | Printers, then right-click your IR-capable printer from the list of devices. From the pop-up list, select Properties. Then choose the Details tab of the printer's Properties sheet. From the Print to the Following Port drop-down box, select your IR port. Or, if it's not listed, click the Add Port button and follow the instructions to append it to the list.

> **TIP** IR ports do not require "line of sight" positioning. IR transmissions bounce off walls and still reach their destination intact. Just try to keep the two IR devices within the same room and they should communicate successfully.

3. Finally, you'll need to ensure that your IR-ready printer is "within range" of your PC. Windows 98 includes a utility called Infrared Monitor that scans for IR devices within range of your PC's IR port. To activate it, select Start | Settings | Control Panel | Infrared. Then choose the Preferences tab and put a check next to Display the Infrared Monitor Icon on the Taskbar. Click OK to close the Infrared sheet. Then right-click the Infrared icon on the Taskbar and check Search for Devices in Range.

With the above configuration, you can print wirelessly from any application whether or not your PC is attached to the LAN.

Proficient Printing

TIP The Add New Hardware Wizard can search your computer to find a newly added infrared port. But the installation process will go faster if you select the new port from Windows 98's hardware list. Choose the hardware list if you have a driver diskette from your IR port's manufacturer.

On the third screen of the Add New Hardware Wizard, select No, I Want to Select the Hardware from a List. Then click the Next button (see Figure 2.11.1).

Figure 2.11.1

For a faster installation, choose your IR port from the Hardware Wizard's list of products.

In the Hardware Types list, choose other devices. Then click the Next button.

From the Manufacturer's list, choose Infrared COM Port or Dongle. Then choose the model type from the Models list. For most ports, the correct choice is Infrared PnP Serial Port (see Figure 2.11.2).

Figure 2.11.2

Pick your type of IR port from the Wizard's categories.

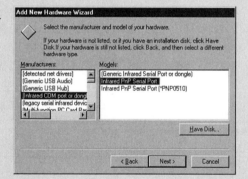

Finally, insert your manufacturer's diskette into your floppy drive. Then click the Have Disk button.

2.11.3 Solve Print Problems with the Print Troubleshooter

What always makes the Top 10 list in computer technical support calls? Printer problems. No matter how far technology progresses, we still can't seem to achieve the mythical "paperless" office.

Before you spend the time and money calling for outside help for your printer problems, launch the Windows 98 Print Troubleshooter (see Figure 2.11.3). Give this tool a try even if you were dissatisfied with Windows 95's Print Trouble-shooter. The revamped and expanded Windows 98 utility can solve most common printer problems with a quick question and answer session.

Figure 2.11.3
The Print Troubleshooter will find and fix most common printer problems.

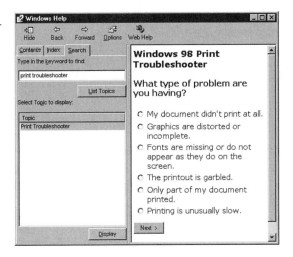

You'll find the tool in the Windows Help System. Choose Start | Help and enter **Print Troubleshooter** in the keyword box. Then select the Print Troubleshooter topic and click the Display button. Windows 98 will activate the tool.

2.11.4 Enhance the Control over Network Printing

When printing to a locally attached printer, your Windows 98 system has complete control over the print queue. It can pause and restart printing as well as cancel items waiting in the queue. If, however, you're using a network printer attached to a Windows NT print server, your PC has no such control over the print queue. That is, unless you install the Remote Procedure Call Print Provider (RPCPP) utility.

Proficient Printing

RPCPP adds the required Win32 APIs to your system so that it can control a Windows NT print server. Follow these steps in install RPCPP:

1. From the Start menu, choose Start | Settings | Control Panel.

2. Select the Network object from the Control Panel.

3. Choose the Configuration tab. Then click the Add button.

4. On the Select Network Component Type dialog box (see Figure 2.11.4), choose Service. Then click the Add button.

Figure 2.11.4

Add remote printer control through the Network dialog box.

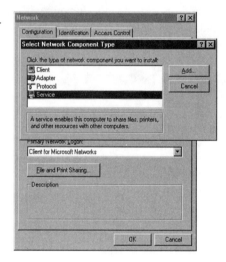

5. On the Select Network Service dialog box, click the Have Disk button.

6. At this point, you should place your Windows 98 CD into your CD-ROM drive. Then, in the Copy Manufacturer's File From field enter the following path: **[CD–ROM drive letter]:\TOOLS\RESKIT\ NETADMIN\RPCPP**. Click the OK button.

7. In the new Select Network Service dialog box, choose Microsoft Network RPC Print Provider. Click the OK button.

8. Click OK to close the Network object. This will begin the installation of the RPCPP files.

9. After the copy, Windows 98 asks you whether or not you want to restart your computer. Click the Yes button.

To access the print queue for your remote printer, choose Start | Settings | Printers from the Start menu. Then pick your remote printer from the list. You'll find the Pause Printing and Cancel Printing options under the Document menu of the printer's print queue.

Chapter

2.12

Internet Productivity

Windows 98 Internet Explorer and Active Desktop features are amazing—and complicated. With default settings, the Active Desktop might hold your system hostage by slowing things down and deciding, on its own, when to dial out on your modem. In this chapter, find out how to tame your dial-up connection, expand Explorer's capabilities, keep in touch with friends and colleagues, and more.

2.12.1 Make Internet Explorer's Autocomplete Work Harder

Windows 98 makes it easier to type in those long cryptic Web URLs through Internet Explorer 4.0's Autocomplete feature. With Autocomplete, you type in just the middle section of the URL, and Internet Explorer searches for a matching address. So, what's the catch? Autocomplete only searches for addresses that end in .COM (corporations), .ORG (non-profit organizations), and .EDU (universities).

A quick Registry hack will expand this list to include .GOV (government) and .NET (miscellaneous) addresses as well. By expanding Autocomplete's search capabilities, you'll end up spending less time entering URLs.

Follow these steps to expand Autocomplete's search feature:

1. Launch the Registry Editor by entering **Regedit** at the Start | Run prompt.

2. Navigate to the Registry key: My Computer\HKEY_LOCAL_ MACHINE\SOFTWARE\Microsoft\Internet Explorer\Main\ UrlTemplate.

3. Beneath this key you'll see six strings with the values: "www.%s.com," "www.%s.edu," "www.%s.org," "%s.com," "%s.edu," and "%s.org." After selecting Edit | New | String Value from the menu, you can enter the following new strings:

Value Name	Value Data
7	www.%s.net
8	www.%s.gov
9	%s.net
10	%s.gov

4. Choose Registry | Exit from the menu to close the Registry Editor.

This change will take place immediately. However, the first time you enter a new .NET or .GOV address, you'll still need to type the whole address.

2.12.2 Download Free Internet Explorer Tools

For billionaires, being generous comes easy. Microsoft gave away utilities, called PowerToys, for Windows 95; and now they're doing the same for Internet Explorer 4.0, which just so happens to be the version included with Windows 98.

So, drop what you're doing and browse Windows Magazine's Free Windows 98 software site (`http://www.winmag.com/win98/software.htm`). There you'll find a file called PowerToys for Internet Explorer 4. Download the file to your hard drive. It's an executable file, so just click on the filename under Windows Explorer and the installation routine will begin.

What do these tools do? They increase your productivity while browsing! Here's a description of the included PowerToys:

- **Image Toggler:** Unless you're riding a high-speed Internet connection, downloading image-filled Web pages slows you down. Unfortunately, Turning off "show pictures" (and turning it back on), under Internet Options, requires several clicks of the mouse. The Image Toggler performs this action in just one mouse click. After it's installed, you'll find this tool on the Links bar.

- **Links List:** Are you tired of scrolling up and down a Web page looking for a link? Just right-click on a page, select Links List from the pop-up menu, and Internet Explorer will display all the page's links in a new Window. Then just click and go.

- **Open in New Window:** Browser frames have taken over the Web. On a page with multiple frames its sometimes difficult to see what's going on. Use this feature to open a single frame in its own window. Just right-click inside the frame and choose Open in New Window.

- **Text Highlighter:** You can mark up Web pages with a virtual yellow highlighter pen. To highlight text, right-click and choose Highlight. So what's the downside? There's no way to remove highlights.

- **Quick Search:** Make searches faster by entering a search engine alias *and* keywords simultaneously in the address bar. For example, "av cloning" activates an Alta Vista search with the keyword "cloning."

- **Web Search:** Web designers often post hyperlinked words or phrases that branch to more detailed descriptions; but, they don't always please everyone with their choices. If you need more information on a non-hyperlinked word or phrase, just highlight it, right-click and choose Web Search to create your own hyperlinks.

- ■ **Zoom In/Zoom Out:** No matter what resolution a Web master uses for embedded images, you can make them larger or smaller for better viewing. Right-click an image, then choose Zoom In or Zoom Out from the pop-up menu.

Keep in mind, these are unsupported tools. Microsoft offers them as freebies, but they are not official parts of the Internet Explorer product.

2.12.3 Move Forward and Backward Faster

Did you know you can right-click Internet Explorer's Forward and Back buttons? Neither did I. Larry Passo, another Macmillan author, passed on this elegant and easy timesaving tip.

How often have you clicked the Forward and Back arrows multiple times in a row desperately trying to get to a Web page you were looking at moments ago? Everyone does this. But you don't need to. Right-click on either the Forward and Back buttons and Internet Explorer 4 will display a list of sites you've just seen. Just move your mouse down the list and select the Web page you want. Explorer will take you directly there.

Also, try the following keystroke for quick transitions. Pressing the F4 key anywhere in Explorer pops up a list of Web sites you've recently visited. Select a site from the list and Explorer will transport you there.

2.13.4 Treat the Address Bar like a DOS Command Line

You probably know you can place an Internet Explorer Address Bar just about anywhere, including the Taskbar, inside Windows Explorer, or even in the middle of the desktop. But you might not know that the Address Bar acts a little like a DOS command line.

Enter DOS's change directory symbols in the Address Bar to move up in your directory hierarchy. Two periods (..) moves up you one level. Four periods with a forward slash in the middle (../..) moves up two levels.

Type the name of a folder in your current directory to open it (see Figure 2.12.1).

Figure 2.12.1

Enter a folder name within your current directory in the Address Bar to open it.

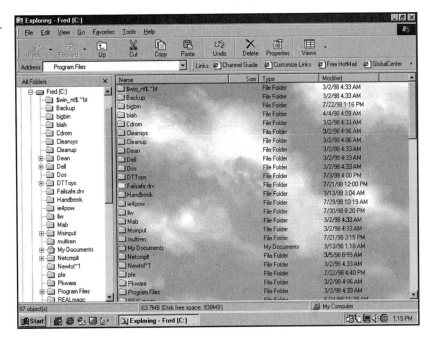

Enter the name of a text file, document, or image and Windows will automatically launch the application associated with that file and open it. When you type in executable and batch filenames, Windows will run them immediately.

2.12.5 Save Your Dial–Up Networking Password

Saving your Dial-Up Networking (DUN) password is a good way to speed up your connections to the Internet and remote-connections to your office network. To do this, simply select My Computer | Dial-Up Networking, and choose your connection from the list of entries. Then put a check next to Save Password in the Connect To dialog box.

> **WARNING** Saving your Dial-Up Networking password reduces your security. If an intruder gains access to your PC, he can log onto the Internet or your office Network by simply selecting the Dial-Up Networking connection. For security-risk environments, take the extra time and enter your password.

You should be aware, however, that this command doesn't always work. Even with Save Password checked, you might find yourself still forced to enter your password with each logon. Windows forums and even Microsoft's online support database offer pages of information describing this bug and what to do about it.

If DUN won't save your password, step through these solutions:

■ **Are you logged on to Windows?** You must be logged on for Dial-Up Networking to save your network password. If you pressed Cancel at the Enter Windows Password dialog box, without entering a password, you are not officially logged on. Check your logon status by opening the Start menu. If you see Log Off... without a username following it, you are not logged on. You can set a null password by choosing Start | Settings | Control Panel | Passwords. Then, in the Change Passwords tab, click the Change Windows Password button. Just leave the New Password and Confirm New Password entries blank (without spaces) and click OK.

■ **Launch the Policy Editor (poledit) at the Start | Run prompt.** (Read the introduction if you haven't installed the Policy Editor). From the menus, select File | Open Registry. Choose Local Computer. Select Windows 98 Network, then choose Passwords. Beneath this policy you'll find an entry reading Disable Password Caching. If there's a check if front of this entry, remove it.

■ Finally, try removing and reinstalling the Dial-Up Networking components of Windows 98. From the Start menu, choose Start | Settings | Control Panel. Then select Add/Remove Programs. Choose the Windows Setup tab, select Communications, and then remove the check next to the entry Dial-Up Networking. Click the OK button to begin the removal process. After it completes, go back to the same entry, place a check in front of it, and click OK to reinstall Dial-Up Networking.

2.12.6 Keep In Touch Online

You've probably heard about the real-time Internet messaging features that some Internet Service Providers (ISPs) offer. America Online, for example, provides this service. Real-time messaging services alert you when your friends and colleagues log on to the net. From there, you can communicate directly with each other in real-time as opposed to the delay of email transactions.

The downside of these services is that your "circle" of associates must all use the same ISP, much like the phone company circle calling programs. But, a company called Mirabilis offers a product that features real-time messaging across ISPs. This product, called ICQ, is available as a time-limited free beta. There's also a specialized version of ICQ for Windows 98's NetMeeting application. With it, you not only have real-time messaging but collaboration capabilities as well.

To get ICQ, browse CNET's Download.com Web site (www.download.com). Search the site with the keyword "ICQ," then select the version you want and follow the instructions for downloading and installing the application.

2.12.7 Stop Unwanted Dial Up

What's the most notable difference between computing at home and computing in an office? Internet connections. In the office, Internet access likely routes through a LAN. At home, in general, Internet access comes through a dial-up connection over your phone line. This difference matters when you use Windows 98 Active Desktop, which regularly and automatically updates your desktop from channel and Web sites subscriptions.

By default, Internet Explorer allows regular subscription updates. This means your PC might suddenly dial out for an update even if you're in the middle of some important task. The first of the following methods describes how to stop Internet Explorer's auto-dialing, which will stop all automatic downloads. The second method shows you how to reschedule subscriptions to a more suitable time.

Follow these steps to end Internet Explorer's auto-dialing:

1. Launch Internet Explorer (under Start | Programs | Internet Explorer).

2. From the menus, choose View | Internet Options.

3. Select the Advanced tab. Then, scroll down and open the Browsing entry. This displays a list of browser settings. Scroll down and remove the check next to Enable Scheduled Subscription updates (see Figure 2.12.2).

Figure 2.12.2

Stop Active Desktop auto-dialing by disabling scheduled subscription updates in Internet Explorer.

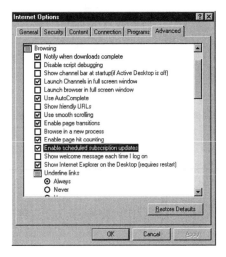

4. Click OK to close the Internet Options sheet.

To alter the update schedule for channel and Web site updates, use the following procedure:

1. Launch the Internet Explorer browser (under Start | Programs | Internet Explorer).

2. Choose Favorites | Manage Subscriptions from the menus.

3. Right-click the channel or Web site that you want to modify from the list of subscriptions. Then choose Properties from the pop-up menu.

4. Choose the Receiving tab from the Properties sheet. If you want only email notification of updates rather than actual page downloads, select Only Notify Me When Updates Occur in the Subscription Type box. Then in the Notification box, put a check next to Send an Email Message to the Following Address. If the email address showing in the box is not your correct address, click the Change Address button to modify it.

5. If you'd rather maintain automatic downloads, but shift the update schedule, skip step 4 and choose the Schedule tab of the Property sheet instead. Modify the schedule as desired or simply put a check next to Don't Update This Subscription When I'm Using My Computer.

6. Click OK to close the subscriptions Property sheet.

In the end, it's much better for you to decide when your system receives updates. The Active Desktop should help, not hinder, your work.

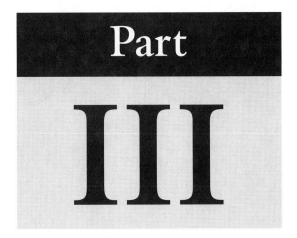

Part III

Performance

Microsoft promised only modest performance improvements with Windows 98. Their main goals for the new operating system were to add hardware support, supplement software features, and make computing easier. In terms of performance, Microsoft simply claimed that Windows 98 would launch applications faster and startup and shutdown in less time than Windows 95.

If you read computer magazine test reports on Windows 98—such as those found in *PC World* and *PC Magazine*—you'll find that, for the most part, Microsoft succeeded with these performance goals. However, Windows 98 is larger than Windows 95; therefore Win98 startup and shutdown times usually only break even with Win95 systems overall.

Most importantly, though, you'll see almost no performance improvement if you just install Windows 98 and then forget it. Like a sports car, you need to tweak and tune the operating system to eke out all the speed potential that lies underneath the hood.

In this section, I'll cover ways to improve your system performance by converting to FAT32, diagnosing and benchmarking your PC, tuning Win98 device parameters, and more. Everyone should scan through this section for speed-up tips. Then read the chapters that relate to the components your PC contains.

Don't be afraid to adjust a setting more than once. You might not find the optimal choice on your first try.

Chapter

3.1

Faster Printing

In most offices, printing consumes an inordinate amount of computing time and resources. Here, you'll learn how to reduce your overall printing time by printing in the background and adjusting your printer's memory settings and graphics mode.

3.1.1 Print in the Background

Quick, what's the best way to improve your printer's performance? If you said "add RAM to your PC," then step up to the head of the class.

During setup, Windows 98 checks your PC's amount of RAM and automatically turns background printing on or off depending on what it finds.

For background printing, Windows 98 creates a printer-ready file, using a format called EMF, before it sends the job to the printer. With sufficient RAM, Windows will spin off this procedure as a separate process and return control to your application so that you can continue on with your work more quickly. The print job proceeds after the EMF file processing completes. If your system doesn't have enough RAM, this process is not spun off as a separate task and ties up your system while you wait for it to finish.

> **NOTE**   Believe it or don't, you'll notice better printing performance when you use a printer that's attached to a Windows 98 file or print server. Why? Because your PC will let the Windows 98 server create the printer-ready EMF file rather than doing it itself. If you use a Windows NT print server, a NetWare print server, or a locally attached printer, your local PC must do all the preprocessing. If you print frequently, mention this performance tip to your office IS manager.

To enable background printing, you need to do two things. First, run your PC with at least 32MB of RAM. Although Microsoft lists only 8MB of RAM as Windows 98's minimum system requirement, you'll notice all-around improved performance as well as faster printing with 32MB. Second, check your print spooling settings and set them according to your needs.

Use the following procedure to check and adjust your print spooling settings:

1. Choose Start | Settings | Control Panel from the Start menu. Then select the Printers icon.

2. Right-click on the printer you want to check. Then choose Properties from the pop-up list.

3. Select the Details tab on the printer's Properties sheet.

4. Click the Spool Settings button at the bottom of the printer's Properties sheet.

5. In the Spool Settings dialog box (see Figure 3.1.1), select Spool Print Jobs So Program Finishes Printing Faster. If you want Windows to return control to your application faster, also select Start Printing After Last Page Is Spooled. Otherwise, if getting the printed pages out faster is a greater concern than returning control to your program, select Start Printing After First Page Is Spooled.

Figure 3.1.1

Use Windows 98's Spool Settings to improve your printing performance.

6. Click OK to close the Spool Settings dialog box. Then click OK again to close your printer's Properties sheet.

After you have completed these software changes, take a moment and review your hardware set up. In most new PCs, you can set your parallel (printer) port for different speed modes such as ECP, EPP, and bi-directional. If your printer is capable of communicating in these faster modes, it's worth adjusting these settings in your PC's BIOS. Read your PC's documentation to determine the appropriate setting for your parallel port.

3.1.2 Modify Your Printer's Memory Settings

Companies such as Hewlett-Packard offer memory modules that let you increase the amount of memory within their printer products. Just like more RAM in your PC, more printer memory means faster printing for you—your PC can send larger chunks of data to your printer and get through a print job and on to other tasks more quickly.

Whether or not you take advantage of these memory modules, you should investigate your printer's memory settings under Windows 98. Why? Depending on your printer's communication capabilities, these settings might or might not be correct. If not, your print jobs might be unnecessarily slow. In fact, with incorrect settings, you might be receiving false Out of Memory error messages from your printer.

Faster Printing

Before you view this setting, perform a self-test on your printer (read your product's documentation for instructions). The self-test should list the amount of memory installed in the printer.

Follow these steps to view and adjust your printer's memory settings:

1. Choose the My Computer icon on your desktop, then open the Printers folder by double-clicking it.

2. On the list of printers, right-click on the printer you want to examine and choose Properties from the pop-up list.

3. Choose the Device Options tab (see Figure 3.1.2). Then choose the amount of memory your printer contains from the Printer Memory drop-down box. See the note about properties sheets if your sheet has no Printer Memory drop-down box.

Figure 3.1.2

Use the Device Options tab of your Printer's Properties sheet to view and modify its memory settings.

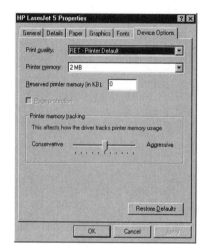

> **NOTE**   Properties sheets don't all look the same for every printer. Some printers won't let you manually modify certain settings. In fact, you might not have all the tabs and options that I list in these hints. I chose to use the Hewlett-Packard LaserJet 5 printer for these examples because it's one of the most popular printers. If the settings I mention are not visible, or are grayed out, on your sheet, don't panic. Your printer probably just doesn't offer these options. Read your printer's documentation for more details.

4. While you're here, you should also check the Printer Memory Tracking setting. For a potential performance boost, move the slider bar a little to the right of center toward Aggressive (but not all the way to the stop). This way, your printer driver will do less preprinting work on your print jobs and just send them on to the printer. So what's the downside? You

might get some Printer Out of Memory error messages when Windows sends a print job that's beyond the printer's capabilities.

Be sure to modify these settings whenever you add or subtract memory to and from your printer.

3.1.3 Send the Correct Graphics Data to Your Printer

Graphics processing can make a computer run as slow as molasses. The pretty images look innocent enough, but the calculations required to render them is tremendous.

The dumbest of printers only understands *rasterized* graphics, where the image is completely processed by the host computer and spewed out as a big file of pixels that fully describe the image. For raster graphics, a printer doesn't need to do any thinking, it just lays out the data pixel by pixel.

Smarter printers support the more efficient *vector* graphics mode. With vector graphics, only lines (vectors), not pixels, define the image.

Take a blue square, for example. With raster graphics, the printer file would include hundreds of "blue" dots laid out in a square format. In vector mode, the four border lines and one reference to the fill-in color "blue" would describe the same square. Vector graphics processing produces very small data files. These small files put less strain on your PC and off-load most of the processing to the printer itself.

Read your printer's documentation to determine if it supports vector graphics. If it does, use the following steps to set vector mode for your printer:

1. Open My Computer, then select Printers.

2. Right-click the printer you want to modify, then choose Properties from the pop-up list.

3. Select the Graphics tab. Again, as in the last hint, your printer might not have a graphics tab. If not, your printer might not support graphics mode adjustments.

4. In the graphics mode box, choose Use Vector Graphics if your printer supports that mode (see Figure 3.1.3).

If you've used raster graphics mode in the past, you should notice your graphical print jobs complete more quickly after you've adjusted this setting.

Faster Printing

Figure 3.1.3

Set Vector Graphics mode for faster printing of graphical pages.

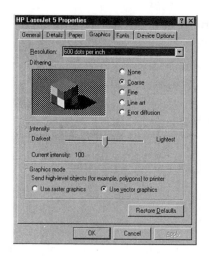

Chapter

3.2

Revving the Disk and RAM

Your hard drive separates your PC from networked computers (NCs) and other "dumb" terminals. It's one of the three linchpins—the other two being RAM and processor—of your overall system performance. When you purchase a new PC or a hard drive upgrade, make sure the hard drive's data transfer rate, disk rotational speed, and access times meet the current standards. Then, read this chapter for information on revving the hard drive's Windows 98 settings.

3.2.1 Convert to the FAT32 File System

One great way to improve your overall system performance is to make the most of your hard disk space. The best way to do that is to convert to the FAT32 file system, if you haven't already done so.

For years, the Windows operating system used only the FAT16 file system to organize data on the hard drive. Unfortunately, FAT16 wastes space, particularly on larger disk partitions. The wasted space results from oversized clusters; a cluster being the smallest chunk of disk space that the file system consumes to store a file. Depending on the size of your files and the size of your disk partition, FAT16 can waste as much as 32K *per file*. These small losses add up and become significant lost storage over time. Additionally, FAT16 restricts disk partitions to a maximum of 2GB. This becomes a serious problem when new hard drives store 8GB or more of data.

With the later versions of Windows 95 and the release of Windows 98, Microsoft included a revamped and more efficient file system, FAT32. FAT32 wastes significantly less space than FAT16 and supports disk partitions of 8GB and larger. But, simply installing Windows 98 doesn't mean you're running FAT32. The upgrade process leaves your file system untouched. Even newly manufactured Windows 98 systems might or might not be running FAT32 when they ship from the factories.

How can you tell if your drives are FAT16 or FAT32? It's easy. Just ask the Drive Converter Wizard. From the Start menu choose Start | Programs | Accessories | System Tools | Drive Converter (FAT32). This launches the Drive Converter. Click the Next button to move past the initial screen. The next screen displays a list of your hard drive partitions and their file systems (see Figure 3.2.1).

WARNING   There are serious downsides to converting to FAT32 and the conversion might not suit everyone. Here are some things you need to understand before you convert a drive:

- You can't go back. Windows 98 does not include a utility to take you back to FAT16. For $69.95, PowerQuest's (www.powerquest.com) PartitionMagic 3.0 performs conversions both ways.

- Dual boot options, where you choose among several operating systems at startup, don't work on FAT32 drives.

- Some older software might not run on your FAT32 drive. Windows 98 keeps a list of suspects in this Registry key: My Computer\HKEY_LOCAL_MACHINE\SYSTEM\CurrentControlSet\Control\SessionManager\CheckBadApps400. Browse it to determine how the conversion will affect your software.

- DriveSpace 3 can't compress FAT32 drives. Fortunately, you probably won't need to compress your new file system. It will already provide more space than you had before the conversion.

- You might not be able to uninstall Windows 98 and return to your previous operating system. Most versions of Windows 95 and all versions of Windows 3.1 cannot read FAT32 drives.

- The FAT32 conversion might set off your antivirus software's alarms. The process changes the Master Boot Record of your hard drive, a key indication of virus infection. Microsoft suggests removing your antivirus software before you convert. You can reinstall it afterward.

FAT32 brings with it many benefits, but as you can see, the conversion has its consequences. I recommend only experts perform this hint. For novices and even intermediate users, the potential pitfalls could be lethal for your PC.

Figure 3.2.1

If you're not sure which file system you're currently using, ask the Drive Converter Wizard

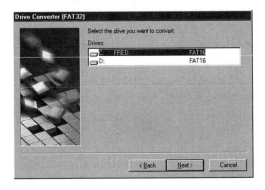

If you've decided to convert, continue on with the wizard, following its instructions. The process is straightforward; and, before the conversion begins, the wizard estimates the amount of wasted storage the process will likely recover.

Revving the Disk and RAM

> **TIP** Some people have had trouble accessing their FAT32 drives when booting from the Windows 98 Emergency Startup disk. If you're one of these people, try Windows 98 FAT32 Emergency Boot disk creator. It also resides on the Win98 CD-ROM. Insert the Win98 CD-ROM into your CD-ROM drive and browse the folder TOOLS\MTSUTIL\FAT32EBD. Read the text file FAT32EBD.TXT for a description of the tool. Then launch FAT32EBD.EXE to create your FAT32 emergency disk.

3.2.2 Use Write-Behind Caching

With write-behind caching, your disk appears to run faster. How does this work? Windows returns control to your applications even though data is still being written to disk. Windows stores this "left-over" data in a disk cache and it steals idle cycles of your processor to finish the disk writes when it can.

You can enable disk caching for both hard disks drives and removable storage drives. Both types of drives show performance improvement with a cache.

There's only one situation in which you might want to disable write-behind caching—that's in brownout, blackout, and other volatile power conditions. With sudden power loss, your computer might shut down before the cache data is written to disk. If this happens, you lose data. And that's bad. Read more about disabling write-behind caching in Chapter 3.5, "Tune Your Operating System," hint 3.5.5.

Follow these steps to check the write-behind cache settings for your hard drive and removable storage drive:

1. From the Start menu, choose Start | Settings | Control Panel. Then select the System object.

2. Choose the Performance tab of the System Properties sheet.

3. Click the File System button in the Advanced Settings box.

4. Pick the Troubleshooting tab of the File System Properties sheet.

5. In the settings box, find the entry labeled Disable Write-Behind Caching for All Drives. Make sure this item *is not* checked (see Figure 3.2.2).

6. Next, pick the Removable Disk tab of the File System Properties sheet.

7. In the settings box, place a check next to Enable Write-Behind Caching on All Removable Disk Drives (see Figure 3.2.3).

8. Click the OK button to save your changes on the File System Properties sheet.

9. Click the Close button on the System Properties sheet.

Windows asks if you want to restart your system. Click the Yes button.

Figure 3.2.2

Control write-behind caching on the Troubleshooting tab of the File System Properties sheet.

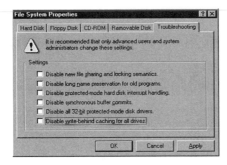

Figure 3.2.3

Click the Removable Disk tab to find the setting for your Zip (or other model) removable storage drive.

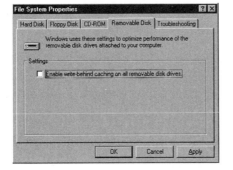

3.2.3 Get Your Hands on WinAlign.exe

This is the only hint in this book that discusses a tool not available on the Windows 98 CD-ROM or on the Web. The tool is called WinAlign.exe and I thought you'd like to know it exists. The only place you'll find this tool is in the Windows 98 Resource Kit (that expensive book/CD-ROM combo package I mentioned in the introduction), not the sample kit included on the Win98 CD-ROM. In a corporate setting, ask your administrator if they have a copy of this product. Otherwise, you should probably suffer without it. The Resource Kit is not worth buying just for this utility—almost, but not quite.

WinAlign.exe speeds up your hard disk performance by optimizing the executable code of your applications on the disk. It re-writes the header information of the binary files and then formats the files into 4K chucks, just the same size as memory pages. This formatting enables Windows 98 to swap the application in and out of memory at lightning speed. You should notice the performance improvement with every application you optimize.

Window 98 loads a similar tool called Walign.exe, but it only optimizes Microsoft Office version 7.0 for Windows 95 and Microsoft Office 97 programs.

Chapter

3.3

Free Space

The amount of free space on your hard drive directly affects your PC's performance. With plenty of free space, Windows 98 can swap memory pages to and from your hard drive as needed. With limited space, memory swapping becomes a painfully slow procedure and your system performance drops like a stone.

How can you increase the amount of free space on your disks? Read this chapter. You'll find information on deleting unneeded files that you've already accumulated and tips on keeping your disk clean.

The amount of free space you need depends upon your PC and the tasks you perform. In general, if you multitask several applications simultaneously, you need more empty room on your hard disk. Systems with 64 megabytes (or more) of RAM need less swap room on the disk. PCs with 32 megabytes (or less) need more swap space. Generally, try to maintain *at least* 50 to 100 megabytes of free space on your drive.

3.3.1 Limit Your Landfill (a.k.a. Recycle Bin)

By default, Windows 98 reserves 10 percent of every hard drive, or drive partition, for Recycle Bin use. Did you catch that? Ten percent! With a 10-gigabyte drive, that's 1 gigabyte of trash.

I don't know about you, but I'm not *that* concerned about recovering deleted files. I can make better use of that much storage. This percentage might have worked a few years ago when hard drives topped out at about 2 gigabytes. But now an average hard drive holds 5 gigabytes. Besides, using a percentage measure to configure your Recycle Bin only makes sense from Microsoft's perspective—they want Windows 98 to work across a wide range of computer makes and models, all with different size drives. I, personally, would never use more than 100 megabytes for the Recycle Bin.

Limit your Recycle Bin's hold over your hard drive by modifying its Properties sheet. Right-click on the Recycle Bin icon and choose Properties from the pop-up menu. You can either set a maximum percentage across all hard drives with the Global tab (see Figure 3.3.1), or configure the Recycle Bin on each drive or drive partition by choosing the lettered tabs and adjusting the settings.

Figure 3.3.1

Use the Global tab of the Recycle Bin's Properties sheet to configure the Recycle Bin across all your hard drives and disk partitions.

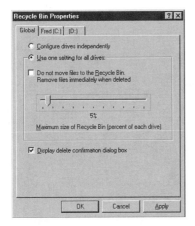

3.3.2 Find and Delete Useless Files

Using the Windows Maintenance Wizard (see Figure 3.3.2) to schedule regular disk cleanup sessions is a great idea. I highly recommend it. It's not, however, a complete solution for eradicating unneeded files.

Figure 3.3.2

Use the Maintenance Wizard's disk cleanup to remove unnecessary files on a regular basis.

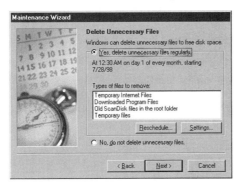

Windows itself, and other software, often backs up files on your hard drive before modifying them. The most common method is saving a copy of a file by changing the file extension to .BAK, .$$$, or some other three-character combo. These backup files aren't needed after you know the change hasn't adversely affected your system.

Zip files are another common waste by-product of computing. Often, people download compressed Zip files from the Web, decompress the file, but still leave the original .ZIP file hanging around.

Don't worry, you don't need to individually search for and remove each of these file types separately. Arcana Development's Dustman shareware utility (see Figure

Free Space

3.3.3) can do it all for you. With Dustman, you define search and destroy "jobs," then Dustman removes the unneeded files for you on a regular schedule.

Figure 3.3.3

Tell Arcana Development's Dustman to automatically find and remove your unneeded files.

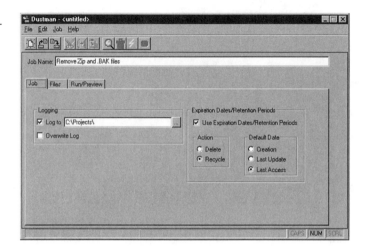

You can download Dustman and try it free for 30 days. After that, a $15 one-time registration fee makes it yours.

Follow these steps to download and install Arcana Development's Dustman utility:

1. Launch your Web browser and point it toward PC World Online's FileWorld site (`www.fileworld.com`).

2. Using the Search FileWorld entry box, enter **dustman** and search. Follow the instructions to download the file DUSTMN20.EXE into a temporary directory on your hard drive.

3. From Windows Explorer, select the file DUSTMN20.EXE. Because it's a self-extracting Zip file, it will automatically decompress the file and then launch Dustman's installation routine.

Unless you specify otherwise, Dustman will add a shortcut to the Accessories branch of your Start menu. Read through the excellent help screens for additional instructions.

3.3.3 Delete the Online Service Starter Kits

Hollywood is notorious for "product placement" deals in which a certain company's product is used overtly in exchange for cash or some commodity.

James Bond's use of BMW automobiles in two of the recent 007 films comes to mind as a good example.

Someone should do a product placement review of Windows 98.

In addition to the blatant Active Channel bar (that presents full-blown commercials when you click on objects), Windows 98 is also weighed down by over 30 megabytes of online service starter kits, if you chose to add Online Services when you installed Windows 98. The odds that you'll need them all are very slim.

Follow these steps to remove the unneeded online service startup programs:

1. Launch Windows Explorer (under Start | Programs).

2. Navigate to the folder: C:\Windows\Options\Cabs.

3. Delete the following files:

Filename	Service
SETUP25I.EXE	AOL
SETUP32.EXE	AOL
CS3KIT.EXE	CompuServe
WOWKIT.EXE	CompuServe

Removing these files saves you over 30 megabytes of space. Perform a few more of these hints and you might not need to buy a bigger hard drive after all, huh?

3.3.4 Remove Your Old Operating System

Did you upgrade to Win98 from a previous version of Windows? If you did, I'm betting you took the installation option to save your previous operating system. I know I did. It's a common sense move.

The theory behind this, of course, is that you have an escape route. If you ever get fed up with Windows 98, you can quickly blow it away and return to your old setup.

But now is the time to answer the question: Are you happy with Windows 98? After about a month of using it, I decided I was never going back. If you haven't made your decision yet, you should do so now. Your hard disk still suffers under the extra 60-megabyte load used to store your old operating system.

> **NOTE** Did you convert your boot drive to FAT32? If so, your Windows 98 uninstallation files might be useless anyway. Most versions of Windows 95 (and all versions of Windows 3.1) do not support FAT32 drives. And Windows 98 does not include a utility to convert back from FAT32 to FAT16.

Free Space

Free up this space, and you'll improve your overall system performance. Extra disk space enables the Windows swap file to expand, if needed, to fill the unused space.

Follow these steps to delete your previous operating system files:

1. From the Start menu, choose Start | Programs | Accessories | System Tools | Disk Cleanup. Then select the drive you want to clean from the Drives drop-down list. For most users, this would be drive C. Then click OK.

2. Select the Disk Cleanup tab.

3. Scroll down the Files to Delete list until you find the entry Delete Windows 98 Uninstall Information (see Figure 3.3.4). Put a check next to this entry. On this line, you'll see the total storage Windows reserves for your old operating system. Quite a bit, isn't it?

Figure 3.3.4

Use the Disk Cleanup Utility to remove your old version of Windows.

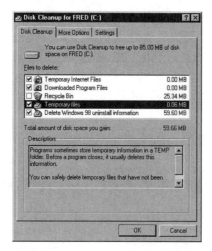

4. Click OK to begin the process. A warning message will appear. Click Yes to continue. If you do perform this action, these files will not show up in the Disk Cleanup list again.

Will you regret this move? I seriously doubt it. But, if you do, there's a brute force way to remove Windows 98 and reload your old operating system. Read the administration section of this book for instructions.

3.3.5 Eliminate Doppelganger Files

You don't need any duplicate files on your hard drive. I'm not talking about backup files; store backups on removable media, not the hard drive. And I'm not talking about document revisions; they're not true duplicates, and they probably differ slightly in size and content. Duplicate files are truly identical, evil twins, except perhaps in name. And all they do is waste space.

Usually, file duplication occurs by accident. You might have mistakenly downloaded the same file more than once, storing it in different folders each time. Or, you might have reinstalled an application into a new folder, not realizing that it still resides in an old one.

Finding duplicate files is the key problem. Eyeballing file details in the Windows Explorer would take an eternity. Windows 98 includes one file comparison tool called Windiff. It's part of the Sample Resource Kit. But, unfortunately, Windiff only searches for ASCII text files. Software developers who need to sort out programming files are the ones who are most likely to use it.

What's a regular user to do? Download a shareware tool called CloneMaster from SoftByte Labs. It specializes in finding and removing duplicate files of all types.

Follow these instructions to download and install CloneMaster.

1. Browse PC World Online's FileWorld site (`www.fileworld.com`).

2. In the Search FileWorld box, enter the name **CloneMaster**. Click the Search! Button.

3. Click the CloneMaster hyperlink to branch to the download page. Follow the instructions to download the 1-megabyte CLONEMASTER.EXE file onto your hard drive. Store it in a temporary folder.

4. The CloneMaster download is a self-extracting Zip file. So simply select it in Windows Explorer to begin the extraction and installation routine.

5. CloneMaster sets up its own menu item on your Start Bar.

CloneMaster can search one or all of your drives (see Figure 3.3.5). The unregistered version works, but SoftByte Labs asks that you register the copy for extended use.

Figure 3.3.5
Use the CloneMaster shareware to find and remove duplicate files.

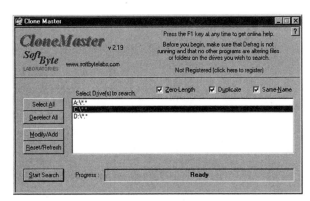

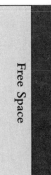

Run Clone Master all by itself, without any other programs running in the background. This enables the tools to search and compare all files on the disk.

3.3.6 Graph Files by Size

To get rid of your largest space-wasting files, you first need to find them. But using the Windows Explorer for this task will only lead to frustration. Why? Explorer's sort feature (right-click a folder, choose Arrange Icons | By Size) is almost useless. It doesn't sort subfolders. So, it would take hours to determine which folders are really taking up the most space.

For a better tool, browse the Web and download Choice Computing's freeware utility DiskFrontier. DiskFrontier was designed specifically for assistance with hard drive cleanup. It not only sorts folders *and* subfolders, but it also displays bar graphs, percentages, last-used dates, and more. You only need a few seconds with DiskFrontier to ferret out your most wasteful files.

Follow these instructions to download and install DiskFrontier:

1. Browse PC World Online's FileWorld Web site (`www.fileworld.com`).

2. In the Search FileWorld box, enter **DiskFrontier**. Click the Search! Button.

3. Click the hyperlink for DiskFrontier to display the download page.

4. Follow the instructions to download the file DISKFRNT.ZIP to a hard disk folder of your choice. This file is compressed with the Zip format, so you'll need a utility such as PKWare's PKZip for Windows (at `www.pkware.com`) to decompress it.

5. After downloading, decompress the file with an "unzip" utility. Read the README.TXT file for instructions on installing DiskFrontier (see Figure 3.3.6). You just need to select the file DISKFRNT.EXE. It installs itself into your Explorer's right-click pop-up menu.

Spend a few minutes investigating DiskFrontier's options. With a few clicks, you'll be able to locate not only your largest files but your least-used files as well.

Figure 3.3.6

The freeware tool DiskFrontier shows you a bar-chart view of your space-wasting files.

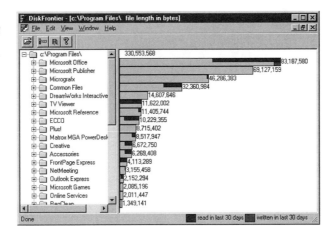

Chapter

3.4

Prudent Power Management

Most modern computer hardware offers sophisticated power management capabilities. But to take full advantage of these capabilities you must be proactive in setting and maintaining these features. Power settings can affect your desktop's performance and your notebook's battery life. In this chapter, learn the tips and tricks of Windows 98 power management.

3.4.1 Modify Your Power Management Settings

Smart computer users adjust their PC's power management settings. Whether you are a desktop or notebook user, these settings determine whether your system will run at its maximum performance potential.

For mobile computing, power management can extend your battery's life by conserving power and temporarily slowing internal devices. For desktop sessions, your tradeoff becomes conserving energy (lowering your energy bill and helping the environment) versus running at top speed.

Whatever you do, don't use the default power management settings without first examining them. If you do, you'll be relying on your PC manufacturer and/or Microsoft to make the correct choices. And, it's very unlikely they've tuned the settings for your particular work style.

Follow these steps to adjust your power management settings:

1. On the Start menu, choose Start | Settings | Control Panel. Then select the Power Management icon.

> **TIP** Most modern personal computers include power management options in BIOS. Don't forget to investigate these in addition to the settings under Windows 98. Both levels of power management affect your system. Read your system's documentation regarding power management and instructions on how to enter the BIOS setup program.
>
> **Desktop users:** Set the BIOS for maximum performance and include little or no power conservation. This doesn't make you an energy hog. You can conserve power through Windows 98's power schemes.
>
> **Mobile users:** First determine which devices Windows 98 will let you control (by following the steps in this hint). Then enter your PC's BIOS. If Windows cannot control your notebook's input–output ports (parallel, serial, modem, and so on), you might consider shutting them off in the BIOS until you need them. Active ports consume battery power and decrease your overall battery life.

2. Choose the Power Schemes tab of the Power Management Properties sheet.

Desktop Users: To be flexible, create two Power Schemes: one for regular work conditions and one for maximum performance. For regular work, adjust the device settings on this page to turn off your monitor and hard drive after some period of inactivity. Then create a maximum performance scheme that keeps all components always on. This way you can quickly choose your power scheme to fit your work mode.

Mobile Users: Create at least two power schemes. One for when you're connected to AC power and one when running on battery. Your AC power scheme should shut down devices less frequently (maybe never), while your battery scheme should turn off devices after a very short period of inactivity. You might also create a third scheme if you have a docking station. Your docking station probably features more devices that you can configure.

3. Before you exit, select the Advanced tab. In the options box, put a check next to Show Power Meter on Taskbar. This loads a Power Meter icon into your Windows 98 System Tray. From there, you can select different power schemes with just a click of the mouse. Also, for mobile users, the Power Meter icon changes from an electrical cord to a battery when you unplug your notebook.

4. Choose the OK button to close the Power Management Properties sheet.

As you add components to your system, go back and modify these settings to include them. Also, feel free to tune these settings after a little experimentation. Many people change their monitor shutdown time two or three times before it feels comfortable.

3.4.2 Find Out Which Software Wastes Power

Is battery life critical to your mobile computing? If so, consider downloading one of the tools used by the pros to ferret out power-squandering software. Intel created the Power Monitor utility to help software developers tune programs to conserve energy, but you can use it to test your applications.

How does it work? Power monitor searches through your software's low-level system calls looking for those that run devices that draw large amounts of power. Then it generates a report ranking your software on power conversation.

Follow these steps to download and install Power Monitor:

1. Browse CNET's Download.com Web site (`www.download.com`).

2. In the Quick Search box, enter **Power Monitor** and click the Search button.

3. Click on the Power Monitor 3.0 hyperlink and follow the instructions to download the file POWERMON.EXE.

TIP	Download Power Monitor during off-hours. It's a 3.7MB file, and it takes several minutes to copy to your hard drive.

4. POWERMON.EXE is a self-extracting Zip file, so you don't need any other tools to decompress it. Just select the file within Windows Explorer to decompress the file and begin the installation process.

WARNING	In its "spy" mode, Power Monitor will actually slow down your system's performance. So don't run it frequently. Just pick one day when you have time to test your software and let Power Monitor do its thing.

After Power Monitor evaluates your software, take its report to heart. To extend your battery life, postpone work with power-wasting software until you're plugged in to an AC outlet. Or, for really bad performers, consider switching applications to more power-thrifty products.

3.4.3 Force Windows 98 to Install ACPI

The latest standard in PC power management is called Advanced Configuration and Power Interface (ACPI). ACPI works as a liaison between your hardware and your operating system to control devices and conserve power. Through ACPI calls, your computer's BIOS passes control of low-level components—such as communication ports, modems, hard drives, and so on—to Windows 98. Windows will shut down or slow down devices (based or your power management settings) to increase your notebook's battery life or to decrease your desktop's power consumption.

The Windows 98 CD contains a list of PCs that are known to have ACPI power management support. During the setup process, Windows 98 checks your PC's vital statistics against this list. If there's no match, the ACPI component of Windows 98 is not installed. If a match is found, Windows installs the ACPI component.

If you don't already have ACPI support, obtaining it makes good sense. You might be able to add ACPI support through a simple BIOS update. Contact your PC manufacturer about getting a new BIOS version for your system.

> **NOTE**   ACPI is the heir to the power management standard kingdom. The predecessor, and still reigning king, is a standard called Advanced Power Management (APM). Microsoft would love for APM to go away. Why? Because with APM, the computer's BIOS, not the operating system, controls the device-level power management of a computer.
>
> Microsoft argues that it's the operating system, not the BIOS, that really "knows" when a computer is idle and can shut down devices without interrupting work.
>
> APM advocates, however, say that PC manufacturers want their computers to have power conservation capability regardless of what operating system a PC is running. And, therefore, the BIOS is the best administrator for slowing down or shutting off devices.
>
> Fortunately, you don't really need to choose when you buy a PC. Most new computers support both standards. My advice, though, is to pick one of the two schemes and let it do all your power management. For APM, set all your power management in the computer's BIOS setup and shut off the settings in Windows 98's Power Management object. For ACPI, set the BIOS to run your computer at full-power all the time, and then adjust Win98's power scheme to shut down your system when appropriate.

After you install your new BIOS, you can hack the Registry and force Windows 98 to detect it. Follow these steps to force Windows 98 to detect your ACPI BIOS:

1. Launch the Registry Editor by entering **regedit** at the Start | Run prompt.

2. Navigate to the following Registry key: My Computer\HKEY_LOCAL_ MACHINE\SOFTWARE\Microsoft\Windows\CurrentVersion\Detect.

3. Beneath this key, add a new string called ACPIOption and set the value to "1." To add a new String, right-click on the key name and choose New | StringValue from the pop-up menu. Then enter **ACPIOption** and press Enter. To set the value, select the string and enter **1** into the Value Data field of the Edit String dialog box. Then click the OK button.

> **NOTE**   In Windows 98 Registry-speak, the ACPIOption with the value of "0" means check this PC against the Win98 CD's list of ACPI-capable systems and install ACPI support on a match. This setting is the default that Win98 assumes even if there is no ACPIOption string. With ACPIOption set to "1," Win98 will check your BIOS and install the ACPI component. If ACPIOption is set to "2," Win98 will remove the ACPI component.

4. From the menus, choose File | Exit to close the Registry Editor.

You'll need to reboot the system before you notice this change. To see the ACPI settings, investigate your Power Management object in the Control Panel (under Start | Settings | Control Panel). The Power Management object's Power Schemes tab lists the devices you can control.

Chapter

3.5

Tune Your Operating System

Windows 98 makes several assumptions about your computer setup. Some of these assumptions might be wrong and they might be costing you in terms of computer performance. In this chapter, you learn how to relocate your Windows swap file, adjust your hard drive settings, prepare for lightning storms, and more.

3.5.1 Relocate the Windows Swap File

Windows doesn't limit its active memory to your PC's RAM. If the operating system needs more memory, it uses free space on your hard drive as a temporary repository called "virtual memory." A swap file, WIN386.SWP, on your hard drive holds the extra data that Windows swaps in and out of RAM during a computing session. This file continually expands and contracts as you use your system.

In the old Windows 3.1 operating system, you could improve your PC's performance by manually setting the size of the swap file. However, Windows 98 does a good job sizing the swap file on its own. So don't mess with the size settings.

To improve your Win98 system's performance, just make sure your swap file resides on a fast hard drive that has plenty of free disk space. Read the other hints in the section regarding freeing up disk space. Here I'll list the steps for relocating your swap file.

If you have more than one hard drive in your PC, make sure the swap file resides on the fastest drive. Fast access to the swap file enables Windows 98 to move memory pages to and from the disk quickly and speeds up your overall session. If you have multiple logical partitions on one physical hard drive, consider moving the swap file to the partition that has the most free disk space.

> **NOTE** At some point, you might boot your PC and notice, right off the bat, that your system's swap file is extremely large. That's OK! It's just the swap file left over from your last computing session. Windows 98 does not delete your last session's swap file during startup, and neither should you. Windows will shrink the swap file automatically, if it isn't needed in your current session.

Use the following steps to relocate your swap file:

1. Select Start | Settings | Control Panel from the Start menu. Then choose the System icon.

2. Select the Performance tab of the System Properties sheet.

3. Click the Virtual Memory button in the Advanced Settings box. This displays the Virtual Memory dialog box.

> **TIP**   If your swap file already resides on a fast drive with plenty of free space, make sure that your Virtual Memory setting has Let Windows manage my virtual memory settings checked.

4. To relocate the swap file, choose Let me specify my own virtual memory settings (see Figure 3.5.1).

Figure 3.5.1

Relocate the swap file by choosing Let me specify my own virtual memory settings.

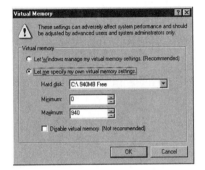

5. Click the drop-down arrow for the Hard Disk field. Choose the drive (or disk partition) in which you want the swap file to reside.

> **WARNING**   Do not modify the Minimum and Maximum settings for your swap file. If you select a new location for the swap file, Windows will list the current amount of free space for that drive in both the Hard Disk field and the Maximum field. *But* it will exceed this maximum, if required, as more space becomes available. Manually setting a maximum size for your swap file rigidly restricts the size to the limit you set. This could negatively affect your system performance.

6. Click OK to close the Virtual Memory dialog box. Windows will display a warning regarding modifying virtual memory. Click Yes to continue. Then click Close to exit the System Properties sheet.

Windows will restart your computer before this change takes effect. The next time you check your virtual memory settings, you'll see that Windows has reselected Let Windows manage my virtual memory settings, even though it has moved the swap file to a new drive.

3.5.2 Remove Unwanted Startup Files

In the pre-release hype, Microsoft touted Windows 98's faster startup capability. Post-release real-world testing, though, showed the improvement was actually very slight, perhaps due to the larger size of the new operating system. The good

Tune Your Operating System

news is that you can speed up your PC's startup process all by yourself. All you need do is remove the startup programs that secretly nest themselves in your Registry.

Software installation routines frequently insert programs into your StartUp folder (C:\Windows\StartUp). Their goal is to make their software very visible on your desktop. Fortunately, removing these programs is easy. Just right-click on the item's StartUp folder and choose Delete.

Other programs use a more secretive route. During setup, some programs will install themselves directly into your Registry and instruct Windows to launch their routines during the startup process.

The easiest way to find and remove these programs is through the System Configuration Utility. Follow these steps to launch the utility and remove unwanted startup programs:

1. From the Start menu, choose Start | Programs | Accessories | System Tools | System Information. Microsoft hides the System Configuration tool underneath the System Information program.

2. From the Tools menu of the System Information tool, select System Configuration Utility.

3. Choose the Startup tab of the System Configuration Utility. This displays a list of all your designated startup programs, whether they result from the Registry or from the Windows StartUp folder (see Figure 3.5.2).

Figure 3.5.2

The System Configuration Utility contains a list of all your startup programs, even if they've been hidden in the Registry.

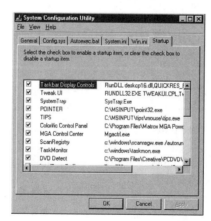

4. Remove the checks next to any unwanted entries. This process does not delete the programs from your computer. You'll still be able to launch them at anytime. This procedure simply stops them from loading during Windows startup.

5. Click OK to close the System Configuration Utility.

Windows 98 will restart your system so that these changes can take affect.

3.5.3 Stop Searching for New Floppy Drives

Did you know that Windows 98 searches for newly installed floppy drives every time it boots up? I consider this a Windows design error. This error slows down your startup process every day—the search takes a good second or two every time. Luckily, you can fix it.

Microsoft included this search because of all the notebook computers out there. Many notebooks let you attach and detach a floppy drive whenever you want. Checking for new floppies makes sense for notebooks configured in this way. But Windows 98 performs this check for all computers—notebooks, desktops, or file servers. Microsoft should have had the setup program only mark this setting if you picked a Portable installation for Windows 98. But they goofed. When's the last time you installed a new floppy drive on your desktop computer? I'll guess never!

Follow these steps to halt Windows 98's pointless search for newly installed floppy drives:

1. From the Start menu, choose Start | Settings | Control Panel.

2. Select the System object.

3. Pick the Performance tab.

4. Click the File System button.

5. Pick the Floppy Disk tab.

6. In the Settings box, remove the check next to Search for new floppy disk drives each time your computer starts (see Figure 3.5.3).

Figure 3.5.3

By default, Windows 98 checks for newly installed floppy drives each time you power up.

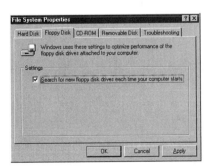

This change will take effect upon your next startup.

3.5.4 Adjust Your Hard Drive Settings

Windows 98 makes several assumptions about your hard drive based on one seemingly innocuous setting buried deep in the Control Panel. Some of these guesses might be wrong and they might be costing you in terms of performance.

The setting asks you to choose the "typical role" of your computer and presents three choices: Desktop Computer, Mobile or Docking Station, and Network Server. Here are Win98's assumptions broken down by choice:

- **Desktop Computer:** Windows 98 assumes you have 32MB or more of RAM and that you're running on AC power, not battery power. It creates two medium-sized disk caches for filenames (8KB) and filepaths (32 paths stored), predicting that you will have average disk access needs.

- **Mobile Computer or Docking Station:** Windows 98 thinks you'll be running with a low amount of RAM, roughly 8MB to 16MB, and that you frequently run from battery rather than AC power. It sets your system to frequently flush the disk cache so that you don't lose any data if your battery dies. Windows 98 creates small disk caches for storing filenames (4KB) and filepaths (16 paths stored).

- **Network Server:** Windows 98 assumes this PC is not a user's station, but rather a non-user file or print server. Because servers normally have a high level of disk activity, Win98 creates large disk caches for filenames (16KB) and filepaths (64 paths stored).

Using these definitions, you might want to alter your "typical role" setting. For example, if your desktop runs only 8MB of RAM, you should switch to the Mobile Computer or Docking Station setting, rather than the Desktop Computer setting. Or, if you primarily run disk intensive database applications on your desktop, you might consider changing to the Network Server setting to benefit from the larger disk caching.

Follow these steps to change the "typical role" setting:

1. From the Start menu, choose Start | Settings | Control Panel.

2. Select the System object.

3. Pick the Performance tab.

4. Click the File System button.

5. On the File System Properties sheet, pick the Hard Disk tab.

6. In the settings box, use the drop-down arrow next to the line Typical Role of This Computer to make your new selection.

7. Click the OK button to close the File System Properties sheet.

8. Click Close to exit the System Properties sheet.

Windows will ask if you want to restart your computer. Click the Yes button to activate your change.

If these "typical role" settings don't suit your setup exactly you can fine-tune them a bit. For example: You might keep your Desktop Computer setting but increase just the filename disk cache to 64KB (the size used for a Network server).

Follow these steps to fine-tune your "typical role" settings:

1. Launch the Registry Editor by entering **regedit** at the Start | Run prompt.

2. Navigate to the following Registry key: My Computer\HKEY_LOCAL_ MACHINE\SOFTWARE\Microsoft\Windows\CurrentVersion\FS Templates.

3. Beneath this key, you'll find three keys (Desktop, Mobile, and Server) corresponding to the three "typical role" choices. These keys store the filename (NameCache) and filepath (PathCache) disk cache values for the File System settings.

   You can alter these disk cache settings to your liking. For example, to perform the filename disk cache change mentioned above, create a new binary value named NameCache under the Desktop key with the same value as the Server keys NameCache (40 00 00 00). In most systems, the Desktop key will have no NameCache or PathCache values to begin with; its values are default in the operating system, so you'll need to newly create those keys and then set their values. To create the key, right-click on the Desktop key and choose New | Binary Value from the pop-up menu.

4. When you've finished your changes, choose Registry | Exit from the menus to close the Registry Editor.

You'll need to restart Windows before you'll notice any change. Feel free to reset these settings if you notice no performance improvement.

3.5.5 Survive Lightning Conditions and Power Loss

Here's an interesting case. In areas with frequent lightning conditions and blackouts, you should consider sacrificing a little performance to save your data.

I recently had a conversation with an engineer in the Underwriters Laboratory (UL) (the same folks that defined the UL 1449 standard for surge protectors). He said that people are often confused by (or even misled about) the protection afforded by consumer-level surge protectors, the kind of devices sold in computer and electronics stores.

The UL 1449 standard, which surge protectors meet, actually just protects consumers from fire and shock hazards resulting from power surges. The rating really doesn't promise your computer equipment will be safe from damage, as some of the marketing material might lead you to believe. The engineer went on to say that the only real way to protect your computer equipment during lightning storms is to power down and unplug your system from the electrical outlet.

That's great advice if you can afford to stop working whenever lightning conditions or storms occur. But, many people live and work in areas where lightning is commonplace during the summer months.

If you can't stop working in bad weather, you should turn off your write-behind disk caching. This way, your data will be written out to disk more frequently. Your chances of losing work because your power goes down will drop dramatically. However, you will notice slight performance degradation. The frequent disk writing steals computer cycles from other tasks. But, for saving critical data, this performance loss is worthwhile.

Follow these steps to disable write-behind disk caching on your system:

1. From the Start menu, choose Start | Settings | Control Panel.

2. Select the System object.

3. Pick the Performance tab of the System Properties sheet.

4. Click the File System button.

5. Pick the Troubleshooting tab.

6. In the settings box, put a check next to Disable Write-Behind Caching for All Drives.

7. Click the OK button.

8. Click the Close button on the System Properties sheet.

Windows will ask if you want to restart you system. Click the Yes button.

Be sure to re-enable disk write-behind caching when the weather clears up.

Chapter

3.6

Improve Device Performance

Closing your PC case isn't the last step of a device installation. For the best performance, tune your device with Windows 98's settings.

3.6.1 Use Protected-Mode Device Drivers

Your devices—PC cards, hard drives, CD-ROMS, removable storage, and so on—use either 16-bit real-mode or 32-bit protected-mode drivers. To maximize performance, you should update most, if not all, of your devices to protected-mode drivers. Protected-mode drivers run faster, use memory more efficiently, and make devices easier to manage.

How do you know if any of your devices are using real-mode drivers? To be thorough, you should check three different locations. Follow these steps to hunt down your real-mode drivers:

1. First, check the System object of the Control Panel (under Start | Settings | Control Panel). Select the System object. Then pick the Performance tab. Check the list under Performance Status, looking for anything listed as 16-bit.

2. Next, browse your CONFIG.SYS file. You can enter **sysedit** at the Start | Run prompt. This launches the System Editor and displays CONFIG.SYS, AUTOEXEC.BAT, and other configuration files. You'll find real-mode drivers listed in the CONFIG.SYS file beginning with the phrase "DEVICE=." Protected-mode drivers use the Registry to store configuration information, not CONFIG.SYS. Don't worry about any listings that begin with "REM." These lines were commented out by Windows 98 when it found and replaced them with protected-mode drivers.

3. Finally, open the file IOS.LOG, if it exists, in Notepad. Windows creates this log file in the C:\Windows directory if it's forced to use a real-mode driver for any device. The file also lists a reason why Windows could not replace the driver with a protected-mode version. If the file doesn't exist, Windows 98 isn't running any real-mode drivers. For drivers you do find in IOS.LOG, check the related file IOS.INI, which lists known real-mode drivers and whether any protected-mode replacements exist for them.

After you find a real-mode driver you should replace it, if possible. Ask the product manufacturer or search their Web site for new drivers. After you obtain a protected-mode replacement, follow these steps to activate the Update Driver Wizard:

1. From the Start menu, choose Start | Settings | Control Panel.

2. Select the System object.

3. Pick the Device Manager tab.

4. Mark View Devices by Type.

5. Choose the device category from the list beneath Computer. For example, if the device is a graphics accelerator card, select Display Adapter.

6. Beneath the device category you will find an entry for your device. In the display adapter example, it might be Matrox MGA Millennium II PowerDesk. Select the device entry to display its Properties sheet.

7. Choose the Driver tab from the device's Properties sheet (see Figure 3.6.1).

Figure 3.6.1

On the Driver tab of the device's Properties sheet, you'll find the Update Driver Wizard's button.

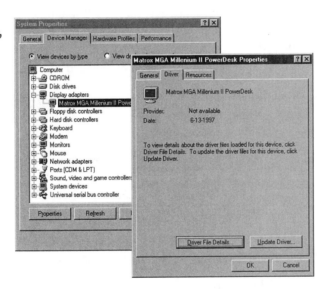

8. Click the Update Driver button to launch the Update Driver Wizard. Follow the instructions to update the driver from the Win98 CD-ROM, floppy, a file on your hard drive, or the Web.

9. When you finish with the wizard, click OK to close the device's Properties sheet, and click it again to close the System Properties sheet.

Windows will ask you to restart your system for these changes to take effect.

Improve Device Performance

3.6.2 Let Your Graphics Card Share the Workload

The chips aboard most modern graphics cards help accelerate both 2D and 3D graphics. These chips process most of the graphics work formerly done by your PC's central processor. Make sure the Windows 98 lets these chips do their job.

There's a setting buried in the Windows Control Panel that is really a hold-over from times past when the cooperation between the central processor and the graphics chips didn't work as smoothly as it does today. The setting enables you to limit the graphics tasks sent on to the graphics accelerator. You should only limit these tasks if you're having a serious problem with your display, such as jittering pixels or error messages. Otherwise, make sure this hardware acceleration setting is at its maximum.

Follow these steps to check your graphics hardware acceleration setting:

1. From the Start menu, choose Start | Settings | Control Panel.

2. Select the System object.

3. Pick the Performance tab.

4. Click the Graphics button.

5. In the Graphics box, examine the Hardware Acceleration setting. Unless you're experiencing some problem, slide the bar to the far right (Full).

6. Click the OK button.

7. Click the OK button to close the System Properties sheet.

Windows will ask if you want to restart your system. Click the Yes button.

3.6.3 Optimize Your CD-ROM Settings

I was disappointed that Microsoft didn't update Windows 98's CD-ROM performance settings. They remain the same as in Windows 95. The problem with the current CD-ROM performance settings is that CD-ROM drives are much faster now than they were in 1995. The fastest drives run at 32X speeds or even faster. But, Windows settings still only focus on 1X, 2X, 3X, and 4X speed drives. Microsoft could have fine-tuned these settings so that you could optimize the supplemental cache and access pattern for faster CD-ROMs (12X, 24X, 32X, and so on).

Nevertheless, you should examine Windows 98's CD-ROM performance settings and adjust them to suit your drive.

Follow these steps to modify Windows 98's CD-ROM performance settings:

1. From the Start menu, choose Start | Settings | Control Panel.

2. Select the System object.

3. On the System Properties sheet, pick the Performance tab.

4. In the Advanced Settings box, click the File System button.

5. On the File System Properties sheet, pick the CD-ROM tab.

6. In the Settings box, find the Supplemental Cache Size slider bar (see Figure 3.6.2). Windows 98 uses this cache exclusively for your CD-ROM drive. Unlike the file and network caches, Windows 98 can page the CD-ROM cache out to your hard disk. So, you needn't be concerned about consuming RAM with this setting. The size options on the slider bar range from 214KB (kilobytes) to 1,238KB (a little over a megabyte). If you've just about run out of room on your hard drive, you can use the smaller cache sizes. However, I recommend that you clean up your hard drive and set this setting at its maximum (Large). You'll notice a performance improvement during CD-ROM software installation and when copying files from CD-ROM to your hard disk.

Figure 3.6.2

The CD-ROM tab contains outdated Windows 95 CD-ROM performance settings.

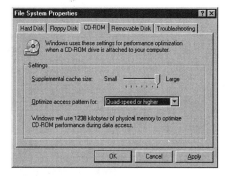

TIP   CD-ROM performance can be a confusing subject. Software developers optimize most CD-ROM software (including games and multimedia titles) for playback on 4X speed drives. Their intent is to deliver smooth video and audio playback no matter what speed drive you have. Thus, you won't really notice any performance improvement when you play multimedia discs on a faster drive.

The benefits of 12X and faster CD-ROM drives only become obvious when you install software from a CD or when you copy files from CD to your hard disk. During these tasks you CD-ROM drive will transfer data as fast as it can.

7. Find the Optimize Access Pattern setting. Here your choices are fairly clear. If your CD-ROM is 4X or faster, choose Quad-Speed or Higher from the drop-down list. Otherwise, select the setting that matches your drive speed. If you do have a slow CD-ROM drive, I highly recommend upgrading to at least an 8X-speed drive.

8. Click the OK button to save your changes and close the File System Properties sheet.

9. Click the Close button on the System Properties sheet.

10. Windows will ask you if you'd like to restart your computer. Click the Yes button.

Your new cache and access pattern settings will take effect when Windows restarts.

3.6.4 Load a SuperDisk Cache

The manufacturers of LS-120 drives are trying to "re-invent" their 120MB removable storage product. The first difference you'll notice is a name change. Now, LS-120 drives are called SuperDisk drives. Several manufacturers—such as Imation and Hi-Val—offer them. The second difference will be a performance improvement. These drives rate rather low on the charts during performance comparisons against other removable storage drives. At the end of 1998, Imation plans to release a SuperDisk drive that runs twice as fast as the original model.

If you own one of the current SuperDisk (LS-120) drives and you're suffering from the slow performance, there is an option. Imation (`www.imation.com`) offers an accelerator software package for SuperDisk drives running under Windows 95 and 98. The software creates an exclusive SuperDisk cache that stores data temporarily as it moves from hard disk to SuperDisk and back. Your SuperDisk drive won't really be running any faster, but it will appear to be, because the operating system will return control to you and your applications more quickly. Windows completes the data transfer using a background process.

You can purchase the SuperDisk Accelerator and part of the SuperDisks Tools on Imation's online store.

Chapter

3.7

Better Benchmarks and Diagnostic Tests

How fast is your computer? There's much more to a computer's performance than its processor chip. Benchmarks, the computer's equivalent of speed tests, can help you determine the performance level of your computer's individual components, software, and your overall system. Diagnostic tests will help you find trouble before a problem arises. Read this chapter for resources on both benchmarks and diagnostic tests.

3.7.1 Use the Sandra Benchmark and Diagnostic Tool

SiSoft Software distributes a set of component-level benchmarks and diagnostic utilities called Sandra. These tests check the performance of your hard drive, floppy drive, Zip drive, CD-ROM drive, and system RAM. The Sandra software also includes detailed diagnostic information for your system, mouse, keyboard, sound board, printer, and other devices.

Helpfully, Sandra package compares your system to "average" Windows systems, so that you have some way to relate your PC to other PCs. Still, it's always more accurate to run the same benchmark on several PCs and compare the results directly against one another.

If you need a general "health check" on your system, you'll find the Sandra software useful. You can quickly analyze several components and determine which ones slow down your system.

SiSoft makes the Sandra package available as shareware in PC Magazine's Software Library. If you plan to continue using the software after a 30-day trial period, you'll need to pay $29.

Follow these steps to download and install the Sandra software:

1. Launch the Internet Explorer browser by choosing Start | Programs | Internet Explorer | Internet Explorer. Or, start your alternative browser.

2. In the Address bar, enter the URL for PC Magazine's Online Software Library: **www.hotfiles.com**.

3. In the Search field, enter **Sandra**. Then click the Search button.

4. Click on the Sandra v98.4.1 hyperlink.

5. On the Sandra page, select the Download Now hyperlink.

6. Save the download file SANDRA.ZIP (a 2MB file) to a temporary folder on your hard drive. This file is compressed with a "zip" utility. You'll need a "zip" decompression utility, such as PKWare's PKZip for Windows (www.pkware.com), to extract the data files from the download file.

7. Extract the files from the download file. You can extract them to the same temporary folder in which it resides.

8. In the Windows Explorer, select the SETUP.EXE.

9. On the Welcome screen, click the Next button.

10. Read the Software License Agreement. Then click the Next button.

11. Read the Information screen. Then click the Next button.

12. The destination folder for the Sandra software is C:\SiSoft Sandra 98 Standard. If you'd like to change this location, click the Browse button. Otherwise, click the Next button.

13. In the Setup Type dialog box (see Figure 3.7.1), I recommend choosing the Typical option. The Sandra software requires about 1.5MB. If you're short on hard disk space, choose the Custom option and remove individual components of the package. After you choose an option, click the Next button.

Figure 3.7.1

If you're short on hard disk space, choose the Custom option and remove components of the package.

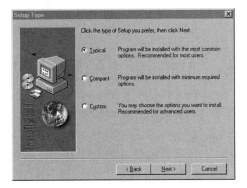

14. On the Select Program Folder screen, examine the destination folder, then click the Next button.

15. Check the software settings, then click the Next button to start copying files to your hard drive.

16. Click the Finish button to complete the installation.

To launch the application, choose the SANDRA.EXE file from within Windows Explorer. It resides in C:\Program Files\SiSoft Software\SiSoft Sandra 98 Standard.

The SiSoft Sandra dialog box will remind you of the Windows 98 Control Panel (see Figure 3.7.2). It contains objects for system diagnostics and the component-level benchmarks.

Better Benchmarks and Diagnostic Tests

Figure 3.7.2
Choose the individual diagnostics and benchmarks from the SiSoft Sandra dialog box.

3.7.2 Compare Your System to Others Using Ziff-Davis's Benchmarks

Ziff-Davis (ZD)—publisher of *PC Magazine, PC Computing, PC Week,* and other computer magazines—posts their benchmark tests online, free for you to download. While you're online, you can also access the results of other PCs tested with these same benchmarks for comparison purposes.

The ZD benchmarks encompass both synthetic- and application-based tests. Application-based benchmarks use real software products, running automatically at high-speed, to measure overall computer performance. Synthetic benchmarks are generally low-level software programs created specifically to test one or more components of the computer.

A division of ZD called the ZD Benchmark Operation (ZDBOp) created the three Windows tests that will be most useful to Windows 98 users. The ZDBOp Web site (`www.zdnet.com/zdbop/`) is where you'll find the tests (see Figure 3.7.3).

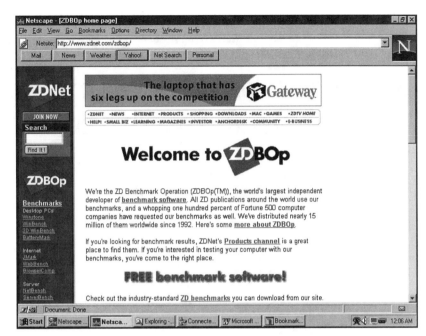

Here's a quick breakdown of the ZDBOp benchmarks:

WinBench 98: This synthetic benchmark tests your hard drive and
processor. An expanded version, which also rates your graphics/video and
CD-ROM subsystems, is available on CD by mail for a $5 shipping and
handling charge. WinBench is a popular test among graphics board manufacturers. You'll often see WinBench scores posted on their own Web sites.
Several of ZD's magazines rank computers based on WinBench results.

3D WinBench 98: Another synthetic benchmark that focuses on the PC's
3D-graphics processing. The hardware components stressed in this test
include: your graphics card or integrated chipset, your monitor, and the
graphics bus (PCI or AGP).

Winstone 98: This application-based benchmark tests overall computer
performance. Due to its size, Winstone 98 is only available on CD by mail
(for a $5 shipping and handling charge). Winstone 98 uses common
business applications running automatically through scripted tasks.

NOTE· You'll also find a battery test for notebook computers at the ZDBOp
Web site called BatteryMark, but I don't recommend this test.
BatteryMark requires a separate $300 mechanical "finger" device that's used to keep the
notebook "awake" during the test.

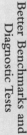

Better Benchmarks and
Diagnostic Tests

To compare your computer's performance against other computers' performances, browse the ZDNet Web site (`www.zdnet.com`). ZDNet posts computer product reviews from all of ZD's computer magazines (see Figure 3.7.4).

Figure 3.7.4

Look for comparative benchmark scores at ZDNet online.

Need more? ZD's online Virtual Labs (`www.zdnet.com/vlabs/`) also offer free tests for your monitor screen, your printer, and your Web browser (see Figure 3.7.5).

Figure 3.7.5

Use ZD's Virtual Labs for other interactive tests.

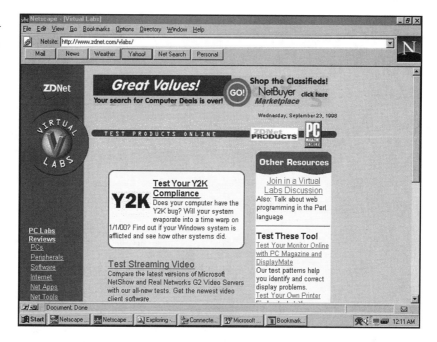

3.7.3 Monitor Your System

Windows 98 offers a powerful diagnostic tool called System Monitor. System Monitor "watches" components of your system and presents real-time charts showing you what these components are doing. With System Monitor, you can stealthily observe your modem, hard drive, processor, RAM, and even your network server. If your PC seems busy for no apparent reason, System Monitor will pinpoint the culprit that's slowing things down.

You might need to install this utility from the Windows 98 CD. It isn't included in the typical installation. You'll know it's not installed if you can't find System Monitor referenced under the Start menu at this location: Start | Programs | Accessories | System Tools.

Follow these steps to install System Monitor:

1. On the Start menu, choose Start | Settings | Control Panel.

2. Select the Add/Remove Programs object.

3. In the Components list, use the arrows to scroll down. Find the System Tools component and double-click it.

4. In the System Tools Components list, use the scroll arrows to scroll down. Find the System Monitor reference and put a check next to it (see Figure 3.7.6).

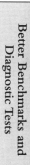

Better Benchmarks and Diagnostic Tests

Figure 3.7.6

Put a check next to System Monitor in the Components list.

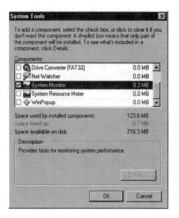

5. Click the OK button to close the System Tools dialog box.

6. Click the OK button on the Add/Remove Programs Properties dialog box.

Windows 98 will copy the file to your hard drive and automatically update the Start menu.

System Monitor offers very little documentation and online help. So, I'll walk you through launching and using the tool.

Follow these steps to launch and use System Monitor:

1. From the Start menu, choose Start | Programs | Accessories | System Tools | System Monitor.

2. The utility launches with a blank screen. Only the menus and toolbar are visible. You need to tell System Monitor which system elements you want to observe. To do this, choose Edit | Add Item from the menus. This action displays the Add Item dialog box (see Figure 3.7.7).

Figure 3.7.7

Add an item for System Monitor to observe.

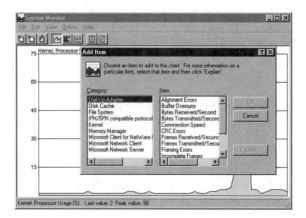

3. The Add Item dialog box contains 9 categories of system items. Each of these categories breaks down into separate items that you can monitor. By setting various charts, you may observe several elements simultaneously. Here's a breakdown of the categories:

Dial-Up Adapter: Scout out your modem with this category. For checking modem speed, watch Bytes Received/Second, Bytes Transmitted/Second, Connection Speed, Total Bytes Received, and Total Bytes Transmitted. To monitor error and recovery, select Overrun Errors, Timeout Errors, Framing Errors, CRC (Cyclic Redundancy Check) Errors, Buffer Overruns, and Alignment Errors.

Disk Cache: Check your hard disk's caching process with this category. To check your cache's efficiency select Cache Hits (higher is better), Cache Misses (lower is better), Maximum Cache Pages, and Minimum Cache Pages.

File System: Use this category to observe your hard disk's speed and error rates. For speed, select Bytes Read/Second, Bytes Written/Second, Reads/Second, and Writes/Second. To observe hard drive data errors, choose the aptly named Dirty Data.

IPX/SPX Compatible Protocol: Watch your network connection with this category. For speed observations, choose IPX Packets Received/Second and IPX/Packets Sent/Second. To track errors, select IPX Packets Lost/Second.

Kernel: Check your processor with this category. Perhaps the most useful of all System Monitor's items is Processor Usage (%). This shows what percentage of the processor is consumed by the current tasks. A Processor Usage Chart will give you a good idea of whether your CPU is being loaded down or not.

Memory Manager: Monitor Windows 98 Virtual Memory (swap file) and RAM with this category. To track the size of your hard drive's swap file, select Swapfile Size. To determine whether or not your computer is "thrashing" (swapping memory pages in and out constantly and thus slowing your system down), choose Page-Ins, Page-Outs, and Page-Faults.

Microsoft Client for NetWare; Microsoft Network Client; Microsoft Network Server: These three categories let you monitor your network software and network server.

For more information on any individual System Monitor item, select the item, then click the Explain... button (see Figure 3.7.8).

Better Benchmarks and
Diagnostic Tests

Figure 3.7.8
Ask System Monitor for more information by clicking the Explain... button.

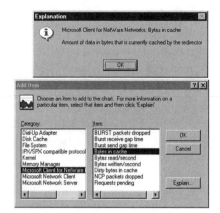

For this example, choose the Kernel category, then select Processor Usage (%). Click the OK button to load the item into System Monitor.

4. System Monitor provides three chart types: Line, Bar, and Numeric. When you use System Monitor, experiment with the different charts and find which one you like best. I, personally, find the Line graphs to be most useful—the charts seem to give me a better sense of changes over time. To select the Line Chart for Processor Usage, choose View | Line Charts from the menus at the top of the screen.

5. System Monitor updates its chart on a regular basis. You can adjust this time interval from 1 second up to 1 hour. For most computer events, a shorter interval is better. To set the update interval to 1 second, choose Options | Chart from the menus. Then slide the Update interval slider bar all the way to the left, toward faster (see Figure 3.7.9).

Figure 3.7.9
For useful observations, make the update interval as short as possible (1 second).

6. At this point, you should have a System Monitor screen that looks similar to Figure 3.7.10. The line chart shows the transitions of your processor's usage as you move the mouse, type at the keyboard, start, run, and stop applications, and so on. A status bar at the bottom of the System Monitor windows shows the Peak Value and the Last Value of your processor's usage.

Figure 3.7.10

*System Monitor's
status bar, at the
bottom of the
window, shows
the Peak Value
and the Last
Value of the
current item.*

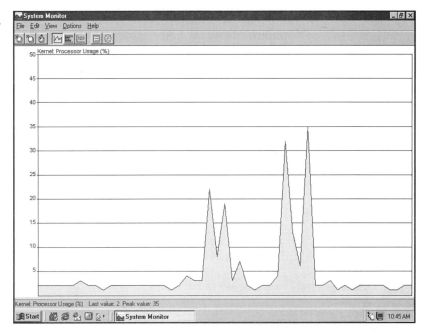

> **T**IP   Create a System Monitor log file if you need to track and save the
> utility's data. From the menus, choose File | Start Logging. This action
> displays a Save As dialog box. Select a folder and choose a name (or use the default
> SYSMON.LOG). Logging begins as soon as you click the Save button.
>
> No matter what chart type you use in the tool itself, System Monitor writes numeric
> data to the text-based log file. However, the logging process does use your choice of
> update interval. In this Processor Usage example, the log file looks like this:
>
> Kernel: Processor Usage (%)
>
> 8
>
> 3
>
> 3
>
> 12
>
> 12
>
> 51
>
> 20
>
> 4
>
> 49
>
> ...
>
> Each line marks the percentage of processor used a 1 second intervals.

7. You'll notice the percentage scale, at the left of the window, adjusts automatically, growing larger or smaller, as more or less activity occurs. For comparison purposes, you can set this scale to a specific range. From the menus, choose Edit | Edit Item. In the Edit Item dialog box, select the item you want to edit. Which in this case is Kernel Processor Usage (%). Then click the OK button.

> **TIP**   You can also use the toolbar to edit an item's chart. Click the Edit button, which looks like a page with a pencil hovering over it. It should be the third button from the left.

8. On the Chart Options dialog box (see Figure 3.7.11), in the Scale box, choose the Fixed radio button. Then in the Value field, set the upper limit for your chart. In this example, enter **50**. Click the OK button to close the Chart Options dialog box and save your changes.

Figure 3.7.11

For comparisons, fix the upper limit of the chart.

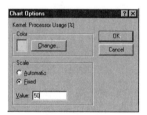

9. To add an item to the chart, select Edit | Add Item from the menus. In this example, in the Add Item dialog box, select Memory Manager as the Category. Then choose Page-Ins as the Item. You'll probably have to scroll down to find it. Or can type in the first letter of the Item name, in this case "P," to jump to the first item beginning with that letter. Click the OK button to close the Add Item dialog box. You'll now have two observations running simultaneously on the screen. It should look something like Figure 3.7.12. You can add over 30 items to one screen of System Monitor (see Figure 3.7.13), but, to make room, the utility removes the scale numbers from each chart when running more than 9 items simultaneously.

Figure 3.7.12

Run two observations side-by-side by adding items to System Monitor.

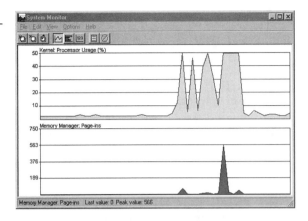

Figure 3.7.13

Add several charts to get an overall sense of your system's performance.

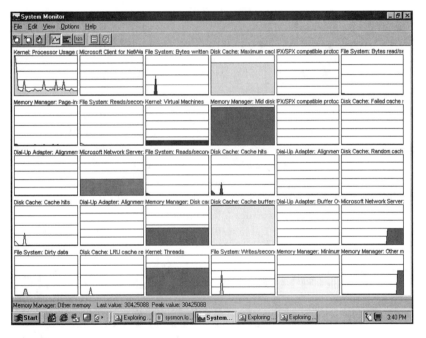

> **TIP** For remote observations, choose File | Connect from the menus. In the Connect dialog box, enter in the ID of the networked computer that you want to monitor.

10. To close System Monitor, choose File | Exit from the menus.

Why do you need System Monitor? It's handy for quickly analyzing both hardware and software. The System Monitor can help you choose among a group of hardware products or just debug your software setup.

Here's an example from my own experience. Several months ago I reviewed DVD-ROM drives for *PC World* magazine. In the review, most of the DVD-ROM upgrade kits included hardware cards that decoded the encrypted MPEG-2 data from DVD discs. One kit—I don't want to name names in the forum, so I'll call it Kit X—did not provide a decoder card. Kit X decoded the MPEG-2 data using software rather than a hardware chip. I wanted to determine how this software decode affected the overall system performance and how the software approach compared with the hardware approach.

> **TIP** For testing, perform other tasks while running System Monitor. But, to make sure you can see what System Monitor analyzes, choose View | Always on Top from the menus. With this setting, System Monitor will "stick" to the desktop, always within view, no matter what tasks you perform.

On the test PC, I used the System Monitor utility to analyze the percentage of processor used during playback for all the DVD-ROM drives. Kit X used about 42 percent of the processor just to playback DVD movies. All the other hardware-card drives used from 9 to 24 percent of the processor to play the same movies. Kit X required much more processor power to get its job done. If we multitasked other applications while playing a DVD title, Kit X dragged down the overall system performance much faster than the other drives. In this situation, System Monitor was the best diagnostic tool for the job.

3.7.4 Compare CD-ROM Drives

TestaCD Labs offers a CD-ROM benchmark called CD Tach. It's available from their Web site (`www.tcdlabs.com`) for $35. If you need to compare your CD-ROM drive's performance against the performance of others, this benchmark can help.

Why? Because CD Tach is the closest thing to a standard in CD-ROM benchmarks. Just about everyone—CD-ROM manufacturers, computer makers, and computer magazines—use it to compare CD-ROM drive speeds.

You can't download the CD Tach Benchmark; the CD it comes on is part of the test mechanism. But you can order it from the Web site.

CD Tach performs nine separate tests that analyze random access reads, sequential reads of differing sizes, reading from the inner-most and outer-most tracks, different levels of processor utilization, and more. And it graphs the results for easy interpretation (see Figure 3.7.14).

Figure 3.7.14

CD Tach's graphs help you interpret its test results.

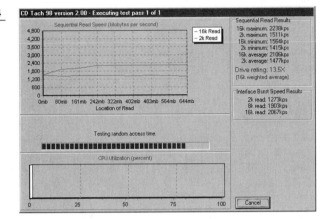

In the end, it provides an overall CD speed rating (in addition to plenty of individual test results) similar to the X rating that most CD-ROM manufacturer's provide. There's just one difference. CD Tach is a harsh grader. Recently, I ran CD Tach on a 20X CD-ROM. It resulted in an 18.4X CD Tach rating.

If you do run CD Tach, make sure you follow the included instructions about disabling the Windows 98 CD cache and read-ahead scheme. These actions force the CD-ROM drive to work without the aide of a hard drive cache, which might artificially increase the drive's performance.

Follow these steps to disable the Windows 98 CD cache and read-ahead scheme for testing purposes:

1. From the Start menu, choose Start | Settings | Control Panel.

2. Select the System object.

3. Pick the Performance tab on the System Properties sheet.

4. In the Advanced Settings dialog box, click the File System button.

5. On the File System Properties dialog box, pick the CD-ROM tab.

6. In the Settings box, slide the Supplemental Cache Size bar all the way to the left (towards Small). Then, in the Optimize Access Pattern For drop-down box, select No Read-Ahead (see Figure 3.7.15).

Figure 3.7.15

Disable Windows 98 CD cache and read-ahead scheme in preparation for the CD Tach test.

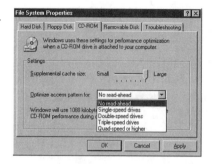

It's best to compare CD-ROM drives when they're attached to the same computer rather than attached to different computers. The computer system has some impact on a drive's CD Tach scores. Still, you can get a general sense of how your CD-ROM stacks up against others by reading computer magazine CD-ROM drive reviews that list the CD Tach benchmark.

Be sure to reset the CD cache and read-ahead schemes for your CD-ROM after you finish testing.

3.7.5 Browse for More Benchmark Resources

Do you need more information about benchmarking Windows 98 systems? There are several resources available on the Web. Here are some samples:

BAPCo (www.bapco.com): The acronym stands for Business Application Performance Corporation. This non-profit organization is made up of PC makers, software companies, and computer press entities. BAPCo develops its own application-based tests and makes them available for a fee. Their latest benchmark, called Sysmark 98 for Windows 98, might be of some interest to Windows users. It tests computers, using the latest Windows applications, for performance in the following areas: Internet, multimedia, content creation, voice recognition, and more. Better still, companies send in their test results, and the scores are posted up on the BAPCo Web site (see Figure 3.7.16). If you're shopping for a new Windows 98 PC, check here and do some PC research.

Figure 3.7.16

Find out how the latest PCs perform with the latest Windows applications.

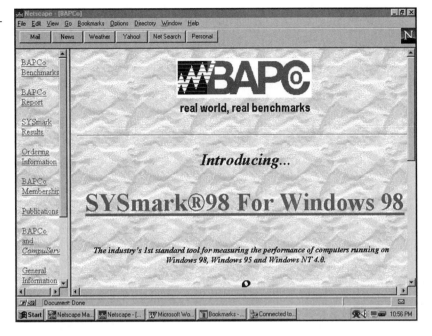

Tom's Hardware Guide (www.tomshardware.com): For the nitty-gritty nerd view of benchmarks and computer hardware, browse this Web site (see Figure 3.7.17). Tom doesn't mince words about the latest processor chips, video cards, or motherboards. And he tests most of them himself. He also critiques benchmarks (which almost no one else does) such as Ziff-Davis's 3D WinBench 98.

BenchmarkResources.Com (www.benchmarkresources.com): Select the PC Performance hyperlink at this Web site (see Figure 3.7.18) for a list of links on PC benchmarking resources on the Web. You'll find new tests for downloading, links to computer magazines, hardware resources, and computer troubleshooting and diagnostic sites. The main page also features benchmarking articles.

Better Benchmarks and Diagnostic Tests

Figure 3.7.17

Tom pulls no punches about PC hardware or benchmarks.

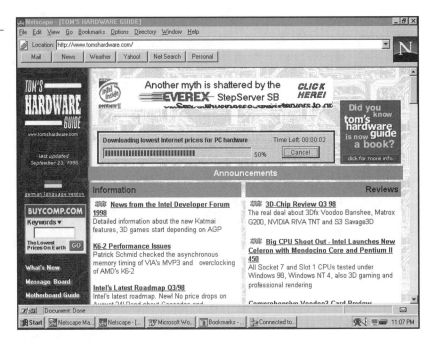

Figure 3.7.18

Select the PC Performance button for a list of benchmarking resources on the Web.

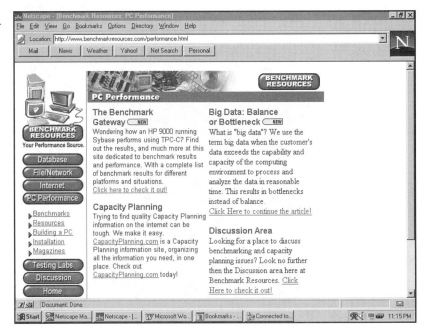

Chapter

3.8

Internet Performance

Who doesn't need faster access to the Internet? A speedy modem is a good first step, but Windows 98 also has a say in how fast you drive on the information superhighway. In this chapter, learn how to tune your Internet cache, adjust the Internet Protocol (IP) packet size, search Microsoft's Software Library offline, and more.

3.8.1 Find and Remove ActiveX Controls

The Internet Explorer often feels like a mixed blessing. With its ActiveX controls, browsing the Web can be a true multimedia experience. But without strict security settings, you end up constantly downloading new ActiveX controls that clutter up your hard drive.

Depending on how often you browse, your ActiveX Cache folder might be filled to the brim. Using the Disk Cleanup utility to remove all the files from these folders is one option. But, if you remove controls that you'll need later, you're shooting yourself in the foot. You'll probably need to download the same controls again on a subsequent Web visit.

Your best bet is to selectively delete ActiveX controls that you don't need.

Follow these steps to remove ActiveX controls from your system:

1. From the Start menu choose Start | Settings | Control Panel. Then select the Add/Remove Programs icon. Some of your ActiveX controls might be listed on the Install/Uninstall tab. Choose the entries you want to delete, and then click the Add/Remove button and follow the instructions. Click OK to close the Add/Remove Programs Properties sheet afterward.

TIP   Where are your ActiveX controls hiding? Use the Registry Editor (Regedit) and navigate to the following key: My Computer\
HKEY_LOCAL_MACHINE\SOFTWARE\Microsoft\Windows\CurrentVersion\
Internet Settings\ActiveX Cache. The strings below this key point to the folders that store your ActiveX controls. If you upgraded from Internet Explorer version 3.0 to version 4.0 when you installed Windows 98, you'll probably see these two entries:

```
"0"="C:\Windows\OCCACHE"
"1"="C:\Windows\Downloaded Program Files"
```

Those who started fresh with Internet Explorer 4.0 will only see the last entry.

2. Not all ActiveX controls can be purged that easily, though. Use the preceding tip to find out where your ActiveX controls reside. Then launch Windows Explorer (under Start | Programs) and browse one of your ActiveX Cache folders. You only need to browse one of them. All your ActiveX controls appear there even if they reside in other directories.

3. Right-click on the controls you want to remove, and then choose Delete from the pop-up menu. Windows 98 installs the following controls by default. Do not delete them.

> DirectAnimation Java Classes
> Internet Explorer Classes for Java
> Microsoft XML Parser for Java
> Win32 Classes

These controls enable Java support; removing them limits your ability to browse Web sites that use Java code.

4. From Explorer's menus, select File | Close to exit, when you've finished removing ActiveX controls.

Through the TweakUI utility, you can display your ActiveX Cache right on your desktop. This way you can access the folder whenever you like. Use these steps to display the ActiveX Cache on your desktop:

1. From the Start menu choose Start | Settings | Control Panel. Then choose the TweakUI icon. If you haven't already installed TweakUI, read the introduction for instructions on loading Microsoft's Sample Resource Kit utilities.

2. Choose the Desktop tab. In the Special Desktop Icons box, put a check next to ActiveX Cache folder. Click OK to close TweakUI.

The new icon should immediately appear on your desktop.

3.8.2 Adjust Your Internet Protocol (IP) Packet Size

With Windows 95, Microsoft guessed wrong about dial-up communications. They set the Maximum Transmission Unit (MTU) for IP (Internet Protocol) packets to 1500 inside the Windows Registry. That's a little too high for normal Internet traffic using regular phone line modems. Packets that large are usually broken down into smaller packets as the data passes through servers that have smaller MTUs. This slows your overall Internet performance because the server must re-assemble these fragmented packets at their destinations.

But Microsoft fixed this problem in Windows 98. Now the default MTU for transmissions speeds less than 128kbps is 576. And that's the Internet standard for IP packet sizes using dial-up connections.

> **NOTE**   With Internet connections above 128kbps, such as cable or ASDL modems, Windows 98 uses 1,500 as the MTU regardless of the settings within the Registry.

However, you still might increase your performance by tweaking the MTU setting within Windows 98. Your best bet is to try the Medium and Large Packet Size settings (Automatic is the 576 default) and see if you notice any performance gains.

Follow these steps to adjust your Windows 98 Packet Size settings:

1. From the Start menu, choose Start | Settings | Control Panel. Then select the Network icon.

2. Choose the Configuration tab of the Network sheet.

3. Select Dial-Up Adapter from the list of Installed Network Components. Then click the Properties button.

4. Choose the Advanced tab of the Dial-Up Adapter Properties sheet.

5. Select IP Packet Size from the Property list (see Figure 3.8.1), then click the drop-down button in the Value box and choose your packet size. I recommend trying Medium (1000 MTU) first and experimenting with that setting for awhile. You can also try the Large (1,500 MTU) setting, but in most cases, this won't improve your performance.

Figure 3.8.1

Change your IP Packet Size in the Dial-Up Adapter Properties dialog box.

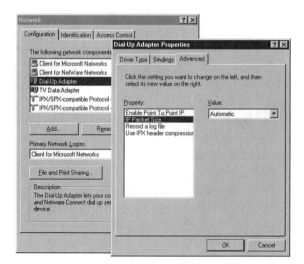

6. Click OK to close the Dial-Up Properties dialog box and then again to close the Network sheet.

If you don't notice any improved performance after days of use, I suggest you reset the packet size to Automatic.

3.8.3 Make Your Cache Faster

Microsoft put so much effort into Internet Explorer's bells and whistles that the program's performance suffers. In terms of caching sites on your hard drive, and recalling them when you click the Back button, Internet Explorer isn't as smart as it could be. Internet Explorer sometimes deletes recently downloaded pages instead of the oldest.

That's where Enigmatic Software's CacheSentry comes in. It's a cache management program written by David Pochron specifically to solve Internet Explorer's performance problems. And, best of all, it's free.

Follow these steps to download and install CacheSentry:

1. Browse Enigmatic Software's Web site (`www.mindspring.com/~dpoch/enigmatic/`).

2. On the home page, you'll see a hyperlink beneath the heading CacheSentry (for Internet Explorer) titled Click Here to Get More Info and Download the Program. Choose this link.

3. Read the next page for installation instructions. If possible, print them out, then click the link titled Click Here Now to Download CacheSentry.

4. Read the license agreement, then click Agree.

5. Choose among the two download options. You can download a full version of CacheSentry along with its documentation, but you'll need an unzip decompression utility such as Pkware's PKZip for Windows (at `www.pkware.com`). Or, you can download a smaller self-extracting Zip file that contains the program itself but no documentation.

6. Follow the download and installation instructions for the file that you choose.

7. Enigmatic Software recommends that you load CacheSentry into your Startup folder (under Start | Programs), so that it will load into memory during Windows startup. It uses no processor cycles until you launch Internet Explorer.

With CacheSentry installed and running, you should notice a performance improvement while browsing the Web, particularly if you backtrack through Web pages and sites.

Internet Performance

3.8.4 Browse Microsoft's Software Library Offline

Microsoft's massive online Software Library offers an incredible array of useful files. There, you'll find bug fixes, quick reference guides, conversion utilities, templates, and a whole lot more. However, searching through this high-traffic site usually takes so long that most people give up before finding what they need.

The good news is that you can download a text version of the site's index. The file includes filenames, descriptions, and posting dates, so that you can quickly find what you need by searching offline right from your hard drive. When you find the file you need, simply logon to Microsoft's site to download the file.

Follow these steps to download the index for Microsoft's online Software Library:

1. The file exists on Microsoft's FTP server, but you can access the server much like you do a Web page via your browser. In the Address field of your browser type `ftp://ftp.microsoft.com/Softlib/`.

2. In this directory, find the file INDEX.TXT. Right-click on the file and choose Save Link As.

3. When the Save As dialog box appears, save the file to a folder of your choice with the name INDEX.TXT.

4. After downloading, simply choose the file from within Windows Explorer. It's too large for Notepad, so Windows will ask if you want to open the file in WordPad instead. Choose Yes.

5. To search, select Edit | Find from WordPad's menus and enter your keywords.

To download specific files, access the Microsoft's Software Library with the following FTP address: `ftp://ftp.microsoft.com/Softlib/MSLFILES`. Then follow steps 2 and 3 to transfer the files to your hard drive.

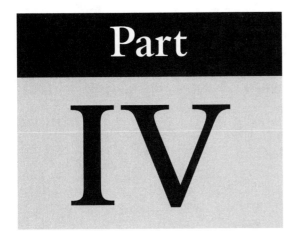

Part

IV

Administration

In this book, I use the term "administrator" loosely. For our purposes, a PC administrator is the person *in charge* of the system. The person saddled with the duties of setup, maintenance, security, new software installations, and so forth. That individual might, in reality, have the title owner, or parent, or Manager of Corporate Information Systems. I'll make no distinctions between these labels in this book.

If you are designated the administrator, I wish you luck. It's become a complex role in modern computing. Sophisticated computer viruses, the Wild West frontier of the Internet, and complicated new software make this job more and more difficult each day. And the difficulties apply both to the home and to the office environment.

I suggest that you scan this section of the book in its entirety. There are some topics here about which you might not have realized you needed to be concerned. This section covers setting up Windows 98, controlling the desktop, security issues, maintaining the PC, fixing known Win98 bugs, the year 2000 problem, and more.

The best administrators find a balance between restricting the computer setup and freeing up users to achieve their own work or play goals. My advice is to ask your users for feedback. Then tune your computer setup to suit both their needs and yours.

Chapter

4.1

Customizing New Installations

If you need to install Windows 98 or other software on any additional PCs, think before you act. The tips in this chapter describe how to prepare for low memory systems, create automated install routines, and handle other situations.

4.1.1 Limit Your RAM to Spot a Memory Hog

Information systems managers say that RAM limitations cause the biggest problems when rolling out applications to a computer workgroup. In many offices, the amount of RAM on-board PCs ranges dramatically—as much as 128MB installed on high-powered systems and as little as 16MB on low-end desktops.

Making matters worse, software vendors sometimes fudge the minimum system requirements that they list on their product boxes, particularly RAM require-ments. An application might run intolerably slow on a PC that actually meets the minimum requirements.

Some administrators test every new application's performance under low RAM conditions before rollout. Most, however, don't attempt this test because they believe it means opening PC cases and physically removing RAM SIMMS. But, guess what? Windows 98 lets you limit RAM for software testing, quickly and easily through the System Configuration utility.

Follow these steps to artificially limit your RAM:

1. Launch the System Configuration utility by entering **Msconfig.exe** at the Start | Run prompt or by choosing it from the Tools menu of the System Information utility (under Start | Programs | Accessories | System Tools).

2. Select the General tab of the System Configuration utility.

3. Choose Normal Startup in the Startup Selection box.

4. Click the Advanced button on the General tab.

5. Put a check next to the Limit Memory To XMB line. Then use the scroll arrows to limit your RAM to your desired amount (see Figure 4.1.1).

6. Click OK to close the Advanced Troubleshooting Settings sheet. Then click OK to exit the System Configuration utility. Windows will ask if you want to restart the computer. Choose Yes.

After you're finished testing your software, don't forget to reset the RAM amount in the System Configuration utility. Otherwise, your system can't access all available RAM.

Figure 4.1.1

*Use the System
Configuration
utility to
artificially limit
your RAM for
test purposes.*

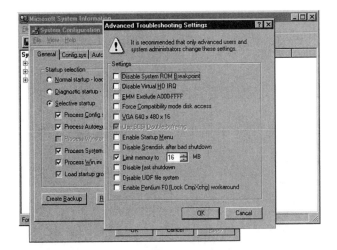

4.1.2 Back Up Your Channel Bar Subscriptions

It might take weeks before you finalize your Channel Bar subscriptions. After receiving the first few updates, many people change their minds, cancel their subscriptions, and subscribe to other channels. But, say you're found a perfect set and you really don't want to lose it. What should you do? Back it up with a Registry hack.

With this hack you can back up your Channel subscription for emergency situations or you can share them with friends and colleagues on other PCs. The Registry Editor's import and export features work their magic here. You'll be exporting two Registry keys. As always, take care when hacking the Registry.

Follow these steps to export your Channel subscriptions for later use:

1. Launch the Registry Editor by entering **Regedit** at the Start | Run prompt.

2. Navigate to the following Registry key:
   HKEY_CURRENT_USER\Software\Microsoft\Windows\ CurrentVersion\NotificationMgr.

3. File the Registry Editor's menus, choose Registry, Export Registry File. This displays the Export Registry File dialog box (see Figure 4.1.2).

4. Make sure the dialog box shows the Registry key mentioned in step 2 and that Selected Branch is marked in the Export Range box. Enter a descriptive filename, such as CHANSUB1.REG, and store it in a folder of your choice. Click the Save button.

Figure 4.1.2

Back up your Channel subscriptions by exporting Registry keys.

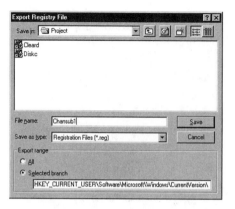

5. Now, navigate to the second key: HKEY_CURRENT_USER\
Software\Microsoft\Windows\CurrentVersion\Taskman. And, export it
to the file CHANSUB2.REG. If you don't see a Taskman key, don't panic.
Depending on your configuration, this key might or might not exist. If
not, just skip this step.

At this point, save these Registry files on your regular backup media. Or, you may
transfer these subscriptions to another PC using Regedit's Import Registry File
menu item.

4.1.3 Use Batch98 for Automatic Installations

If you need to install and configure Windows 98 for more than two PCs, I
strongly advise you to use the Batch98 utility instead of doing it all manually.
You'll save a lot of time, and you'll make far fewer mistakes.

Microsoft hides the Batch98 automated installation tool on the Windows 98 disc,
but tells you nothing about it in the documentation. It's left there for technical
people to discover. It's part of the Windows 98 Sample Resource Kit utilities, so
read the introduction for installation information on the sample kit, if you haven't
already done so.

The Batch98 program is very easy to use. It lets you quickly customize every
aspect of a Win98 installation. You can even copy the Registry from one system to
many others with this tool.

Follow these steps to launch and use Batch98:

1. From the Start menu, choose Start | Programs | Windows 98 Resource Kit |
Tools Management Console. The Management Console should open with
the Windows 98 Resource Kit Tools Sampler already loaded. If not, from

the menus, select Console | Open. Then enter
C:\Win98RK\TMC\Win98tmc.msc in the File Name field. Click
Open.

2. Under the Tools A to Z folder, select the A to C folder. This displays
   Batch98 and other tools in the right-hand pane of the Management
   Console.

3. Choose Batch98 (see Figure 4.1.3).

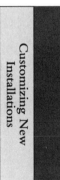

Figure 4.1.3

Use Batch98 to automate and customize multiple Windows 98 installations.

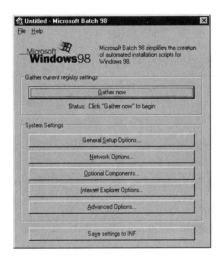

4. To copy the Registry settings of your current system to other PCs, click
   the Gather Now button in the Gather Current Registry Setting box.

5. Click each of the buttons under System Settings and modify the settings
   according to your rollout plan.

6. When you're finished customizing your installation routine, click the Save
   Settings to INF button. This creates a file called MSBATCH.INF on your
   hard drive.

7. Copy this file to the root directory (C:\) of each machine to which you
   will install Win98. Then insert the Windows 98 installation disc into the
   CD-ROM drive of the new PC and enter the following command at an
   MS-DOS prompt: **[CD-ROM drive letter]:setup C:\msbatch.inf**.

Windows 98's Setup program will use your custom settings for the installation.
Not all setup questions get answered by the .INF file, so you or someone else
should watch the installation and respond to any query from the procedure.

4.1.4 Decompress Before Installation

If you've compressed your hard drive with DriveSpace or any other compression utility, you should definitely decompress the drive before installing Windows 98. A compressed drive will slow the installation process dramatically, and the procedure already takes a good 20 minutes on an average PC.

What's more, with a compressed drive you won't be able to take advantage of Win98's FAT32 file system. The Disk Converter Wizard will not convert a compressed drive to FAT32.

If you choose, you can recompress your hard drive with the DriveSpace 3 utility that Windows 98 includes after you've completed the installation.

Chapter
4.2

Controlling
the Desktop

Windows 98 makes restricting and controlling the desktop very easy—just don't abuse the power. Read this chapter for instructions on limiting access to the Control Panel, modifying Registered Owner and Registered Organization information, removing Windows options, and other administrative tasks.

4.2.1 Change the Registered Owner and Registered Organization Settings

Recycling PCs is one of many administrative tasks. As employees transfer from one job to another, their PCs must be cleaned up and shifted to someone new. The normal recycling process includes removing applications, archiving data, and possibly upgrading obsolete components. But, during this makeover, two elements often go untouched—the Registered Owner and Registered Organization settings in Windows. Why? Because Microsoft didn't leave any easy way to change these settings. For that, you must hack the Registry.

Generally, these settings are used during new software installations. Application setup programs often query the Registry for these items and use them to fill in registration profiles and other settings. During a software installation, you'll often see the Registered Owner's name appear as the user name in initial dialog boxes.

Follow these steps to change the Registered Owner and Registered Organization of Windows 98:

1. Launch the Registry Editor by entering **regedit** at the Start | Run prompt.

2. Navigate to the following Registry key: My Computer\HKEY_LOCAL_ MACHINE\SOFTWARE\Microsoft\Windows\CurrentVersion.

3. Beneath this key find the RegisteredOwner string and the RegisteredOrganization string. To modify these items, select them and enter their new values in the Value Data fields of the Edit String dialog box (see Figure 4.2.1).

4. Click OK to close the Edit String dialog box. Then choose Registry | Exit from the menus to close the Registry Editor.

You won't need to restart Windows before you see these changes.

Figure 4.2.1

Modify the Registered Owner and Registered Organization settings directly in the Windows Registry.

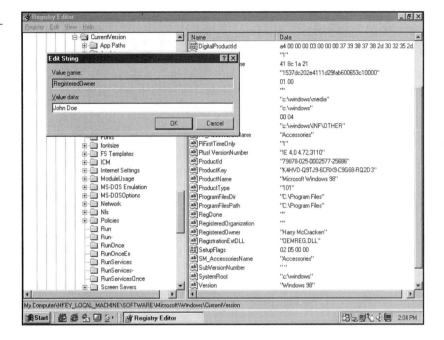

4.2.2 Remove Windows Update Option

Administrators must often manage all the PC software in their department or workgroup. This responsibility includes the controlled rollout of software updates and revisions. Unfortunately, Windows 98's Windows Update feature enables users to update their own software without the administrator's involvement or knowledge.

If this situation applies to you or you don't want your home system updated without your consent, you can remove the Windows Update feature from your PC. But, Microsoft doesn't make it easy for you. You'll need to hack the Registry.

There are three locations through which users can access the Windows Update process: the main menu of the Start bar, under Start | Settings on the Start menu, and through the Update Driver button on any device's properties sheet (see Figure 4.2.2). I'll show you how to remove all of them.

Follow these steps to remove the Windows Update option the Start | Settings menu and the Update Driver Wizard:

1. Launch the Registry Editor by entering **regedit** at the Start | Run prompt.

Figure 4.2.2

*The Windows
Update option is
also available
through the
Update Driver
Wizard.*

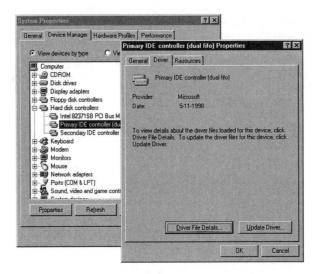

2. Navigate to the following key: My Computer\HKEY_LOCAL_
    MACHINE\SOFTWARE\Microsoft\Windows\CurrentVersion\
    Policies\.

3. Below this key, you might or might not have a key named Explorer. If you
    do, expand it. If you don't, create it by right-clicking on the Policies key,
    choosing New | Key, and then entering **Explorer**.

4. Under the Explorer key, create a new DWORD Value called
    NoWindowsUpdate. Create the DWORD by right-clicking on the
    Explorer key, choosing New | DWORD Value, and entering
    NoWindowsUpdate.

5. Select the NoWindowsUpdate DWORD and enter **1** as the value's data.
    Make sure you have the Base box set to Hexadecimal. Then click OK to
    close the Edit DWORD Value dialog box. This removes the Windows
    Update option from the Start | Settings menu.

6. Follow the same procedures as in steps 4 and 5 to create another
    DWORD value named **NoDevMgrUpdate**. Set its value to **1**. This
    removes the Windows Update check box option from the Driver Update
    Wizard.

You'll need to restart your computer before you'll see these changes. If you need
to turn these options back on, simply change the values from "1" to "0."

Removing the Windows Update item from the main Start Bar is easy. Just right-
click on it and choose Delete from the pop-up menu.

The Windows Update option runs the program WUPDMGR.EXE in the Windows Folder. For the tightest security, you can remove this program. Doing so, however, means you can't turn these options back on.

4.2.3 Modify, Remove, or Add Time Zones Settings

During the setup process, Windows 98 asks you to enter your time zone. This setting helps Windows keep track of your local time, even through the potential hiccups of the daylight savings periods. Microsoft also made every attempt to "internationalize" Windows by listing every time zone in the world, including Eniwetok, Kwajalein.

Administrators, however, might see this long list as more problematic than helpful. With so many choices, it is easy to accidentally choose the wrong one. The Arizona and Mountain Time settings, for example, only differ by the Daylight Savings adjustments.

If your plans only call for shipping PCs within the US, why not delete all of the international choices? Or, even better, why not rename the options to suit your particular business, such as Jittery Café, San Francisco and Jittery Café, Colorado? This will reduce the number of user mistakes during setup.

All this is easy if you use the Time Zone Editor that Microsoft includes on the Windows 98 disc.

Follow these steps to modify the Time Zone choices:

1. Launch the Microsoft Management Console by choosing Start | Programs | Windows 98 Resource Kit | Tools Management Console from the Start menu. If you haven't already installed the Sample Resource Kit utilities, read the introduction for instructions on installing them.

2. Navigate to the following section of the console: Console Root\ Windows 98 Resource Kit Tools Sampler\Tools A to Z\S to T.

3. Select the Time Zone Editor from the list of tools.

4. From the list of Time Zones (see Figure 4.2.3), choose an item you want to delete, highlight it, and then click the Delete button. Unlike other lists in Windows, you cannot select more than one item at one time in the Windows Time Zone Editor.

5. To rename an item with a more meaningful name, highlight the item and press the Edit button. This displays the Edit Time Zone dialog box (see Figure 4.2.4).

Controlling the Desktop

Figure 4.2.3

Use the Time Zone Editor to modify the list of time zone choices.

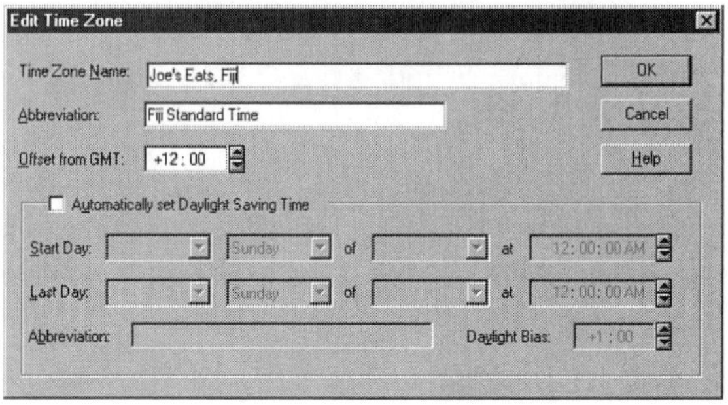

Figure 4.2.4

Rename time zones with more meaningful names.

6. Enter a new name in the Time Zone Name field, adjust the time settings if needed, and then click the OK button.

> **NOTE** You'll find the Windows Time Zone setting in the Registry at the following key: My Computer\HKEY_LOCAL_MACHINE\System\ CurrentControlSet\control\TimeZoneInformation. But you should only adjust the settings in the Control Panel's Date\Time object or through the Time Zone Editor.

7. Strangely, you'll find no exit menu on the utility. To save your changes, click the (X) Close button in the upper-right-hand corner of the window.

You'll need to restart Windows before you see your changes.

How do users access these time zones? As a user, you would choose Start | Settings | Control Panel from the Start menu. Then select the Date/Time icon. Finally, choose the Time Zone tab. The drop-down box (see Figure 4.2.5) displays your edited list.

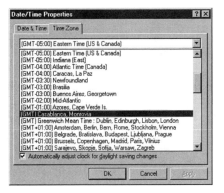

Figure 4.2.5
The Time Zone tab displays your time zone edits.

4.2.4 Hide the Control Panel

The Control Panel is one of the most dangerous areas for unaware users to wander through unattended. In the Control Panel, users can remove device drivers, reset passwords, uninstall software applications and a whole lot more.

As administrator, you don't want to remove the Control Panel completely—it's an integral part of the operating system—but hiding the Control Panel will keep it safely tucked away from an accident-prone novice.

> **NOTE** Parents of children and young adults highly recommend this tip for home computers. Kids quickly pick up the basics of computer use and, from there, their curiosity pushes them to learn more about configuring the system. By hiding the Control Panel you can limit the changes they can make.

> **WARNING** In addition to system settings, the Control Panel stores the TweakUI utility, the very tool you'll use to hide the Control Panel objects. If you hide the TweakUI icon, launching it and restoring the Control Panel's objects will be difficult. Before you hide the Control Panel's object make a shortcut to the TweakUI utility and bury it in a folder on the hard drive about which only you know.

Follow these steps to hide the Control Panel's objects:

1. Launch the TweakUI tool by choosing Start | Settings | Control Panel from the Start menu and then selecting the TweakUI object.

2. Select the Control Panel tab.

3. From the list of objects, remove the checks from those objects you want to hide. If you don't remove all of them, you should at least remove the most dangerous. These include: Add/Remove Programs, System, Passwords, and Internet (see Figure 4.2.6).

4. Click OK to close TweakUI.

Controlling the Desktop

Figure 4.2.6

If you decide not to hide all the Control Panel's objects, at least restrict the potentially dangerous ones.

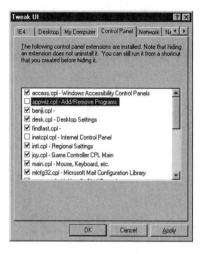

You'll need to restart your system before you see these changes.

For more precise restrictions, use the System Policy Editor. With the Policy Editor, you can disable Control Panel objects—but leave them visible—or you can hide individual tabs within objects and leave the other tabs functioning normally. Read the introduction for instructions on installing the System Policy Editor from the Win98 CD, if you haven't already done so.

Follow these steps to restrict the Control Panel using the System Policy Editor:

1. Launch the System Policy Editor by entering **poledit** at the Start | Run prompt.

2. From the menus, choose File | Open Registry.

3. Select the Local User object.

4. Navigate to the following policy path:
   Local User\Windows 98 System\Control Panel.

5. Beneath this policy, you'll see five sub-policies—Display, Network, Passwords, Printers, and System. Each of these Control Panel objects may be restricted.

   Here's a list of possible restrictions for each policy.

   Display
   Disable Display control Panel
   Hide Background page
   Hide Screen Saver page
   Hide Settings page

Network
Disable Network Control Panel
Hide Identification page
Hide Access Control page
Passwords
Restrict Passwords Control Panel
Hide Change Passwords page
Hide Remote Administration page
Hide User Profiles page
Printers
Hide General and Details pages
Disable Deletion of Printers
Disable Addition of Printers
System
Hide Device Manager page
Hide Hardware Profiles page
Hide File System button
Hide Virtual Memory button

To make these restrictions, open the policy header and place a check next to the corresponding Restrict…Control Panel entry. Then put a check next to each of the restrictions you want to set within the Control Panel object (see Figure 4.2.7).

Figure 4.2.7
Put a check next to each restriction you want within the Control Panel object.

6. Click OK to save the Local User Properties sheet.

7. From the menus, select File | Save to save your changes.

8. From the menus, choose File | Exit to close the System Policy Editor.

You must reboot the PC before these changes take effect.

4.2.5 Hide Your CD-ROM and Other Drives

Electronics stores sell locks that you can install on your PC to secure you CD-ROM drive. But, you don't need to spend the extra money. Through the TweakUI utility, you can hide the CD-ROM drive, and any other drive on the system, from other users.

You might ask why you would want to limit access to the CD-ROM. This is because besides the Internet, the CD-ROM is the main path for new software installation. To stop others from playing computer games or filling up your hard drive with unneeded software, restrict access to the CD-ROM. It's the most effective way to control your PC's setup.

Follow these steps to hide your computer's drives:

1. Launch the TweakUI utility. You'll find the TweakUI object in the Control Panel (under Start | Settings | Control Panel). If you haven't yet installed TweakUI from the Windows 98 CD, read the introduction for instructions.

2. Choose the My Computer tab. This displays a list of drives. Although the list shows the entire alphabet of possible drive letters, all those drives not actually available will have a red "X" over the item (see Figure 4.2.8).

Figure 4.2.8

TweakUI's My Computer tab lists your computer's drives. A red "X" covers those that are unavailable.

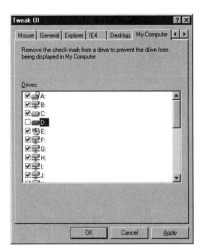

3. Remove the checks next to the drives you want to hide. Your CD-ROM drive would most likely be the letter D or E, but you'll know by the disc icon in front of the correct letter.

> **NOTE**   You might be wondering about Windows AutoPlay feature, where a CD's software automatically starts when a CD is inserted into the drive. Good news: Hiding a CD-ROM drive through TweakUI overrides the AutoPlay setting. With a hidden CD-ROM, inserting a disc will not launch the CD's software.

> **WARNING**   Hiding a drive through TweakUI only affects the Windows operating system. You can still access CD-ROM data by opening an MS-DOS window and entering the drive letter for the CD-ROM.

4. Click the OK button to close TweakUI.

You must restart Windows before you see this change.

4.2.6 Allow Only Certain Programs to Run

Most Windows 98 users think they can run any Windows-compatible program on their system. In truth, that's only because their administrators let them.

With the System Policy Editor, an administrator can specify a list of approved applications. If a particular program isn't on the list, it won't run. Period.

This tip might sound a little fascist. That's because it is. I don't recommend it for most computing environments. In the vast majority of cases, PCs should empower people, not limit them. However, I can imagine scenarios—medical environments, performance-testing labs, the Space Shuttle—where strict application control might be necessary.

Follow these steps to create a list of approved Windows applications:

1. Launch the System Policy Editor by entering **poledit** at the Start | Run prompt. Read the introduction for instructions if you haven't yet installed the System Policy Editor from the Windows 98 CD.

2. Choose the Local User object.

3. Navigate to this policy path: Local User\Windows 98 System\ Restrictions.

4. Beneath this policy, put a check next to the line reading Only Run Allowed Windows Applications. This displays information in the Settings box at the bottom of this page along with a Show… button (see Figure 4.2.9). Click the Show… button.

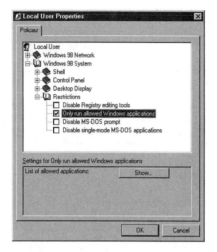

Figure 4.2.9

Build a list of approved Windows applications. Only these applications will run.

5. When it first appears, the Show Contents box will be empty. Click the Add button to start building your list of approved applications. There is no Browse button, so you'll need to enter the exact path of your applications.

> **WARNING**   If you set this policy for all users, you had better include the System Policy Editor (C:\Windows\Poledit.exe) in the list; otherwise, it will be difficult to remove this policy later on.
>
> If you've already made this mistake, run the Registry Editor (regedit.exe). (You might need to boot from the Windows 98 Emergency Startup disk). Navigate to the key: My Computer\HKEY_CURRENT_USER\Software\Microsoft\Windows\CurrentVersion\Policies\Explorer. Below this key you should find the key RestrictRun. Delete it. Then reboot the system.

6. Continue adding applications until you complete your list.

7. Click the OK button to close the Local User Properties sheet.

8. From the menus, choose File | Save to save your changes.

9. From the menus, choose File | Exit to close System Policy Editor.

You'll need to reboot the systems before these changes take affect.

4.2.7 Restrict Registry Access

The hacks mentioned in this book demonstrate the power, and the danger, of editing the Windows 98 Registry. Through Registry edits a user can completely transform, or disable, his PC.

As administrator, you should limit Registry access. Beginners, for example, could accidentally cripple their system within minutes and then require you to spend time troubleshooting the problem. Disabling Registry access is useful for both home and corporate PCs.

Follow these steps to restrict access to the Windows 98 Registry:

1. Launch the Policy Editor by entering **poledit** at the Start | Run prompt. If you haven't already installed the Policy Editor, read the introduction section for instructions and warnings.

2. From the menus, choose File | Open Registry.

3. Click the Local User icon.

4. Navigate to the following policy path:
   Local User\Windows 98 System\Restrictions\.

5. Beneath Restrictions you'll find a list of check-box entries. Put a check next to Disable Registry Editing Tools.

6. Click OK to close the Local User Properties.

7. From the Policy Editor's menus, choose File | Save. Then select File | Exit to close the utility.

You must restart Windows for this hack to take effect. This procedure disables access to both the Registry Editor and the TweakUI utility.

Controlling the Desktop

Chapter

4.3

Software
Modification

Wouldn't it be nice if you could just install software and forget it? Yes, but then the administrator's job would be too easy, and we can't have that.

In this chapter, you'll find the insider hints for managing and maintaining PC software. Learn how to find out more about Windows 98 system files, edit the Add/Remove Programs list, support old Windows 3.1 software, and other useful tricks.

4.3.1 Edit the Add/Remove Programs List

All administrators plan when to add or remove software. Because when a user removes an application spontaneously, either intentionally or by accident, it's likely the administrator's job to restore it.

Fortunately, with a quick Registry hack, you can edit the Add\Remove programs list and make it more difficult to delete software from a PC.

Follow these steps to edit the Add/Remove programs list:

1. Launch the Registry Editor by entering **regedit** at the Start | Run prompt.

2. Navigate to the following key: My Computer\HKEY_LOCAL_ MACHINE\SOFTWARE\Microsoft\Windows\CurrentVersion\Uninstall\.

> **WARNING**   It's much better to export items from the Uninstall keys and save them than it is to just delete them. You might need to restore these keys at a later date when the time comes to remove software from the system.

3. Below this key, you'll find a separate key for each application in the Windows Add/Remove Programs list (see Figure 4.3.1). As mentioned in the Caution text, you should back up the keys you want to remove by exporting them into Registry files. To export a key, highlight it, and then choose Registry | Export Registry File from the menus. The Export Registry File dialog box lets you choose a folder and filename on your hard drive. Make sure you mark Selected Branch in the Export Range box of this dialog box. The procedure will append a .REG file extension, denoting a Registry file. You can import this file later as needed.

4. After exporting all the keys you plan to delete, you can begin removing the keys one by one. To remove a key, right-click on it and then select Delete from the pop-up menu.

Figure 4.3.1

Each entry in the Add/Remove Programs list matches a Registry key at the following location: My Computer\ HKEY_LOCAL_ MACHINE\ SOFTWARE\ Microsoft\ Windows\ CurrentVersion\ Uninstall\.

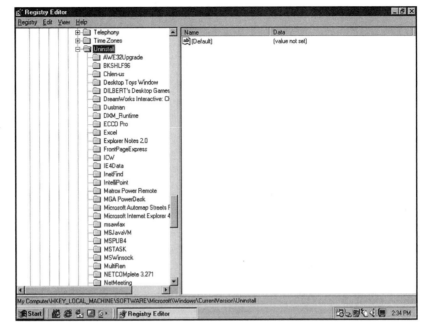

5. Choose Registry | Exit from the menus to close the Registry Editor.

You must restart Windows before you'll see these changes in the Add/Remove Programs list. Be sure to include your exported Registry files with your other important files when you backup your hard drive.

4.3.2 Lie to Windows 3.1 Software

Windows 3.1 software won't die. Even though many software houses revamped and revised their products for Windows 95 and 98, others did not. And even if there is a newer version of an old Windows 3.1 program you own, you might not feel like shelling out the extra cash to pay for it.

The question is: Will your old Windows 3.1 software run correctly on Windows 98? Maybe, and maybe not. It depends on how well the program was written. The only way to know for certain is to install it and try it.

If an error message pops up, it's not the end of the world. Nor does it mean you need to remove your Win3.1 application. First, try lying to it—make it think it's running on a Windows 3.1 computer. That sounds crazy, doesn't it? But it usually works.

Software Modification

Lie to the program by using the Make Compatible utility (MKCOMPAT.EXE). Windows 98 loads Make Compatible onto your hard drive during installation. You'll find it in the C:\Windows\System directory. MKCOMPAT.EXE can fool your Win3.1 software in a number of ways, from lying about the Windows version number to fooling the program with old Win3.1 color palettes.

Launch the Make Compatible tool by entering **Mkcompat.exe** at the Start | Run prompt. Then examine the options under File | Advanced Options on the menus (see Figure 4.3.2).

Figure 4.3.2

Check the Advanced Options of the Make Compatible tool to see all it can do.

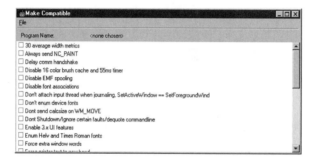

To identify the program you want to fool, select File | Choose Program from the menus. Then use the subsequent dialog boxes to locate your problematic Win3.1 program.

Consider the following tips as you select the Make Compatible options.

- First, try only the Lie About Windows Version option. This solves most cases of misbehaving Win3.1 software.

- Use the Windows error messages, if any, as a guide. For example, if the error message mentions the system memory "stack," then select MKCOMPAT's Increase Stack Size entry.

- Determine the problem category. For example, for problems while printing, use MKCOMPAT's printer-related options such as Disable EMF Spooling or Force Win3.1 Printer Dev Mode Size. For peripheral-related troubles, use MKCOMPAT's Delay Comm Handshake. For display-related problems, use MCKCOMPAT's Enable 3.x UI Features and so on.

■ Don't be afraid to try several options at the same time. You won't do any damage to your Windows 98 system.

Keep in mind, MKCOMPAT can't work miracles. If your Windows 3.1 application isn't a "well-behaved" program, it might never work under Windows 98.

4.3.3 Change Your Windows 98 Source Path

Always keep track of your Windows 98 CD-ROM. You will need it at some point in the future. For example, as you add hardware to your system, you'll likely require software drivers that are only available on that disc. You also might decide to add operating system components from the CD that you didn't originally think you'd need.

Even if you do keep track of the disc, though, there's still a chance you might run into trouble with it. If, for example, you ever change your CD-ROM's drive letter (as you add other devices such as a DVD-ROM drive), your PC won't know where to find your Windows 98 CD. And, you'll receive one of those "can't find file x" messages.

You see, the operating system stores the original location of your CD in a Registry string called the Source Path. So, if you ever change the location of your CD, you need to hack the Registry to let it know.

Follow these steps to change the Windows 98 source path:

1. Launch the Registry Editor by entering **regedit** at the Start | Run prompt.

2. Navigate to the following key: My Computer\HKEY_LOCAL_MACHINE\SOFTWARE\Microsoft\Windows\CurrentVersion\SETUP.

3. Beneath this key, locate the string value SourcePath. Select this entry to display the Edit String dialog box (see Figure 4.3.3).

Software Modification

Figure 4.3.3

Modify the SourcePath string in the Registry to tell Windows where your system files are located.

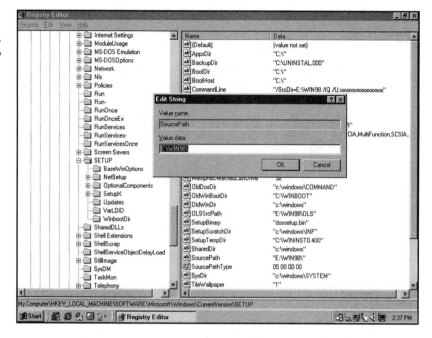

4. Enter the new path for your Windows system files in the Value Data field. Click the OK button.

5. Choose Registry | Exit from the menus to close the Registry Editor.

You must restart Windows for this change to work.

4.3.4 Change File Date and Time Stamps

For administrators, file date and time stamps become very important. These stamps indicate when a file was last modified and they help administrators track system updates and workflow. Even backup routines use these date and time stamps when they collect a list of modified files to include in any current backup jobs.

Normally, the operating system controls time and date stamps; when a user saves a file to disk, the operating system changes the "last modified" time and date stamp to the system's current time and date.

You can view these stamps in the Windows Explorer (but you must select View | Details from the Explorer's menus). There are times, however, when you need to correct errors or rerun backups. Performing these tasks sometimes requires a change to a file's time and date stamps.

To aid administrators with these stamps, Microsoft included a utility called FileWise in the Sample Resource Kit utilities. FileWise lets you alter a file's time and date stamps to whatever you want.

Follow these instructions to launch FileWise and use it to change a file's time and date stamps:

1. FileWise is part of the Sample Resource Kit, but it is not copied to your hard drive when you install the Kit (read the introduction section about installing the Sample Resource Kit). However, you can run it directly from the Win98 CD. Insert the Win98 CD into your CD-ROM drive. In the Windows Explorer, navigate to this directory on the CD: [*Your CD-ROM drive letter*]:\TOOLS\reskit\diagnose. Then select FILEWISE.EXE.

> **NOTE** Attention! Windows 98 Beta Program Users! The "gold" Windows 98 CD does not contain FileWise. It shipped with the Beta 3 CD and the off-the-shelf Windows 98 software, but not the "gold" disc. However, you can download FileWise from the Web. The URL is:
> `http://www.geocities.com/SiliconValley/Pines/5444/`.

2. Open the file that you want to modify. Choose File | Add a File from the menus, and select it through the dialog box.

3. To change the file's time and date, highlight the file's row and then choose Edit | Touch from the menus. This displays the Touch dialog box (see Figure 4.3.4).

Figure 4.3.4
FileWise enables you to alter a file's time and date stamps.

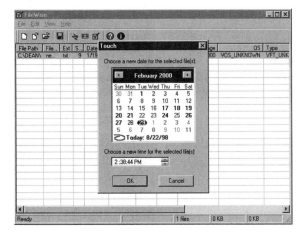

4. Pick a new date from the monthly calendars. You can scroll forward and backward to other months with the scroll buttons at the top of the dialog box. To modify the time stamp, enter a new time in the field at the bottom of the dialog box or use the time field's scroll buttons.

> **NOTE** Changing file date and time stamps might also help you solve the infamous Year 2000 (Y2K) problems for your PC. To determine how your system will work in the new millennium, simply reset the dates of critical files (after a complete system backup, of course) to January 1, 2000.

5. You do not need to save the file. In fact, FileWise's Save menu option has nothing to do with saving the original file you opened. It's only saving the FileWise report itself and there's no need to do that for this situation.

6. To close FileWise, choose File | Exit from the menus. If a file has been opened, FileWise will ask if you want your information to a tab-delimited text file. Click the No button. FileWise will close.

If you did want to keep track of your file time and date changes, feel free to use FileWise's report features to do so.

4.3.5 Track Your System Files

Windows 98's System File Checker utility helps you track changes to your hard drive as you add and remove software to and from your PC. It checks all the system folders you specify and generates a report telling you which files were added, which were modified, and which were deleted.

Why is this important? Not all software cleans up after itself. Some uninstallation routines leave files on your disk, simply because they were poorly written. With the System File Checker's report you'll be able to clean up after misbehaved software.

> **NOTE** If you must rigorously track new software installations, consider purchasing an off-the-shelf uninstaller application. These products load monitor agents into your PC's memory that "watch" new software installations and record all the changes made to your system. These packages start at around $30 and are well worth the money.

System File Checker also checks for corrupted Windows files. If a system file has been damaged, the utility can restore it from the Windows 98 CD.

Follow these steps to launch and run the System File Checker tool:

1. Microsoft hides the System File Checker tool underneath the System Information Utility. So first launch the System Information Utility by choosing Start | Programs | Accessories | System Tools | System Information.

2. From the System Information Utilities menus choose Tools | System File Checker. This displays the System File Checker (see Figure 4.3.5).

Figure 4.3.5

The System File Checker can look for altered files or restore damaged system files from the Windows 98 CD.

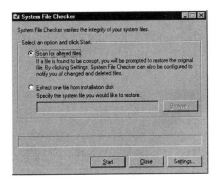

3. To look for changes to the hard drive, choose Scan For Altered Files in the Select an Option and Click Start box. Then click the Settings button.

4. Click the Settings tab. Then make sure that you put a check in front of Check For Changed Files and Check For Deleted Files.

5. Select the Search Criteria tab. Use the buttons in the Select the Folders You Want to Check box to add folders and subfolders to your disk scan. Also add file extensions to search for in the box at the bottom of the page. You aren't limited to system file extensions. You can add any type, including text (.TXT) and (.DOC) Word file extensions.

6. Click OK to close the Settings sheet.

7. Back on the System File Checker's main screen, click the Start button to begin the search.

8. After the scan completes, view the log file. To do this, click the Settings button on System File Checker's main screen. Then select the Settings tab. Click the View Log button in the Log File box of this sheet to open the report in Notepad (see Figure 4.3.6).

Software Modification

Figure 4.3.6

View the log file to review the recent changes to your system files.

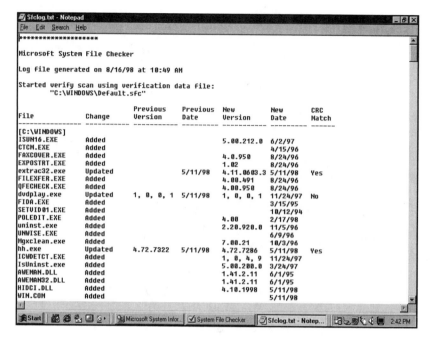

9. Choose File | Exit from the menus to close Notepad. Then click OK to close the Settings sheet. Finally, click the Close button to exit System File Checker.

It's a good idea to run the System File Checker regularly, say, once a week for most systems. You must run the tool after each new software installation to record the system changes of individual products.

4.3.6 Investigate Your System Files

Imagine this scenario: During a disk cleaning session you stumble across a big mysterious Windows system file. You'd like to delete it, but you have no idea what the file does and you're afraid it will cripple some component of the operating system if you remove it. What should you do?

Look the file up and find out exactly what it does! Then you can make an educated decision about deleting it. How? Use the Microsoft File Information utility that's included on the Windows 98 CD. It contains a detailed description of every Windows system file. The utility is part of the Sample Resource Kit utilities. Read the introduction for instructions on installing the Resource Kit, if you haven't already done so.

Follow these instructions to launch the Microsoft File Information utility:

1. From the Start bar, choose Start | Programs | Windows 98 Resource Kit. Then select the Tool Management Console.

2. Navigate to the following console entry: Console Root\Windows 98\ Resource Kit Tools Sampler\Tools A to Z\D to O. Then select the Microsoft File Information utility from the right-hand pane of the console.

3. Select the File Information tab (see Figure 4.3.7).

Figure 4.3.7
The Microsoft File Information utility contains a description of every Windows 98 system file.

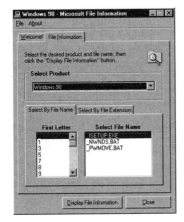

4. Make sure you select the correct Microsoft product in the Select Product drop-down box. If you were part of the Windows 98 beta program (thousands of people were), you'll see entries for the betas as well as your purchased copy of Windows 98.

5. You can search for your file by name or by extension. Click on the appropriate tab and follow the onscreen instructions. When you find your file, highlight it and click the Display File Information button. This brings up the File Information dialog box (see Figure 4.3.8).

Software Modification

Figure 4.3.8

The File Information dialog box tells everything you need to know about a system file

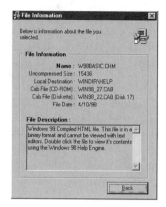

6. Click the Close button to exit the Microsoft File Information utility.

If you can't find a particular file in the Microsoft File Information Utility, then you know some other software product, not Windows 98, loaded that file onto your PC.

Chapter

4.4

Security Issues

Both home and corporate users need secure PCs. Find out how to protect your personal data, create more sophisticated passwords, obtain a digital ID for use on the Internet, and more, in this chapter.

4.4.1 Protect Your Personal Data

Business transactions over the Web are becoming commonplace. Many users now shop, sell things, and deal with financial institutions over the Internet. You've probably worried about crackers prying into your personal data online, but there's a potential security problem much closer to home—your Internet Explorer cache.

The pages that Internet Explorer 4.0 saves on your hard drive might contain your credit card number, your bank account information, a record of your online purchases, or other personal data. Anyone with access to your PC might also have access to these items. Make sure that these pages are not cached using the Advanced settings of Internet Explorer.

Follow these steps to stop Internet Explorer 4.0 from saving personal Internet data:

1. Launch Internet Explorer (under Start | Programs | Internet Explorer).

2. From the menus, choose View | Internet Options.

3. Select the Advanced tab.

4. Scroll down until you see Security settings (see Figure 4.4.1).

Figure 4.4.1

Protect your personal data by modifying settings in the Internet Explorer.

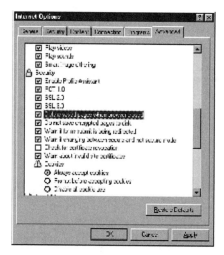

5. Put a check next to Delete saved pages when browser closed and another next to Do not save encrypted pages to disk.

Browsing forward and backward through your recently viewed Web pages might be slowed somewhat by these settings, but this will only occur when you browse encrypted Web pages.

4.4.2 Get a Digital ID for Outlook Express

The latest wave in Internet security is the digital ID. As more business transactions shift from "snail" mail to email, digital signatures increase in importance.

With a digital ID, recipients of your email will know with certainty that a message with your ID came from you, not an impostor. Digital IDs also enable you to send email fully coded with a public key/private key encryption method.

Currently, VeriSign, Inc. (`www.verisign.com`) issues digital IDs for as little as $9.95 per year. As of the time of this writing , VeriSign offers a free 60-day trial of their service. For more information, contact VeriSign directly or browse the Digital ID section of Microsoft's Web site (`www.microsoft.com/ie/ie40/oe/certpage.htm`) for other options.

Follow these steps to configure Internet Explorer with a digital ID:

1. Purchase your ID from an online service such as VeriSign and download the certification file.

2. Launch Internet Explorer (under Start | Programs | Internet Explorer).

3. From the menus, choose View | Internet Options.

4. Pick the Content tab of the Internet Options sheet.

5. In the Personal Information box, click the Edit Profile button.

6. Choose the Digital IDs tab.

7. Assign the signature to an email address by clicking the drop-down arrow in the Digital IDs box. (see Figure 4.4.2).

> **NOTE** A digital ID can only be assigned to one email account and must only be used with that account. If you have multiple email accounts that you want to secure, you must obtain multiple digital IDs.

8. Click the Import button.

9. In the Select digital ID file to import dialog box, choose the .P7C or .CER digital signature file and click the Open button. This imports the digital signature file.

Figure 4.4.2

Select the email address to which you will assign the digital ID.

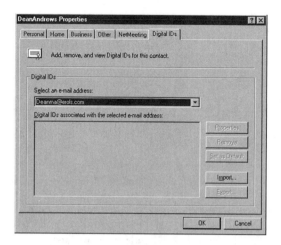

10. Click OK to close the Properties dialog box.

11. Click OK to close the Internet Options dialog box.

After you obtain and import an ID, configure Outlook Express for digital signatures using these steps:

1. Launch Outlook Express (under Start | Programs | Internet Explorer).

2. From the menus, choose Tools | Options.

3. Pick the Security tab.

4. In the Security box (see Figure 4.4.3), put a check next to Digitally sign all outgoing messages and Encrypt contents and attachments for all outgoing messages.

Figure 4.4.3

Digitally sign your email in Outlook Express.

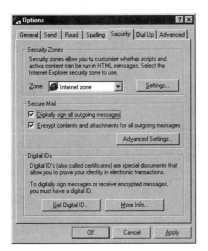

4.4.3 Check File and Print Sharing Settings while on the Net

Connecting to the Internet is very similar to connecting to a massive corporate Wide Area Network (WAN)—except that the Internet is filled with strangers instead of colleagues. PC Administrators often protect servers against external invasion, through the use of firewall security schemes, but sometimes administrators forget about those users who dial out over regular phone lines. Dial-Up Networking connections to the Internet expose the same file sharing privileges to the outside world that they do on the LAN or WAN. For a more secure Dial-Up Networking session, make sure you disable file-sharing privileges before you connect.

Follow these steps to disable file-sharing privileges on your Win98 PC:

1. From the Start menu, choose Start | Settings | Control Panel.

2. Select the Network object.

3. Choose the Configuration tab of the Network sheet.

4. Click the File and Print Sharing button.

5. Remove the check next to I want to be able to give others access to my files (see Figure 4.4.4).

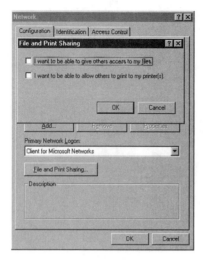

4.4.4 Manage Web Cookies

By now, you've probably heard of *cookies*, the innocent-sounding but devilish little files that Web sites place on your hard drive to find out more about you and your browsing patterns.

Face it. Cookies are an invasion of your privacy, no matter what perspective you take on the issue. Unfortunately, so many sites now use this traffic-monitoring device that it's almost impossible to surf the Web without receiving these un-wanted "treats."

One way to combat this is to set up your browser so that it automatically ex-cludes all cookies or prompts you every time you're about to receive one. To do this in Internet Explorer, choose View | Internet Options from the menus. Click the Advanced tab. Scroll down until you see the Cookie item. Then select either Prompt Before Accepting Cookies or Disable All Cookie Use.

This isn't, however, a perfect solution. With the previously mentioned settings, your Web surfing will become a minefield of prompt screens and rejection notices (some sites block access if they can't place cookies).

My advice is to accept the cookies at the outset. Then throw off the Web masters by selectively deleting the ones you don't want when you're offline. Their tracking procedures won't be fast enough to track you.

NOTE   Not all cookies are bad cookies. Some Web sites use cookies to save your preferences. For example, you might set up a profile that defines your favorite news topics, sporting events, and music artists. On your next visit, the Web site automatically shows you your preferences. In these cases, deleting the cookies means deleting the profile.

Internet Explorer lets you examine and delete cookies through its menus. To do this, choose View | Internet Options from the menus. Select the General tab. Then click the Settings button in the Temporary Internet Files box. On the subsequent Settings sheet, click the View Files button. This action displays both your cookies and the .CDF setup files used by Active Channels. You can remove files from this list if you like.

But I have a better idea. Download a freeware tool called Cookie Cruncher from RBA Software. Cookie Cruncher gives you more control over cookies. Follow these steps to download and install Cookie Cruncher:

1. Launch Internet Explorer and browse *PC World* Online's FileWorld site (www.fileworld.com).

2. Use the search box to locate the file "Cookie Cruncher." Don't use quotation marks during the search. Click the Cookie Cruncher hyperlink to proceed to the download page.

3. Follow the instructions to download the file COOK211.ZIP. You'll need a Zip decompression tool such as PKWare PKZip for Windows (www.pkware.com) to extract the data files from the download file.

4. Extract the files to a temporary directory. Then run the SETUP.EXE installation program. By default, the program installs into the C:\Program Files\Cookie Cruncher 4 directory. In the Cookie Cruncher Setup dialog box, tell the tool which browsers you have installed on your system (see Figure 4.4.5).

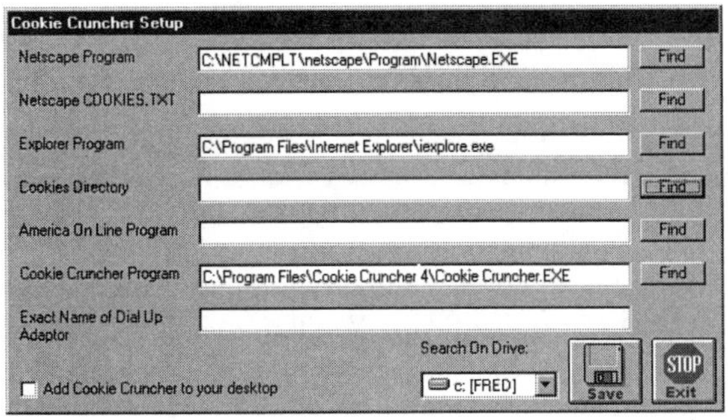

Figure 4.4.5

The Cookie Cruncher dialog box looks for all your browsers.

5. Run the application by launching the COOKIECRUNCHER.EXE file. This displays the main screen of the tool (see Figure 4.4.6).

The main screen of Cookie Cruncher presents all the cookie files, regardless of whether they arrived through a Netscape browser or a Microsoft browser. The right-hand panel describes which Web site delivered the cookie and when it sent it. You can delete individual cookies or all of them by using the buttons at the bottom of the screen.

Figure 4.4.6

*The Cookie
Cruncher
freeware tool lets
you manage
cookies from
either Netscape
or Microsoft
browsers.*

4.4.5 Hide Files from Windows, DOS, and Other Users

Very personal documents require an extra measure of security. Windows 98, however, is not the most secure operating system in the world. So, you might want to consider hiding the files from Windows 98 as well as other users.

How? With a shareware download from the Web called Magic Folders, you can hide files from Windows and DOS. You can also protect these files with a password. And for even greater security you can download a version that encrypts the files as well as hides them.

Follow these steps to download and install Encrypted Magic Folders:

1. Point your browser to the following Web site:
    `http://www.pc-magic.com/`

2. For the encryption version of the program, select the Encrypted Magic Folders hyperlink. If you prefer the cheaper, unencrypted version, use the Magic Folders hyperlink.

3. Follow the instructions to download the file EMF.ZIP to a temporary directory on your hard drive. You'll need a decompression tool such as PKWare's PKZip for Windows (`www.pkware.com`) to extract the data files from this download file.

4. Extract the data files. For the installation, you'll need a blank formatted floppy disk —which is used in case you forget your password.

5. In Windows Explorer, run the program INSTALL.EXE by selecting it.

6. During the installation, Magic Folders will ask you to enter a password, confirm it, and insert a blank floppy.

7. After the installation, run Magic Folders by selecting the file,
MAGIC.EXE from Windows Explorer. This displays the Encrypted Magic
Folders dialog box in which you can add and remove folders and files (see
Figure 4.4.7).

Figure 4.4.7

*Encrypted Magic
Folders will
password-protect,
encrypt, and
make your
personal files
invisible to
Windows and
DOS.*

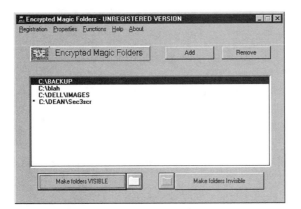

Magic Folders and Encrypted Magic Folders are free to use for 30 days. After that,
you must register or the programs will stop working. You can purchase Magic
Folders for $29 and the encrypted version for $58.

4.4.6 Make Passwords More Secure

How wimpy is your password? If it's a variation on your name, a family member's
name, your birthday, an anniversary, or any other easy memory trigger, you might
as well not use a password. With a little background research, crackers can break
through such common passwords in minutes.

With its default password settings, Windows 98 is extremely flexible—a little too
much so. Passwords can be any length, even as short as one character. They can be
text or numbers, or a combination of both. They can be saved, so users don't need
to re-enter them. You can even bypass the password dialog box in default mode.

As an administrator, it's important to educate users to the realities of password
security. But sometimes education isn't enough. With the help of the System
Policy Editor, you can force users to implement more complicated—and less
vulnerable—passwords.

Follow these steps to implement more secure passwords:

1. Launch the System Policy Editor by entering **poledit** at the Start | Run
prompt. Read the introduction section for instructions if you haven't
installed the System Policy Editor from the Windows 98 CD.

2. From the menus, choose File | Open Registry.

3. Pick the Local Computer object.

4. Navigate to this policy path: Windows 98 Network\Password.

> **NOTE** Windows 98 passwords are actually too secure for some network operating systems. By default, Windows 98 sends encrypted passwords to network servers for authentication. Unfortunately, some Server-Message-Block (SMB) network operating systems, such as IBM LAN Server and LAN Manager for UNIX Systems, only process unencrypted passwords.
>
> You can configure Windows 98 to use unencrypted passwords so that it can network with these servers, but this requires a Registry hack.
>
> Use the Registry Editor to navigate to the following Registry key: My Computer\ HKEY_LOCAL_MACHINES\System\CurrentControlSet\Services\VXD\VNETSUP.
>
> Beneath this key, insert a new DWORD value (right-click on key, choose NEW | DWORD Value), named EnablePlainTextPassword and give it the value **1**.
>
> You'll need to reboot the system to activate this change.

5. For the highest level of password security, place a check next to each of the following policy entries: Hide Share Passwords with Asterisks, Disable Password Caching, Require Alphanumeric Windows Password, and Minimum Windows Password Length. In the Settings for Minimum Password Length, use the scroll buttons to increase the length to 7.

6. Click OK to close the Local Computer Properties sheet.

7. Choose File | Save from the System Policy Editor's menus to save your changes.

8. Select File | Exit from the menus to close the System Policy Editor.

You must reboot your system to activate these password changes.

4.4.7 Monitor Application Use

I don't advocate spying on people. However, there are times when monitoring PC activity seems reasonable. If, for example, you suspect someone is tampering with your PC, or you need to gather usability information for a software development effort, then monitoring application use might help you.

Believe it or not, Windows 98 monitors you all the time. Every time you run an application, Windows 98 logs it. The Task Monitor process uses these logs to help improve the performance of your hard drive. The Disk Defragmenter runs a program called CVTALOG.EXE to collate the log files and reorganize your disk so that your most frequently used programs run efficiently.

Unfortunately, interpreting these log files is difficult; they're coded in a way that makes them hard to read. If, however, you don't want to download or buy any special monitoring software, you can use the logs to get a sense of what's happening to your system.

You'll find the log files in the C:\Windows\Applog directory. Each application on your drive has its own file listed with a special .LGX file extension (X will be the drive letter on which the application resides). For example: the log for a Microsoft Word application residing on the C drive will be called WORD.LGC.

For more precise, easy to understand monitoring, download the Boss Everyware shareware tool from PC Magazine's Software Library. Alexander Jmerik wrote the program.

Follow these steps to download and install Boss Everyware:

1. Browse *PC Magazine*'s Web site (`www.pcmag.com`). Navigate to the Software Library section of the site.

2. Use the search box to find Boss Everyware.

3. Follow the instructions to download the compressed BSSEVRWR.ZIP file to a temporary folder on your hard drive.

4. Decompress the file with an unzip tool such as PKWare's PKZip for Windows (`www.pkware.com`).

5. Run the INSTALL.EXE program that your Zip program extracts from the download file.

6. The installation routine installs the program by default into the C:\Program Files\Boss Everyware folder. Launch the program by selecting BEWMAN.EXE from this folder.

7. Choose Service | Options from the menus. This displays the settings for when to run the program and where to store the log file (see Figure 4.4.8).

Figure 4.4.8

Use Boss Everyware to watch your system while you're away.

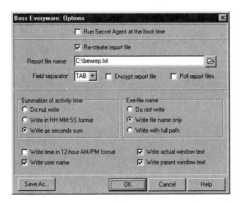

By default, the log file is stored in a file called BEWREP.TXT in the root directory of your C drive. You'll find the log clear and easy to read. For each program, you'll see a time stamped listing. You must register Boss Everyware online if you plan to use it more than 30 days.

Chapter

4.5

Multiple Users

Don't repeat the same setup work for multiple PCs that you use for multiple users. Share settings for the Internet Explorer and the Task Scheduler with the hints described here. You'll also find out how to cut down on frivolous email on your network.

4.5.1 Auto-Configure Internet Explorer

As administrator, you can configure Internet Explorer 4.0 once and then set up others users automatically with the same profile. The profile includes settings for home pages, connection information, security levels, mail and news software, and more.

You'll need Microsoft's Internet Explorer Administration Kit (IEAK) software. You can download it free from Microsoft's site (`www.microsoft.com/IE/IEAK/`), but you must register before you install it. And you must use Internet Explorer 4.0 to complete the download and installation of IEAK. Netscape's browsers won't work.

The IEAK configuration produces a set of .INF files for individual, group, and default profile settings. After you've created these files, you must post them on your corporate Intranet or on a LAN server. Your users will then step through the following instructions to auto-configure Internet Explorer 4.0 on their PCs.

Follow these steps to auto-configure Internet Explorer 4.0 based on an administrator's IEAK profile:

1. Launch Internet Explorer 4.0 (under Start | Programs | Internet Explorer).

2. From the menus, choose View | Internet Options.

3. Select the Connection tab.

4. In the Automatic Configuration box, click the Configure button. This action displays the Automatic Configuration dialog box (see Figure 4.5.1).

5. Enter the URL supplied by the administrator. Then click the OK button.

This process transfers profile files from the administrator's server to your PC.

Figure 4.5.1

Auto-configure your Internet Explorer setup using an administrator's profile.

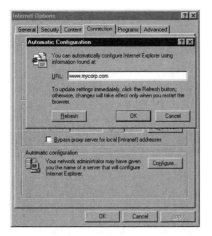

4.5.2 Shift Users from Email to Winpopup for Frivolous Messages

Let's admit it, shall we? Even in a corporate environment, a lot of email messages are personal, not business related. It's human nature to gossip as well as transact business over this fast, easy, communication mechanism.

For administrators, though, frivolous email can be a problem. Namely, it takes up too much space. People seldom manage their inboxes effectively, and so with a large network, non-business related email could fill gigabytes of storage.

What to do? As administrator, you should persuade your users to shift from email to Winpopup messages for non-business messages.

The Winpopup utility (see Figure 4.5.2) lets users send short, real-time text messages to any user on the network. But the messages *can't be saved*. Nor can they include attachments. It's the proverbial win-win situation. Network users can still chat with each other, but the administrator is freed up from storage nightmares.

The WINPOPUP.EXE utility is in the C:\Windows directory. There's no configuration required. It automatically finds network users' IDs. You should, however, put a Winpopup shortcut into your Windows Startup folder. The utility must be running for you to receive messages from another user.

Depending on your system configuration, you might need to install Winpopup first. To do this, locate the WINPOPUP.INF file (in your C:\Windows directory). Right-click on the file. Then choose Install from the pop-up menu.

4.5.3 Share Scheduled Tasks with Other PCs

Setting up a list of Windows 98 scheduled tasks can be time consuming and tedious. Don't waste time re-creating these tasks for multiple users. In a small office, a workgroup, or a corporate LAN you can just copy and paste these tasks to other systems.

You'll find all the scheduled tasks on your system stored in .JOB-type files in the directory C:\Windows\Tasks. The filenames are the same as the task titles you used when you set the tasks up. Simply copy the directory over to another computer on the LAN or just store them on a floppy disk—job definition files are usually only 1 kilobyte in size—and port them wherever you want.

> **NOTE**   A scheduled task can run while a computer is in suspend mode as long as the PC's BIOS supports Advanced Power Management (APM) version 1.2 or Advanced Configuration and Power Interface (ACPI) version 1.0. Read the PC's documentation to determine if it supports one or both of these power management standards. If Windows 98 can't "wake up" a PC when it's time to run a task, it will report that it was unable to complete a scheduled task the next time you power up the system.

There's no additional setup required. Just make sure to copy the files into the new systems C:\Windows\Tasks directory. The Task Scheduler automatically loads any job stored there.

Chapter

4.6

Maintenance
Tips

Maintenance duties consume most of an administrator's time. Read this chapter for hints that will reduce the amount of time you spend keeping PCs running smoothly.

4.6.1 Restore the Registry

The worst problem a user can encounter is a non-booting PC. Fixing this problem immediately becomes the user's number one priority. As administrator, you need a fast, foolproof method for restoring the Registry files. Here it is. And, you won't even need the Emergency Startup disk.

Follow these steps to restore the Windows 98 Registry for a non-booting PC:

1. If the PC is powered up, power it down. Don't concern yourself with the normal shutdown procedures if you can't find a path to the Start menu. Just turn off the power switch.

2. Wait a good 30 seconds then power the system back on again. Hold the Ctrl key down during the boot process. This displays the Windows 98 Startup menu.

> **NOTE**   You no longer need to hold down the F4 or F8 keys to access Windows's Step-by-Step Confirmation mode for interactive boot-up. In Windows 98, this item resides on the Startup menu that you invoke by holding down the Ctrl key.
>
> By the way, Microsoft made this process much smoother by choosing the Ctrl key instead of the function keys. With depressed F4 or F8 keys, you would hear your keyboard chatter as it tried to send multiple keystrokes to the operating system. The Ctrl key is silent.

3. From the Startup menu, choose item number 5—Command Prompt Only. Then press the Enter key.

4. At the C:> prompt enter **scanreg /restore**. This runs the Registry Checker program. The Registry Checker will display a list of Registry backups (Windows 98 backs up the Registry every day during startup) with creation dates. Ask the PC's user which day corresponds to the day the PC was last working properly. Highlight that Registry Backup, and then choose the Restore button (you can use the Tab key to select the Restore button or just press the R key on your keyboard).

5. The next screen tells you that you have restored a "good" registry and, it asks if you want to restart the system. Choose Restart. In fact, it's your only option on this screen.

The PC will reboot and launch Windows with a restored Registry.

4.6.2 Remember Passwords

Windows 98's Dial-Up Networking component lets you save your password. This way, you don't need to re-enter it every time you log on to the Net. For security reasons, the operating system uses asterisks as placeholders for your password. And, therein lies the problem. Many users forget their original passwords over time because they never have to enter them.

Just try to close your Internet service provider account without your password, and you'll understand why you need to remember them.

Windows 98 won't let you decode those asterisks, but a free utility that you can download from the Web will. It's called Snadboy's Revelation, and once you've used it, you'll wonder how you ever lived without it.

Follow these steps to download and install Snadboy's Revelation:

1. Point your browser to this URL: `http://www.snadboy.com/ Revelation.shtml`.

2. Click the Download hyperlink.

3. Choose one of the FTP download sites in your country. Save the file REVEL11.ZIP to a temporary directory on your hard drive. You'll need a Zip decompression tool such as PKWare's PKZip for Windows to extract the data files.

4. After you've downloaded the file and extracted the data files, run the SETUP.EXE program by selecting it in Windows Explorer. This will install Snadboy's Revelation in the folder C:\Program Files\ Snadboy Software\Revelation.

5. Using Revelation is easy. Bring up any dialog box that shows a coded password—such as a Dial-Up Networking Connect To box. Then launch the REVELATION.EXE tool.

6. Drag the Password Field Selector icon from Revelation's main screen (see Figure 4.6.1) over the coded password field. Your decoded password will appear in Revelation's password box.

Revelation is completely free, but the creators ask that you register your program with them if you plan to use it beyond 30 days.

Maintenance Tips

Figure 4.6.1

Like a secret decoder ring, Revelation will tell all about passwords.

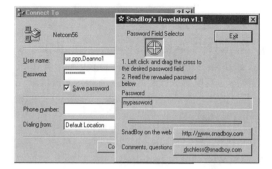

4.6.3 Stabilize Your Desktop

In Windows 98, Internet Explorer and the desktop are intricately linked. Perhaps a little too much so. Misbehaving Web sites, poorly written ActiveX controls, and even bad modem connections might crash your desktop if you use Windows's default settings.

For greater stability, set the Internet Explorer to browse in a separate process from the Explorer desktop shell program. This way, even if the Internet Explorer hangs, freezes, or implodes, your desktop will survive the disaster and continue running as if nothing has happened.

> **NOTE**   To terminate a crashed Internet Explorer session, press the key-combination Ctrl-Alt-Delete. This displays the Close Program dialog box. Select the Internet Explorer task—its name will be the Web page or file which is currently being browsed—then click the End Task button. If you've set your options for Browse in a New Process, this will not shutdown your desktop.

> **WARNING**   Often, administrators trade performance for stability, and that's true in this hint as well. Spinning off a separate browser process might negatively affect your PC's performance, but only very slightly.

Follow these steps to set Internet Explorer to spin off a new process while browsing:

1. Launch the Internet Explorer (under Start | Programs | Internet Explorer).

2. From the menus, choose View | Internet Options.

3. Select the Advanced Tab.

4. Scroll down to the Browsing settings (see Figure 4.6.2).

5. Put a check next to Browse in a new process.

To activate this change, restart Windows.

Figure 4.6.2

Set your Internet Explorer to Browse in a new process for greater stability.

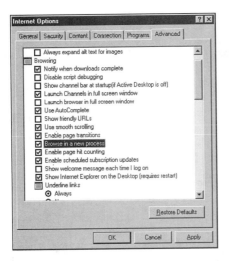

4.6.4 Clear Out the Most-Recently-Used (MRU) Lists

Maintenance Tips

Have you noticed how Windows 98 keeps track of everywhere you've been? For example, the Start menu's Run and Find | Files or Folders items both have drop-down boxes that display your previous entries. Microsoft calls these lists the most-recently-used (MRU) lists.

Most people find the MRU lists helpful; you don't have to do as much typing when you can easily recall previous commands. But, it's nice to have some control over these lists. Administrators might want to clear out the MRU lists, for instance, when recycling a PC from one user to another.

Follow these steps to clear Windows's MRU lists:

1. Launch the Registry Editor by entering **Regedit** at the Start | Run prompt. Or, just pick Regedit from the Run command's MRU list, if you've entered it before.

2. Navigate to the following key: My Computer\HKEY_CURRENT_ USER\ Software\Microsoft\Windows\CurrentVersion\Explorer\.

3. Below this key, you'll find several MRU keys relating to various Windows lists. Here's a table of references:

Key Name	Related Windows Object
Doc Find Spec MRU	Start menu's Find | Files or Folders
FindComputerMRU	Start menu's Find | Computer
PrnPortsMRU	Windows 98's printer ports
RunMRU	Start menu's Run

Open any of the preceding keys and remove all the entries below them except the (Default) string. This will clear the MRU list.

4. Close the Registry Editor.

After these changes, the Find command's MRU lists are immediately cleared. For the other MRU lists, you must restart Windows 98 for the changes to take effect.

4.6.5 Disable the Low Disk Space Warning

Windows 98's low disk space warning is never good news. It means that your drive is very short on free space. You'll see the warning during file creation and copy tasks on a nearly full hard drive, disk, or removable storage drive.

But, there are times when the message does more than make you feel bad. With automated backup and copy tasks, a low disk space warning might actually interrupt a process while it waits for a user to press OK in response. If these automated tasks take place during the night, you might return in the morning, only to find the error message and not a completed backup.

With a Registry hack, you can disable this warning for any drive on the PC.

> **WARNING** Disabling the warning message does not solve your disk storage problem. Make sure to archive data or clean up unneeded files to free up more space.

Follow these steps to disable Windows 98's low disk space warning message for any drive.

1. Launch the Registry Editor by entering **Regedit** at the Start \| Run prompt.

2. Navigate to the following Registry key: HKEY_LOCAL_MACHINE\ System\CurrentControlSet\control\FileSystem.

3. Below this key, you should see a DWORD value named DisableLowDiskSpaceBroadcast which is set to 0, meaning that the

warning is enabled. If you don't have this DWORD, create it. To create it, right-click on the FileSystem key and choose New|DWORD Value from the pop-up list.

Use the following table to enter a value for this DWORD value referencing a specific drive letter. Entering **8**, for example, disables the warning for drive D.

Drive Letter	DWORD value
A	1
B	2
C	4
D	8
E	16
F	32
G	64
H	128
I	256
J	512
K	1024
L	2048
M	4096
N	8192
O	16384
P	32768
Q	65536
R	131072
S	262144
T	524288
U	1048576
V	2097152
W	4194304
X	8388608
Y	16777216
Z	33554432

4. To disable more than one drive, you need to create additional DisableLowDiskSpaceBroadcast DWORDs and enter in the corresponding drive letter number as the value. To create additional DWORDs, right-click on the FileSystem key and select New|DWORD Value from the pop-up list.

5. Choose Registry|Exit from the menus to close the Registry Editor.

You must restart Windows to complete the change.

Maintenance Tips

Chapter

4.7

Managing the Registry

Hacking the Registry is one thing, but working with it on a daily basis is another. Administrators should make friends with the Windows 98 Registry and understand how it behaves. In this chapter, you learn how to import and export Registry files, track changes, and observe the Registry in action.

4.7.1 Import and Export Registry Files

One of the best features of Windows 98 is that it gives you the ability to import and export Registry files. The export capability enables you to save the entire Registry or just parts of it. With the import feature, you can "patch" the Registry with fixes or enhancements. And, using both, you can share Registry keys and values among several PCs.

The Registry Editor (REGEDIT.EXE) provides the import and export commands under its Registry menu item. Read the introduction for instructions on launching and using Regedit.

When you export a Registry file, you create an ASCII text file. You can edit this file with the WordPad editor (under Start | Programs | Accessories) or any other text editor.

Below is an example of an exported Registry key:`[HKEY_LOCAL_MACHINE\`
`SOFTWARE\Microsoft\Windows\CurrentVersion\explorer\VolumeCaches\`
`Download Program Files]`

`@="{8369AB20-56C9-11D0-94E8-00AA0059CE02}"`

`"Display"="Downloaded Program Files"`

`"Priority"=hex:64,00,00,00`

`"StateFlags0000"=dword:00000002`

In this example, the first line in brackets is the name of the Registry key and its Registry path. The next four lines note the values stored beneath this key. The line beginning with the @ sign shows the value of the string labeled "(Default)" under this key when it is viewed in the Registry Editor. The next line connotes a string named Display and its value "Downloaded Program Files." The next line describes a binary value named Priority with its hexadecimal value "64 00 00 00". And the last line shows a DWORD (Double Word) named StateFlags0000 with its value "00 00 00 02."

You'll find Registry "patches" on Windows newsgroups and forums on the Internet. As always with the Internet, you should be careful about what you download and install into your system. It's best if you trust the sources. It's also a good idea to read over any file (in WordPad) before you import it into your system. Try to understand the changes the new files will make to your Registry before you use them.

Follow these steps to import a Registry file into your Windows Registry:

1. Store the import file somewhere on your hard drive.

2. Launch the Registry Editor by choosing Start | Run from the Start menu. Then enter **regedit** into the Open field. Click the OK button.

3. You don't need to navigate to any particular key. Windows handles all the details for you. From the Registry Editor's menus, select Registry | Import Registry File.

4. The Import Registry dialog box looks just like a standard Open dialog box (see Figure 4.7.1). Browse your hard drive and locate the import file. Highlight the import file and then click the Open button.

Figure 4.7.1

The Import Registry dialog box looks and acts like a standard Open dialog box.

> **WARNING**   The keys and values within the import file override any keys and values currently stored in your Registry. Be sure you want to make these changes.
>
> The import file might also contain new keys and values that don't exist in your current Registry database. Windows will automatically create these new keys and store the new values.
>
> If you do run into any trouble, remember, you can restore a previous version of the Registry. Windows automatically backs up the Registry every time your power up your system.

5. Windows will import the Registry File and set all the keys and values described in it.

Whether or not you have to reboot your PC depends upon the changes the import file has made. Some Registry changes will appear immediately. Others won't take effect until you restart your system. If you're unsure about a particular change, restart your system.

You can also import Registry files in MS-DOS mode. This capability is very handy for crash recovery situations. You can boot your PC from disk and alter the Registry with patches before you launch Windows.

Follow these steps to import a Registry file in MS-DOS mode:

1. With the PC turned off, insert a bootable (system) disk, such as the Windows 98 emergency disk, into the floppy drive. Then power up the PC.

    To follow this example, you can also just open an MS-DOS session (under Start | Programs | MS-DOS Prompt on the Start menu).

2. Change to the directory, either on the disk or the hard disk that holds the import file. Use DOS's CD command to move from one directory to another.

3. Enter the following command at the DOS prompt:

    Regedit *filename*.reg

    In the example, *filename* is the name of the Registry file you want to import.

    For this command to work, you must have the C:\Windows directory in your DOS Path. The complete syntax of the whole command would be:

    C:\WINDOWS\REGEDIT.EXE C:*FILEPATH**FILENAME*.REG

> **NOTE** If you perform this command in an MS-DOS box rather than a full-screen DOS session, a Windows message box will pop up and ask if you're sure to want to add the information in this file to the Registry. Click the Yes button to continue the import.

Windows will import the file and display Importing File (100% Complete) when finished.

There's yet another way to import a Registry file. It relates to the MS-DOS method shown previously.

In the Windows Explorer, you can simply double-click on any file with a .REG extension and Windows will begin to import it into the Registry. It will first ask if want to continue (see Figure 4.7.2).

Figure 4.7.2
Windows asks your permission before it alters the Registry.

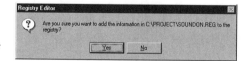

How does this work? It has to do with .REG file types and the actions defined for them.

Follow these steps to examine the actions defined for .REG files:

1. From the Start menu, choose Start | Settings | Folder Options.

2. On the Folder Options sheet, pick the File Types tab.

3. Scroll down the Registered File Types list and find Registration Entries.

> **TIP** Just as you can with other lists in Windows 98, you can quickly search the Registered File Types by keys on the keyboard. Enter **REG** and you'll jump to the Registration Entries item.

4. Highlight Registration Entries and click the Edit button.

5. On the Edit File Type sheet, you'll see three actions listed for Registration Entries: Edit, Merge, and print (see Figure 4.7.3). The Merge action should be in boldface type. This means that Merge is the default action for this file type. Highlight Merge and click the Edit button.

> **NOTE** To change the default action for this or any other File Type, highlight the new action and click the Set Default button.

Figure 4.7.3
Windows 98 offers three actions for Registration Entries.

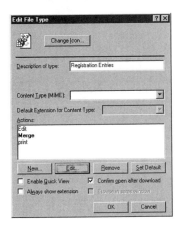

6. You'll see that the Application used to perform action field is the same instruction as the one for importing Registry files within an MS-DOS session (see Figure 4.7.4). The parameter "%1" is replaced by a filename when you double-click a file in the Windows Explorer. I don't recommend altering this action.

Figure 4.7.4

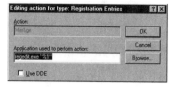

The instruction for merging Registry files in Windows is the same as importing Registry files within MS-DOS.

7. Click the Cancel button to close the Editing action for type: Registration Entries dialog box without saving changes.

8. Click the Cancel button on the Edit File Type dialog box to close it without saving changes.

9. Click the Cancel button on the Folder Options dialog box to close it without saving changes.

The exporting procedure works in a similar way to the import process. Windows performs all the conversions, from the Registry database format to ASCII text, automatically for you.

You can export any Registry key. If the key you choose contains subkeys, those subkeys are also exported. If the subkeys have subkeys, they are also exported. You get the idea. Any keys and values below the key you select are all written out to a Registry file during exportation.

> **NOTE** You cannot export an individual value. If you select a value in the right-hand pane of the Registry Editor and try to export it, the Registry Editor will assume you meant to export the key in which that value resides. And it will write the whole key out to the export file.

Follow these steps to export a Registry key:

1. Launch the Registry Editor.

2. Navigate to the key you'd like to export.

3. Highlight the key.

4. From the menus, choose Registry | Export Registry File.

5. The Export Registry File dialog box looks slightly different than a regular Save As dialog box (see Figure 4.7.5). The Export range box at the bottom of the dialog box asks whether you want the entire Registry exported (All) or just your Selected Branch. Make sure you mark Selected Branch.

Figure 4.7.5

*The Export
Registry File
dialog box
includes an
Export range
box.*

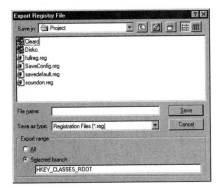

> **NOTE** Can you really export the entire Registry? Yes, you can. On my
> system, the resulting .REG file is about 5MB in size. WordPad has a
> difficult time, but it does manage to read this file.
>
> If you have a removable storage drive or other high-capacity backup medium, you
> might save a copy of this file for crash recovery purposes. As mentioned in the MS-
> DOS instructions above, you could restore the entire Registry by booting to MS-DOS
> and importing your saved Registry database in real-mode.
>
> By marking All in the Export range box, you can export the entire Registry database.
> Another way is to highlight My Computer, the top of the Registry tree and choose
> Registry | Export Registry File from the menus.

6. Enter a filename in the File name field. Make it a descriptive name. Do
   not use a file extension (.XXX) on the name. When you click the Save
   button, Windows will append .REG to the name.

7. Click the Save button. If the key contains a lot of information, this process
   might take a while. Saving the entire Registry, for example, takes over a
   minute on some PCs.

8. To exit the Registry Editor, choose Registry | Exit from the menus.

As an administrator, you can save Registry keys (from hacks in this book, for
example) and quickly configure other PCs with the same settings.

4.7.2 Make Notes in the Registry

What's the best way to track the Registry changes you make? Make notes right in
the Registry itself. Think of a note as a programmer's comment field. It's hard to
interpret the Registry keys and values by themselves—most are cryptic. But, by
including notes, disguised as Registry strings, you can stay on top of the fixes,
modifications, and enhancements you make to your operating system.

The notes should include your name, the date and the time, and a description of the change. Because the Registry sorts everything alphabetically, it's a good idea to make the note's name similar to the keys and values you add, so that they will appear next to these changes when you view the Registry.

Below is a sample of adding a note, saying that you've modified the Registered Owner string of the Registry (a hack from this book).

Follow these steps to add notes to your Registry:

1. Launch the Registry Editor by entering **regedit** at the Start | Run prompt.

2. Navigate to the following key: My Computer\HKEY_LOCAL_MACHINE\SOFTWARE\Microsoft\Windows\CurrentVersion.

3. Among the values listed under this key, you'll see RegisteredOwner (see Figure 4.7.6).

Figure 4.7.6

Find the RegisteredOwner string beneath the CurrentVersion key.

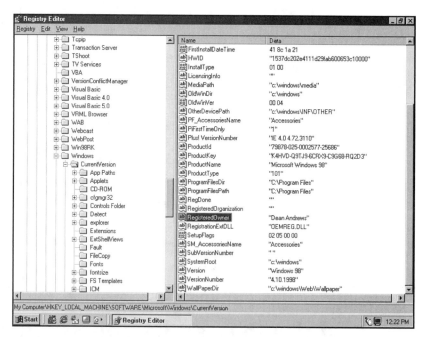

4. To add the note, right-click on the CurrentVersion key and choose New | StringValue from the pop-up list.

5. The new string will appear at the bottom of the list of values. Enter the name **RegisteredNOTE**. Then click the Enter key to set the name.

6. Double-click on the RegisteredNOTE string. This action displays the Edit String dialog box. Enter **Modified RegisterOwner String on 12/12/98 – DA** into the Value Data field (see Figure 4.7.7). Click the OK button to set the value.

Figure 4.7.7

Enter the note into the Edit String dialog box.

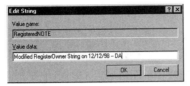

7. Initially, your new note will stay at the bottom of this key's list of values. For the alphabetical sort, you need to refresh the screen. Press the F5 function key or choose View | Refresh from the menus. At this point, Windows will sort the list and the note should appear near the RegisterOwner string (see Figure 4.7.8).

Figure 4.7.8

After a refresh, the string will appear near the RegisteredOwner string.

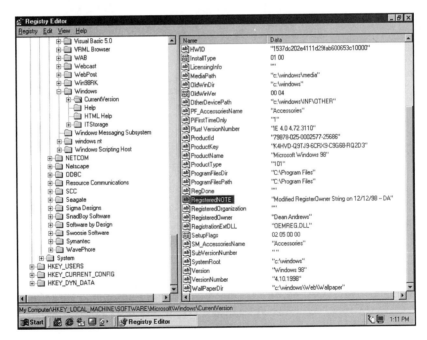

You can also track changes by exporting them, with notes, to a folder on your hard drive.

It's best to remove this sample note from the Registry before you close the Registry Editor. To remove the string RegisteredNOTE, right-click on it with your mouse. Then choose Delete from the pop-up menu. To close the Registry Editor, select Registry | Exit from the menus.

Managing the Registry

4.7.3 Spy on the Registry

Examining the Windows 98 Registry with the Registry Editor is one way to figure out how the Registry works. But there's a better way. Systems Internals (www.sysinternals.com) created a utility called Regmon that lets you spy on the Registry while it's processing data. With Regmon, you can observe how and when individual Registry keys and values are accessed and manipulated.

Regmon uses a *virtual device driver* to attach itself to Registry access calls. Whenever Windows opens, reads, and writes to the Registry, Regmon captures the information and sends it out to its own utility window for you to see.

With Regmon, you can "watch" software installs or just monitor how your work affects the Registry database.

Systems Internals offers the tool, for free, on their Web site.

Follow these steps to download and install the Regmon utility:

1. Launch the Internet Explorer by choosing Start | Programs | Internet Explorer | Internet Explorer. Or, launch your alternative browser.

2. In the Address bar, enter the URL: **www.sysinternals.com**.

> **NOTE**   Because the Registries for Windows 95 and Windows 98 are virtually identical, Regmon functions on both operating systems.

3. Select the Utilities for Windows 95 hyperlink.

4. Scroll down and find the Regmon for Windows 95 hyperlink within the list of utilities. Select the Regmon hyperlink.

5. Download the REGMON95.ZIP file to a folder on your hard drive. You'll need a "zip" decompression tool such as PKWare's PKZip for Windows (www.pkware.com) to extract the data files from this download.

6. Extract the files to a folder on your hard drive.

7. That's it for the installation. To run the program, select the REGMON.EXE file from within Windows Explorer.

8. Regmon's main screen will automatically start listing Registry events after you launch the utility (see Figure 4.7.9). The # column simply assigns a number to each new event. The Process column notes the application that is querying the Registry. The Request column names the event currently being processed. The Path column lists the Registry key involved in the request. The Result column tells whether the request was successful or not successful. And the Other column notes any Registry values involved in the Request.

Figure 4.7.9

Regmon begins listing Registry events automatically.

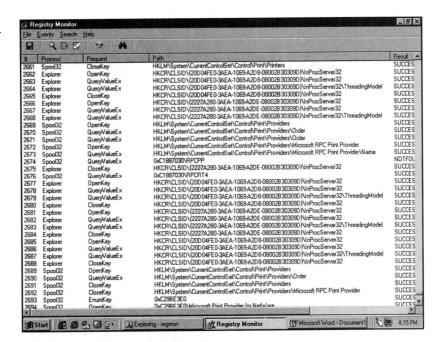

| | TIP | Use Regmon's Search menu item to find particular Registry keys, applications, or values. |

9. To exit Regmon, choose File | Exit from the menus.

You'll find that Regmon's event list grows quite rapidly. To focus on a particular part of the Registry, you can narrow down the events that the tool displays. To do this, choose Events | Filter from the menus.

The Regmon Filter dialog box lets you narrow by Process name (for example, Mspaint, Explorer, Winword, and more) or by Registry path (see Figure 4.7.10). In Regmon, the root key names are abbreviated as follows:

Root Name	Regmon Abbreviation
HKEY_CLASSES_ROOT	HKCR
HKEY_CURRENT_USER	HKCU
HKEY_LOCAL_MACHINE	HKLM
HKEY_USERS	HKU
HKEY_CURRENT_CONFIG	HKCC
HKEY_DYN_DATA	HKDD

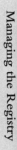

Managing the Registry

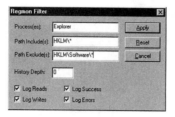

Figure 4.7.10
*Narrow down
Regmon's event
list with filters.*

You'll need to use these abbreviations when specifying Registry paths to include
in or exclude from the event list. Regmon supports "★" wildcarding. The asterisk
means any characters and any number of characters. You can also use multiple
paths in one filter and separate them with a semicolon. Here are some examples
of potential Regmon filters:

Regmon Filter	Meaning
HKLM\Software\★	The HKEY_LOCAL_MACHINE\Software key and everything below it
HKCC\S★	The HKEY_CURRENT_CONFIG\Software and HKEY_CURRENT_CONFIG\System keys and everything below them
HKU\★; HKLM\★	The HKEY_USERS and HKEY_LOCAL_MACHINE keys and everything below them

Finally, you can save Regmon's event log to an ASCII text file. To do this, choose
File | Save As from the menus. The Save File Info Dialog box will append an
.RGD file extension to whatever file name you choose. However, you can open
an .RGD file in the WordPad tool (or any other text editor).

4.7.4 Optimize the Registry

As you could see in this chapter's import/export hint, the Registry's files are large.
They might, however, be a little larger than they need to be. As you modify, add,
and delete keys, the Registry ends up with unused "dead" space. This wasted space
actually slows down your overall system performance because a larger Registry
takes longer to access. Fortunately, you can compress the Registry, and optimize it
for performance, with a special feature of the Windows Registry Checker.

The Registry Checker comes in two flavors, a Windows version (SCANREGW.EXE) and an MS-DOS version (SCANREG.EXE). But only the MS-DOS version offers the special optimization parameter. You can't run SCANREG.EXE within a DOS box, so you must either boot your system to DOS or shut down to DOS to execute this hint.

Follow these steps to optimize your Registry:

1. Boot up your system and hold the Ctrl key down during the power-up sequence. This action displays the Windows 98 Startup Menu.

> **NOTE** You can also shut down to DOS to run SCANREG. To do this, select Start | Shut Down from the Start menu. Then, in the Shut Down Windows dialog box, mark the option reading Restart in MS-DOS Mode and click the OK button.

2. Choose the option reading Command Prompt Only. Then press the Enter key.

3. At the C:>, change directory to the C:\Windows directory, by entering **CD C:\Windows**. Press the Enter key.

4. Enter the command **SCANREG /OPT**. Press the Enter key. The Registry Checker will optimize the Registry.

5. To start Windows, enter **Win** and press the Enter key. To shut down the system, turn off the power switch.

The differences in your Registry will be very slight, and you probably won't notice any performance improvement. But your system will run more efficiently with an optimized Registry.

Managing the Registry

Chapter

4.8

Installing New Hardware

With the fast pace of the computer industry, PCs become obsolete very quickly. However, few of us can afford a new PC purchase every six months. You can fight obsolescence by upgrading and adding components to your system; and, by installing up-to-date hardware, you can put off a new system purchase for several years.

In this chapter, you'll learn the tips and tricks of installing new hardware on a Windows 98 machine.

4.8.1 Setting Up USB Devices

Windows 98 added support for USB (Universal Serial Bus) devices to the Windows operating system. The theory behind this new technology was to make adding hardware as easy as "plugging in a lamp."

You can Plug and Play up to 127 USB devices on your PC, although, with that many, your desk would be covered with cables. To install a USB product, just plug in one end of a special USB cable to the product and plug in the other end to your PC (or to another USB product sitting in a chain of devices attached to your system). Windows 98 will instantly recognize the new device and enable you to use it. You can also "hot-swap" USB devices. Meaning you can plug in a new USB device (or unplug one) without even powering off your PC.

In addition to USB devices, there are USB *hubs*. A hub is really just a port that lets you plug more USB devices. Hubs provide power to the devices attached to them.

USB devices might also contain hubs. Currently, you'll find USB monitors on the market that have additional USB ports on the back. These monitors act as both devices and hubs. Each USB device must be within five meters (via cable) of a hub.

The *bus* or data path used by USB devices supports two different data transfer rates: 1.2Mbps (megabits-per-second) and 12Mbps. When compared to other PC buses, like SCSI or Firewire (IEEE 1394), USB rates are slow. That's because USB technology was designed for low-bandwidth devices such as keyboards, mouse pointing devices, joysticks, hand-held scanners, monitors, and printers. Devices that send and receive the smallest amount of data—such as a keyboard or a mouse—use the 1.2Mbps data rate. Other devices use the faster 12Mbps rate.

> **NOTE**   Contrary to what computer architects promised, choosing between USB and Firewire devices can be confusing. The Firewire bus, which I'll discuss in the next hint, was designed for high-bandwidth devices such as video capture and editing hardware, video disc players, digital camcorders and so forth. But you will see some of the same products—such as scanners and printers—available in both USB and Firewire interfaces.
>
> Which type should you choose? It depends on your system and your needs. Most PCs purchased in the last two years feature USB ports on the back. However, very few PCs currently offer Firewire ports. Thus you might not really have a choice. You could purchase a Firewire adapter and install it into your PC, but this would add to the expense of the Firewire solution. Read your PC's documentation to find out whether it supports USB, Firewire, both, or neither.
>
> If your PC supports both Firewire and USB, and you had your choice of products, the Firewire device would theoretically offer faster performance. In reality, this isn't always true. Try to find computer press reviews that discuss the performance of the products you're considering. That way, you can make an informed decision.

Because USB is still an emerging technology, you might find some monkey wrenches left in the works. For example, not all the products will be as easy to install as a lamp. You might find some that require the loading of special software drivers. For the best results, read and follow the installation instructions of your particular product.

Here is a list of other potential USB problems and what you should do about them:

Problem: You have USB ports on your PC, but no USB devices work when you attach them.

Solution: It's possible you have an outdated USB host controller. The first PCs that supplied USB capability used an A-1 stepping chip, which is not supported by Windows 98. You can find out for sure by checking the firmware version of your USB host controller.

Follow these steps to check your host controller firmware version number:

1. From the Start menu, choose Start | Settings | Control Panel.

2. Select the System object.

3. Pick the Device Manager tab.

4. Select the View Devices By Type radio button at the top of the Device Manager sheet.

5. Find the item below My Computer that reads: Universal serial bus controller (see Figure 4.8.1). Select it.

Figure 4.8.1

Find your Universal serial bus controller in the Device Manager.

6. Below the Universal serial bus controller, you should see two entries, a Universal Host Controller and a Root Hub. Select the Universal Host Controller. Then click the Properties button at the bottom of the Device Manager sheet.

7. On the Properties sheet for your Universal Host Controller, pick the General tab (see Figure 4.8.2). If the Hardware Version number is "0000," your USB Host Controller is not supported by Microsoft. If this is the case, call your PC manufacturer and ask for a USB Host Controller firmware upgrade.

Figure 4.8.2

Check the Hardware Version of your USB Universal Host Controller.

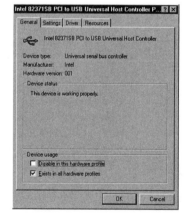

8. Click OK to close the Host Controller Properties sheet.

9. Click OK to close the System Properties sheet.

10. Choose File | Close from the menus to close the Control Panel.

If your Host Controller firmware is supported, but your USB devices don't work, double-check your BIOS settings. Most PCs have a USB port setting within the BIOS that lets you enable and disable USB devices. Make sure to *enable* USB devices within the BIOS.

Problem: Your new USB device doesn't work, but other USB devices do work on your system.

Solution: Check the USB port. Some of the early USB-capable systems had one functioning USB port and another malfunctioning USB port. The test is simple. Just plug your new device into another port (that works with other devices). If the new device starts working, your original port is malfunctioning. If the new device doesn't work after you change ports, then there might be a problem with the device itself.

Problem: Your USB devices work intermittently.

Solution: You might have a power management problem on the USB bus. As I mentioned above, hubs supply power to USB devices. The hubs themselves draw power either from the USB bus itself (called *bus-powered*) or from some other source, such as an electrical outlet or PC power supply (called *self-powered*).

Use the Windows 98 USB Viewer utility to scout out USB power management problems. The USB Viewer lists all the devices and hubs attached to your PC. It also supplies power management information.

> **NOTE** The USB Viewer utility is part of the Windows 98 Sample Resource Kit. You must have the Sample Kit installed before you can use USB Viewer. Read the introduction if you haven't yet installed the Sample Kit.

Follow these steps to launch the USB Viewer utility:

1. From the Start menu, choose Start | Programs | Windows 98 Resource Kit | Tools Management Console.

2. In the Microsoft Management Console navigate to this path: Console Root | Windows 98 Resource Kit Tools Sampler | Tools A to Z | U to Z. The USB Viewer should be visible at the top of the U to Z list (see Figure 4.8.3).

3. Select the USB Viewer utility.

4. Expand the My Computer entry (like you do with Registry Keys) by selecting it or by clicking on the plus sign (+) in front of it.

5. Expand the USB Universal Host Controller entry.

6. Expand the Root Hub entry. The right-hand pane displays the Root Hub configuration and power management information (see Figure 4.8.4).

Figure 4.8.3

The USB Viewer utility is part of the Windows 98 Sample Resource Kit.

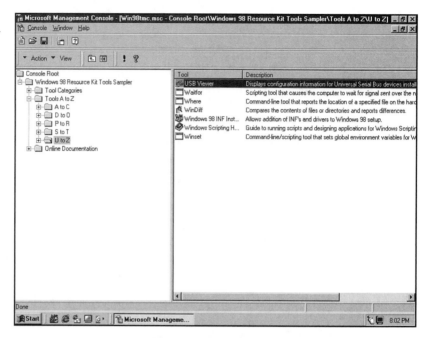

Figure 4.8.4

The USB Viewer displays the power management information for your USB device chain.

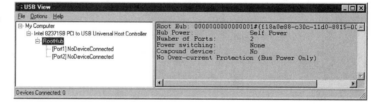

7. Continue expanding items in the USB chain, looking for errors in the power management configuration.

8. To exit the USB Viewer, choose File | Exit from the menus.

9. To exit the Microsoft Management Console, choose Console | Exit from the menus.

For the latest on USB products and technology, browse the USB Developer's Web forum at www.usb.org (see Figure 4.8.5). You'll also find a USB Evaluation utility that will detect whether or not your PC is USB-ready.

Figure 4.8.5

Browse the USB Developer's Forum for the latest USB news and the USB Evaluation utility.

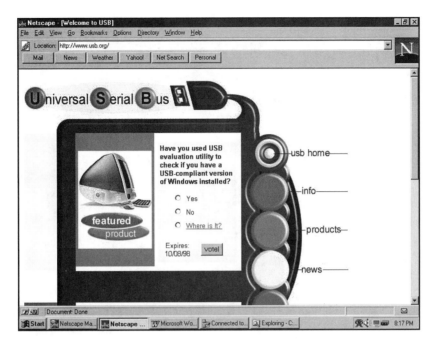

4.8.2 Using Firewire (IEEE 1394) Devices

Firewire (IEEE 1394) technology is similar to USB technology in many ways. Firewire devices are designed for full Plug and Play capability and they can be "hot-swapped" like USB devices. The Firewire bus supports up to 63 devices running concurrently. And, like USB, Firewire supports more than one data transfer rate. However, the Firewire data rates are much faster than USB. Currently, Firewire has three speed modes: 93Mbps (called S100), 196 Mbps (S200), 393Mbps (S300). Developers plan to create even faster rates for Firewire in the coming years.

Unfortunately, at the moment, few PC manufacturers ship Firewire-ready PCs. You should see more PCs preconfigured with Firewire capability in the coming year.

Microsoft does not supply a Firewire "viewer" utility in Windows 98. Thus it's best to stick with your Firewire product's documentation for installation and troubleshooting tips.

For the latest Firewire news and a list of available products, browse the Firewire Trade Association's Web site at `www.firewire.org` (see Figure 4.8.6).

Figure 4.8.6
Browse the Firewire Trade Association's Web site for information on Firewire developments and available products.

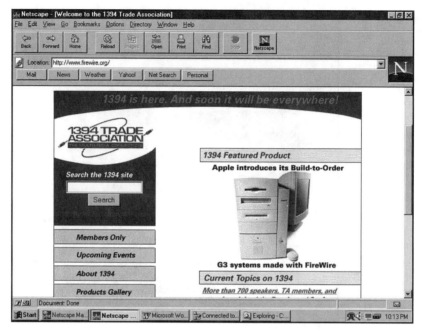

4.8.3 Installing a DVD-ROM Drive

Windows 95 had no internal support for DVD-ROM drives or their Universal Disk Format (UDF) file system. In Windows 95, a DVD-ROM was recognized only as a CD-ROM disc. You had to load special drivers to watch movies or play DVD PC titles. And you had no access to individual files on the DVD disc— Windows 95 couldn't "see" them at all.

Windows 98 offers internal support for DVD-ROM. Now you can Plug and Play the drives and you can access a disc's data files. Microsoft also included a DVD Player utility. With the DVD Player, you can control the playback of DVD movies and PC titles.

However, even with the Windows support, installing a DVD-ROM drive is tricky. The upgrade kits come with several parts: a drive, an add-in playback card (for MPEG-2 video and Dolby Digital audio decoding), and cables for connecting the drive to a sound card and a graphics card.

Make sure you follow your kit's instructions carefully. In general, you should install the playback card first, then the DVD-ROM drive, and then route the graphics and sound card cables. For a detailed set of instructions, browse *PC World* Online and search for Stan Miastkowski's July '98 Upgrade Guide column "Be the First on Your Block With DVD" in the Here's How section. The article's direct URL address is: `http://www.pcworld.com/heres_how/article/ 0,1400,3960,00.html` (see Figure 4.8.7).

Figure 4.8.7
Look for detailed DVD-ROM installation instructions at PC World Online.

Here are some tips for purchasing and installing a DVD-ROM upgrade kit:

■ Look for the latest DVD-ROM drives. As of this writing, DVD-ROM drives have only been out about a year. But they've evolved tremendously in that short time. The first generation kits had compatibility problems with CD-R (CD-Recordable) media and played CD-ROMs at slow speeds. The second generation drives solved both of these problems. The third generation drives, which should arrive by the end of '98, will finally be compatible with some of the rewritable DVD standards such as DVD-RAM, DVD+RW, and so on. Unfortunately, you will probably find all the generations represented on your local computer store shelves. Don't be fooled into buying a flaky first-generation DVD-ROM drive. Do some research before you head to the store.

■ Plan your audio-visual connections. Will you watch DVD video over your computer monitor or a by using a television? Will you attach two speakers (two-channel down-mixed Dolby Digital Sound) or six speakers (six-channel Dolby Digital Surround Sound) to your playback card? You need to make these decisions before you buy a kit, because not all playback cards offer the same output ports.

> **TIP** For the ultimate PC gaming (and movie playback) experience, attach some six-channel Dolby Digital surround sound speakers to your DVD-ROM playback card. These speaker sets currently cost around $500, but they are well worth the money. The speaker sets include four corner speakers (left and right in front of you, and left and right behind you), one front-center speaker, and one sub-woofer unit on the floor. These speakers require a Dolby Digital S/PDIFF (pronounced "speediff") port on the back of your DVD playback board. The S/PDIFF port outputs the raw six-channel Dolby Digital audio stream that the speakers themselves decode and route to the separate speaker units.

- Install the DVD kit components separately, and reboot your system after each one. You'll suffer far fewer troubleshooting nightmares if you treat the playback card and DVD-ROM drive as separate installations. First install the playback card, then reboot your PC and see if Windows 98 recognizes the board. Then go back and install the DVD-ROM drive.

- If possible, hang on to your CD-ROM drive. DVD-ROM drives play both DVD-ROM and CD-ROM media. However, the CD-ROM playback speed of even the latest DVD-ROM drives isn't as fast as state-of-the-art CD-ROM drives. There's a good chance your CD-ROM drive plays CDs faster than your new DVD-ROM drives. So unless you've run out of expansion bays in your system, keep your CD-ROM drive installed. Just add the DVD-ROM drive.

Windows 98 does not install the DVD Player utility during a typical installation. And you might not need it anyway. All DVD-ROM upgrade kits provide some form of DVD player software in the box. However, you might want to examine Microsoft's DVD Player and compare it to whatever your kit vendor supplied.

Follow these steps to install Windows 98's DVD Player utility:

1. From the Start menu, choose Start | Settings

2. Choose the Add/Remove Programs object.

3. On the Add/Remove Programs Properties sheet, pick the Windows 98 Setup tab.

4. Scroll down the list of Components and find the entry labeled Multimedia. Highlight Multimedia, then click the Details button in the Description box toward the bottom of the sheet.

> **TIP** Like other Windows 98 lists, you can quick-search the Components list by pressing the keys on the keyboard. As you type the letters **M U L T I M**, the highlight bar will jump from Microsoft Outlook Express to Multilanguage Support and finally to Multimedia.

5. In the Multimedia dialog box, place a check mark next to DVD Player (see Figure 4.8.8).

Figure 4.8.8

Install the DVD Player utility from Windows 98's Multimedia Component.

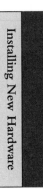

6. Click OK to close the Multimedia dialog box.

7. Click the OK button to Close the Add/Remove Programs Properties sheet and begin the installation routine.

The installation adds a DVD Player item to your Start menu. You'll find it under Start | Programs | Accessories | Entertainment.

4.8.4 Configuring Multiple Monitors

In a first for PC users, Windows 98 supports multiple monitors. Mac users, of course, have had this capability for years. But because this configuration is new to the PC, a little explanation seems appropriate.

Microsoft claims that Windows 98 lets you run nine display adapters and monitors simultaneously, although no one I know has tried installing more than two display adapters and two monitors in one PC. Most users who decide to go with multiple displays will opt for two.

What's the benefit of two monitors? Basically, multitasking applications becomes easier. Instead of switching between tasks via the Taskbar or the Alt+Tab key sequence, you simply need to gaze over at another screen to see what your application is doing. Windows 98 connects two monitors into one large virtual desktop. So you can have two full-screen applications visible simultaneously. The operating system even links the displays logically for the mouse. If you move your mouse off the right side of one monitor, it will appear on the left side of the second monitor.

> **NOTE**   Under Windows 98, your two monitors can run different resolutions. You could set 800x600 on a 15-inch display and 1024x768 on a 17-inch monitor, both running side-by-side on one PC.

Checking email and Web browsing top the list of most useful dual monitor activities. You could run your Internet connection in one screen and your other application in the second display.

Are there downsides to multiple monitors? You bet. The most obvious downside is cost. Graphics cards and monitors are both expensive. You'll spend at least $400-$500 for a second set of these components. Moreover, your current graphics card might not cooperate with a second graphics adapter. Not all do. Graphics card manufacturers now post dual-monitor support information on their Web sites (see Figure 4.8.9). If your current graphics card does not cooperate with others, you'll have to purchase *two* new graphics accelerators. Then you'll really be spending some cash.

Figure 4.8.9

Diamond Multimedia posts multiple monitor information about their graphics accelerators online.

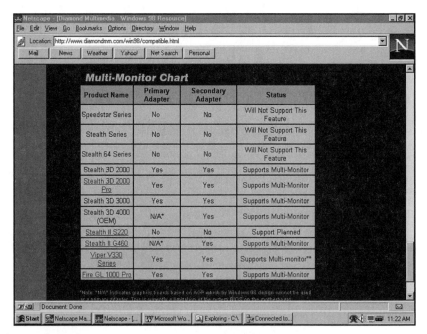

Product Name	Primary Adapter	Secondary Adapter	Status
Speedstar Series	No	No	Will Not Support This Feature
Stealth Series	No	No	Will Not Support This Feature
Stealth 64 Series	No	No	Will Not Support This Feature
Stealth 3D 2000	Yes	Yes	Supports Multi-Monitor
Stealth 3D 2000 Pro	Yes	Yes	Supports Multi-Monitor
Stealth 3D 3000	Yes	Yes	Supports Multi-Monitor
Stealth 3D 4000 (OEM)	N/A*	Yes	Supports Multi-Monitor
Stealth II S220	No	No	Support Planned
Stealth II G460	N/A*	Yes	Supports Multi-Monitor
Viper V330 Series	Yes	Yes	Supports Multi-monitor**
Fire GL 1000 Pro	Yes	Yes	Supports Multi-Monitor

> **NOTE**   Save yourself some money and a PC card slot by investigating graphics accelerators that support two monitors on one graphics card. Several graphics card manufacturers offer such products.

The second biggest concern is processing power. In the Windows 98 documentation, Microsoft admits there is some overhead to multiple display support. Logically linking two monitors gives your processor extra work to do. Besides, even multitasking applications with a single display burdens a processor. If your system slows to a crawl when you run several applications simultaneously, then it's not a good candidate for multiple displays.

The installation procedure depends on your system configuration. For example, installing a single graphics card that supports two monitors would be different than installing a second graphics card. In both cases, follow your product's instructions carefully.

At this point, most users would probably opt for two graphics cards, thus maintaining their investment in their current card.

The process for installing a second graphics adapter and monitor will go something like this:

1. Verify that your current graphics card and your new graphics card both support multiple displays under Windows 98. Check with the manufacturers of your products.

2. Power off your computer.

3. Open the computer case.

> **NOTE**   Both graphics cards must use either the PCI bus or the AGP bus. ISA-based graphics cards do not support multiple displays in Windows 98.

4. Install the second graphics card into a PCI or AGP slot.

5. Connect your second monitor to your new graphics card. Then connect your second monitor to an electrical outlet.

6. Close the PC case.

7. Power up your computer. Windows 98 should automatically recognize your new graphics accelerator and your new monitor. It will install the necessary software drivers. During this process you might need to restart your PC more than once. Follow the directions provided by Windows 98.

8. Right-click a blank space on your desktop and choose Properties from the pop-up list.

9. Pick the Settings tab of the Display Properties sheet.

> **NOTE**
> The full-screen MS-DOS window only displays on the monitor designated as your primary display.

> **WARNING**
> Most screen saver programs were not designed for multiple monitors. You might find your screen saver only displays on one of your two screens. If you use a screen saver as a security barrier (for example, a password-protected screen saver), multiple monitors might disable this feature.
>
> Shop around for a new screen saver that supports multiple monitors.

10. Your original graphics card and monitor will automatically be designated the primary display. Your new graphics card and monitor will be the secondary display.

    On the Settings tab of the Display Properties sheet, highlight the icon for your new monitor. Then put a check next to the line reading: Extend My Windows Desktop onto This Monitor. On the same screen, adjust the virtual coordinates for your new, extended desktop.

> **TIP**
> You cannot drag a maximized window from one monitor to the other. To drag a window, you must first restore it to a regular window size. Click the window tool between the Minimize and Close tools in the upper right-hand corner to restore the window to regular size.

11. Click the OK button on the Display Properties sheet to save your new settings.

Try different resolution settings for your new monitor setup. You might prefer the same resolution settings for both monitors, or you might make more use of one high resolution and one low resolution setting.

4.8.5 Configuring Multiple Modems

In addition to displays, Windows also supports multiple modems. For PCs, this technology, called *channel aggression*, was first used with ISDN (Integrated Services Digital Network) lines. Channel aggression enables two or more separate lines to share the data workload involved in a communication link. In Windows 98, you can use channel aggression for regular (analog) phone line modems as well as digital modems. In the Windows documentation, this technology is referred to as the PPP Multilink protocol.

> **NOTE** Configuring your system for PPP Multilink protocol will do no good if the service or server you dial in to does not support it. Contact your ISP (Internet Service Provider) and ask if they support PPP Multilink protocol before you reconfigure your system.

> **TIP** Like graphics adapters, Windows 98 lets you install more than two modems for PPP Multilink. Unfortunately, the overhead of linking modems grows with each modem you add. For the best performance, stick with two modems, and purchase the fastest modems you can afford.

Before you can configure PPP Multilink, you need to install your second modem.

Follow this procedure to install your second modem:

1. From the Start menu, choose Start | Settings | Control Panel.

2. Choose the Add/Remove Hardware object. This launches the Add New Hardware Wizard.

3. On the first screen of the Wizard, click the Next button.

4. The second screen reads `Windows will now search for any new Plug and Play devices on your system`. If you do have a Plug and Play modem, Windows will find it after you click the Next button. If you have a non–Plug and Play modem, or you have an external modem, Windows won't find it in this initial search. In either case, click the Next button.

5. At this point, Windows will have found a Plug and Play modem and present you with a Finish button. Click it to conclude the modem installation. For other modems, you'll see a screen asking whether or not Windows should search for hardware that is not Plug and Play compatible. This search will take far too long, especially if you already know the brand of your modem. Select the option reading No, I want to select the hardware from a list (see Figure 4.8.10). Then click the Next button.

Figure 4.8.10

Don't let Windows search for your new modem. The search takes forever. First narrow the search by selecting the hardware category from a list.

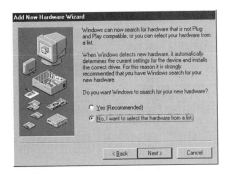

6. On the next screen, Windows presents the Hardware Types list. Scroll down and highlight the Modem entry. Then click the Next button.

7. Now Windows will search only for modems—a much shorter search than it was planning to do a few steps back. Make sure you have the modem attached to the PC and the phone line, and make sure that it is powered on. Remove any check you see in front of Don't Detect My Modem. Then click the Next button.

8. Windows will search all your ports for a modem. This might take a minute or two. When it's finished, it will report what it found and where it found it (see Figure 4.8.11). If the information is not correct, click the Change... button to select the modem from a list. Otherwise, click the Next button.

Figure 4.8.11
Windows reports back when it finds your modem.

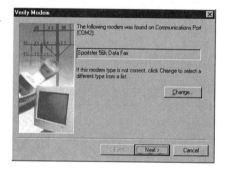

9. Finally! You've reached the final screen of the Modem Wizard. Click the Finish button to close the Wizard.

To enable a PPP Multilink protocol, you must first choose a particular Dial-Up Network connection to which to apply it.

Follow these steps to enable a PPP Multilink protocol for a Dial-Up Networking connection:

1. Select the My Computer icon on the desktop.

2. Choose the Dial-Up Networking object.

3. Right-click on the connection that supports PPP Multilink. Choose Properties from the pop-up list.

4. Pick the General tab of the connection's Properties sheet.

5. The General tab displays the phone number that this connection dials. In the Connect Using box, click the drop-down arrow and select the modem that will be the primary modem in the PPP Multilink (see Figure 4.8.12).

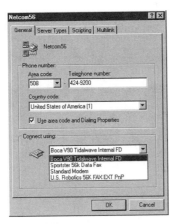

Figure 4.8.12

On the General tab, select the primary modem for the connection.

NOTE In a PPP Multilink session, Windows 98 will first dial and connect the primary modem. Then it will dial and connect the secondary modem.

6. Now you must set the secondary modem. Pick the Multilink tab.

7. On the Multilink tab, choose the radio button labeled Use Additional Devices. This activates the Add button at the bottom of the sheet. The first time you set up a Multilink, the device list will be empty.

8. Click the Add button to add your new modem to the device list. This action displays the Edit Extra Device dialog box.

9. On the Edit Extra Device dialog box, click the drop-down arrow and select your secondary modem from the list (see Figure 4.8.13).

Figure 4.8.13

Choose your secondary Multilink modem on the Edit Extra Device dialog box.

> **NOTE** Your ISP might provide a second dial-in phone number to use with your secondary Multilink modem. If so, enter that number in the Phone Number field of the Edit Extra Device dialog box.

10. Click the OK button to close the Edit Extra Device box. Now your secondary modem choice will be listed in the Multilink Device List (see Figure 4.8.14).

Figure 4.8.14

Your secondary modem will appear in the Multilink Device List.

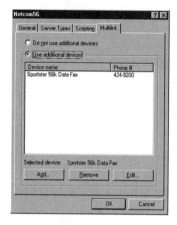

11. Click OK to close the Dial-Up Networking connection's Properties sheet.

Now you can select the Dial-Up Networking connection as you normally would. Windows 98 will dial, negotiate, and connect both modems.

Chapter

4.9

Managing the Internet and Active Desktop

Sometimes the Web feels like an information hurricane. Install some storm windows with the hints in this chapter.

4.9.1 Restrict Changes to the Active Desktop

Windows 98's Active Desktop might negatively affect a system's performance. For example, a system featuring several Web site and Channel subscriptions might grind to a halt as these subscriptions get updated via the Internet.

As the administrator, limiting or restricting the Active Desktop will help you maintain a system's performance level so that important applications will run quickly and smoothly.

By using the TweakUI utility you can either disable the Active Desktop completely or limit changes to it. Follow these steps to control the Active Desktop:

1. Launch TweakUI. Its object resides in the Control Panel (under Start | Settings | Control Panel). If you haven't installed TweakUI, read the introduction for instructions.

2. Select the IE4 tab. This displays several Registry-level Internet settings.

3. To completely disable the Active Desktop, remove the check next to Active Desktop Enabled. If, however, you want to stop any changes to the current settings, remove the check next to Allow Changes To Active Desktop.

4. Click the OK button to close the TweakUI utility.

Both these changes require a Windows restart. To remove the restrictions, simply replace the check marks on the IE4 tab of TweakUI.

4.9.2 Block Web Content

Windows 98's Content Advisor enables you to restrict Web browsing from your PC. The Content Advisor was designed with parents in mind and it uses ratings similar to those used by the movie industry. The Advisor breaks down content into the following categories—Language, Nudity, Sex, and Violence—and lets you set appropriate content "levels" for each one.

Here's the catch: The Content Advisor isn't that effective. Why? Because it relies on Web masters and Web developers to self-regulate sites. For the Content Advisor to work properly, a site must post its own rating using the guidelines provided by the Recreational Software Advisory Council (RSAC).

Microsoft and the RSAC hope to motivate Web masters to use these ratings by asking you to block all content that posts no rating through Internet Explorer's settings (see Figure 4.9.1). Yeah, right. At the moment, blocking all non-rated sites would leave you with about two sites on the entire Web from which to choose— Microsoft's homepage (`www.microsoft.com`) and the RSAC site (`www.rsac.org/ratingsv01.html`).

Figure 4.9.1

Internet Explorer enables you to set content levels by category.

For more effective Web blocking, download the shareware tool called Cyber Patrol. Cyber Patrol works with actual Web site lists, not an honor system. Real users submit block requests to Cyber Patrol's site (`www.cyberpatrol.com`). If a particular site gets several "block" requests, it's added to the database. No, this public opinion method isn't ideal, but it's much more practical than Microsoft's scheme.

Use Cyber Patrol free for 30 days. If you like it, you're asked to register the program and pay a one-time $30 fee.

Follow these instructions to download and install Cyber Patrol:

1. Launch the Internet Explorer and browse *PC World* Online's FileWorld Web site (`www.fileworld.com`).

2. Search for the site by typing **CyberPatrol**. Click on the resulting hyperlink to jump to the Cyber Patrol download page.

3. Follow the instructions to download the file CP-SETUP.EXE. Store the file into a temporary directory on your hard drive.

4. In the Windows Explorer, select the self-extracting executable file CP-SETUP.EXE. The program asks if you want No, Low, or High security on your system. Read about the differences between these levels at the Cyber Patrol site (`www.cyberpatrol.com`). Exit the Internet Explorer application before you begin this installation.

5. After the installation, Cyber Patrol launches automatically when you activate the Internet Explorer. The first time you use it, you'll be presented with a checkpoint dialog box (see Figure 4.9.2). Initially there is no password, so just click the Validate Password button to proceed to the main screen.

Managing the Internet and Active Desktop

Figure 4.9.2

*Friend or foe:
Cyber Patrol's
checkpoint screen.*

6. Use the settings on Cyber Patrol main screen (see Figure 4.9.3) to restrict hours of access, chat rooms, news groups, Web sites and more.

Figure 4.9.3

*The Cyber Patrol
Headquarters
dialog box
enables you to
restrict most
aspects of the
World Wide Web.*

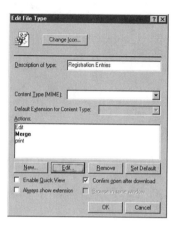

7. To download the latest CyberNOT list (used to block sites), choose File | Update CyberNOT list from the menus.

8. Don't forget to create passwords by selecting File | Set HQ & Deputy Passwords from the menus. Choose File | Exit to close Cyber Patrol.

If, for whatever reason, you become unhappy with Cyber Patrol, use the Uninstall Cyber Patrol option under the program's file menu to remove it.

4.9.3 Use a Child's Interface to the Web

To protect children, Resource Communications' software uses an approach that's different than Cyber Patrol's method. Their Kidnet Explorer shareware program acts as a new interface for the Internet Explorer browser.

The Kidnet software has no Address Bar, so children can do no Web surfing on their own. Five buttons across the top of the screen show the list of "Cool Sites" as prescribed by Resource Communications. Parents can add sites to the cool list or block any sites they deem inappropriate.

Kidnet Explorer is free to try, but you'll have to pay a $20 fee if you plan to keep it.

Follow these steps to download the Kidnet Explorer:

1. Launch the Internet Explorer under Start | Programs | Internet Explorer on the Start menu.

2. Browse *PC Magazine*'s Online Software Library. Enter **www.hotfiles.com** into the Address Bar. Then press the Enter key.

3. In the Search box, enter **Kidnet Explorer**. Then click the Search button.

4. Follow the instructions to download the file KIDNET.ZIP to a temporary folder on your hard drive. This file is compressed with the zip format, so you'll need a zip decompression utility, such as PKWare's PKZip for Windows (**www.pkware.com**), to extract the data files from the download file.

5. After you extract the files, run the SETUP.EXE program, by selecting it in the Windows Explorer. Follow the Setup Wizard's instructions to install the program.

Kidnet Explorer comes with helpful documentation. It's easy to set up and use.

Managing the Internet and Active Desktop

Chapter

4.10

Known Windows 98 Bugs

Do you gnash your teeth and pound your desk when you sit down at the PC? If so, you've probably encountered Windows 98's known bugs. In this chapter, you'll find the solutions to these problems.

4.10.1 Bug: The Mouse Trap

They call you the King of Hardware Upgrades. You've overcome incredible odds and successfully battled through the most heinous upgrades known to man: SCSI host controllers, Network Interface cards, and ISDN terminal adapters. What trouble could a little old mouse pointing device cause you? Plenty!

Many people attempt to Plug and Play their new Microsoft Intellimouse or other pointing device, only to find that Windows 98 won't recognize it. What's up? A few old Registry entries from previous pointing devices are gumming up the works.

Microsoft's technical support team recommends doing a little Registry house cleaning to solve this problem. Use the following steps to prepare your Registry for pointing device Plug and Play capability:

1. Launch the Registry Editor by entering **Regedit** at the Start | Run prompt.

2. Navigate to the following Registry key: My Computer\Hkey_Local_Machine\System\CurrentControlSet\Services\Class\Mouse\.

> **WARNING**   These hacks disable your current pointing devices. Only use this procedure to start fresh with a new pointing device.

3. Below this, you should find keys represented by sequential four-digit numbers beginning with 0000. Delete them all.

> **NOTE**   Depending on your PC configuration, you might not find all of the Registry keys mentioned in these steps within your Registry. If not, just move on the next step.

4. Now navigate to this key: Hkey_Local_Machine\Enum\Serenum.

5. Remove all keys below this key. Depending on your configuration, there might not be any. Do not delete the (Default) string below this key.

6. Now navigate to this key: Hkey_Local_Machine\Software\Logitech\Mouseware.

7. Remove this Registry key.

8. Close the Registry Editor by selecting Registry | Exit from the menus.

9. At this point, you must clear the pointing devices out of the Device Manager. To access it, choose Start | Settings | Control Panel. Then select the System icon. Choose the Device Manager tab. Select each serial mouse pointing device and click the Remove button. Click OK to close the System Properties sheet.

10. From the Start menu, choose Shutdown. Then select Restart and click the OK button. Windows will restart itself.

Upon restart, Windows should recognize and install drivers for the new pointing device that's attached to your PC.

4.10.2 Bug: WebTV for Windows Won't Launch

You've heard the big buzz phrase: PC-TV convergence. In the next few years, this "convergence" will likely occur smack dab in the middle of your living room. The line between home entertainment and home computing will blur until it becomes invisible. And you'll need an extra shelf in your home entertainment console for your PC's system unit. But, for now, WebTV for Windows can give you a taste of the future—if you can get it to work.

Microsoft's online technical support database reports that some Windows 98 users can't launch WebTV for Windows. Follow these steps to correct the problem:

1. Launch the Registry Editor by entering **Regedit** at the Start | Run prompt.

2. Navigate to the following key: HKEY_LOCAL_MACHINE\ SOFTWARE\Microsoft\Windows\CurrentVersion\RunServices.

3. Find the VidSvr string beneath this key and select it. Remove any value that resides in the Edit String Value Data box, leaving it blank. Then click the OK button.

4. Close the Registry Editor by choosing Registry | Exit from the menus.

5. Now you must uninstall and reinstall WebTV for Windows. Select Start | Settings | Control Panel. Then choose the Add/Remove Programs icon. Select the Windows Setup tab. Scroll to the bottom of the Components list and remove the check next to WebTV for Windows. Click OK. Windows will ask if you want to restart the computer. Choose Yes.

6. After restart, re-enter the Windows Setup tab of the Add/Remove Programs sheet and replace the check next to WebTV for Windows. Restart the computer again.

Known Windows 98 Bugs

For full functionality, you'll need to restart your computer one more time. If you don't, you'll see video but hear no sound from the TV broadcasts. Remember, to see TV broadcasts with WebTV, you must have a Windows 98 TV tuner card installed and have an antenna or cable-service cable attached to the back of your TV tuner card. Without a TV tuner card, you are limited to searching through the local TV program listings.

4.10.3 Bug: My Documents Shortcut Displays an Error Message

Windows 98 creates a folder on your hard drive called My Documents. Many applications use this folder as the default when you open or save a new document. This is Microsoft's way of helping you organize your disk, so that you don't have documents scattered all over the place. For easy access, Windows 98 also provides a shortcut to this folder on your desktop.

The trouble is that the shortcut is buggy. Some users have complained of the following cryptic error message when they select the My Documents shortcut `Explorer: This program has performed an illegal operation and will be shut down`.

What's going on? The Registry's reference to the My Documents folder is either missing or incorrect. Microsoft posted this fix on its Technical Support Web site.

Follow these steps to correct the problem:

1. Launch the Registry Editor by entering **regedit** at the Start | Run prompt.

2. Navigate to the following key: HKEY_CURRENT_USER\Software\ Microsoft\Windows\CurrentVersion\Explorer\User Shell Folders.

3. You should see a path to the folder C:\My Documents under this key. If not, you must add it. Add a new string called Personal (by right-clicking the key and selecting New | String Value from the pop-up list). Then insert **C:\My Documents** as the string's data. Click OK to close the Edit String dialog box.

4. Close the Registry Editor by choosing Registry | Exit from the menus.

You should restart your PC before retrying the My Documents shortcut.

4.10.4 Bug: Microsoft's Backup Bugs

Windows 98's Microsoft Backup utility is a vast improvement over the backup tools included with previous versions of Windows. But it's not without problems of its own.

Microsoft's technical support database describes two potentially frustrating bugs. Here are quick descriptions:

1. You've instructed Backup to save your Registry files (by placing a check next to Back Up Windows Registry in the Advanced tab of the Job | Options sheet), but it doesn't save them.

2. You've removed Backup from your system (through the Add/Remove Programs icon's Windows Setup tab), but now when you boot your PC you get the following error message:
   `Backup Exec Agent Communication Transport Failure.`

Follow these steps to solve problem #1:

1. Launch Microsoft Backup by selecting Start | Programs | Accessories | System Tools | Backup from the Start menu.

2. In the backup job that saves the Registry files, make sure you include the entire Windows directory in the What To Back Up list.

3. Additionally, if your job is backing up files that reside somewhere other than the boot drive of your PC, make sure to include at least one file from the boot drive in this backup job.

4. Save your changes by choosing Job | Save from the menus.

5. Close Microsoft Backup by selecting Job | Exit from the menus.

Follow these steps to solve problem #2:

1. Launch the Registry Editor by entering **regedit** at the Start | Run prompt.

2. Navigate to the following key: My Computer\HKEY_LOCAL_ MACHINE\SOFTWARE\Microsoft\Windows\Current\Version\ RunServices.

3. Delete the following string, if it exists:

String Name	String Value
BackupExecAgent	"BkupAgnt.exe"

4. Close the Registry Editor by choosing Registry | Exit from the menus.

Restart your PC to implement either or both of these changes.

Known Windows 98 Bugs

Chapter

4.11

Manage the Year 2000 Problem

You've heard the rumors. On January 1, 2000, computers all over the world will crash due to poorly programmed software. Traffic will snarl. Stock markets will fall. Banks will close. And, we'll all have the week off.

Think globally, but compute locally. Check your PC hardware and software for Y2K bugs with these hints.

4.11.1 Adjust Your Regional Settings for Y2K

Breathe a sigh of relief. Windows 98 won't crash when presented with a date past the year 2000. Both Windows 3.1 and Windows 95 had a couple of nagging bugs related to the infamous Y2K problem—including a problem with Win3.1's File Manager and another in Win95's Microsoft Wallet—but these known problems were fixed in Windows 98.

There is, however, one Win98 setting that you should definitely check—your Regional Date Settings. This setting determines how the operating system responds when given a two-digit year. If it's not set correctly, your Regional Date could throw off your system.

> **TIP** An easy way to test your application software for Y2K problems is to reset your system clock to a time and date after the year 2000. Just choose Start | Settings | Control Panel. Then select the Date/Time object and adjust the calendar. Make sure to reset the Date/Time back to normal after your test.

> **TIP** Use the FileWise utility to reset the date of an individual file to beyond the year 2000. It's a good idea to keep at least one dummy file with a 2000 date sitting around on your hard drive, so that it's easy to test new applications. FileWise is loaded into the C:\Win98RK directory when you install the Sample Resource Kit from the Win98 CD-ROM. Read the introduction section if you haven't yet installed the Sample Resource Kit.

Follow these steps to check Win 98's Regional Date setting:

1. From the Start menu, choose Start | Settings | Control Panel. Then select the Regional Settings.

2. Choose the Date tab.

3. In the Calendar box, use the scroll arrows to adjust the 99-year-span of two-digit years to a reasonable setting (see Figure 4.11.1). If your work requires forecasting far into the future then set the start date higher. Maybe to 1950 or so. Otherwise, any year on or after 1920 should work

for most situations. Do not set the start number to 1900 or 1901. This will throw off sorting and calculating when the system clock rolls past the year 2000.

Figure 4.11.1

Adjust the Regional Settings 99-year-span to correctly interpret a two-digit year.

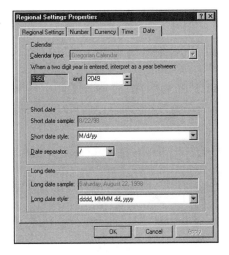

4. Click the OK button to save your Regional Settings.

4.11.2 Check Your Hardware for Y2K

As I've mentioned, with Windows 98 your operating system is in good shape for Y2K, but what about your hardware?

Your system clock and firmware might balk at year 2000 dates.

Luckily, *PC Magazine* Online offers a free download that will test your PC's BIOS for year 2000 problems.

A link to this Y2K tool is found in *PC Magazine* Online's Software Library, in the Year 2000 Resource Center site, and in their "Virtual Labs." The program was co-designed and developed by the McAfee Software Division of Network Associates, Inc. and *PC Magazine*.

Follow these steps to download and run *PC Magazine*'s Y2K BIOS utility:

1. Browse the following section of PC Magazine Online:
   `http://vl1.zdnet.com/scripts/y2k.pl`.

2. Scroll down the page until you see the Y2K Download and Run button. Click it.

3. Set the Save As dialog box to store the file Y2KTEST.EXE in a temporary folder on your hard drive. Start the download by clicking the Save button.

Manage the Year 2000 Problem

4. When the download completes, open the Windows Explorer.

5. Navigate to the Y2KTEST.EXE file and select it to run it. This program automatically extracts the data files and begins running the Y2K test of your hardware.

6. Follow the instructions to complete the Y2K test (see Figure 4.11.2). The program reports whether your system passed the test.

Figure 4.11.2
Use this PC Magazine download to test your BIOS for year 2000 problems.

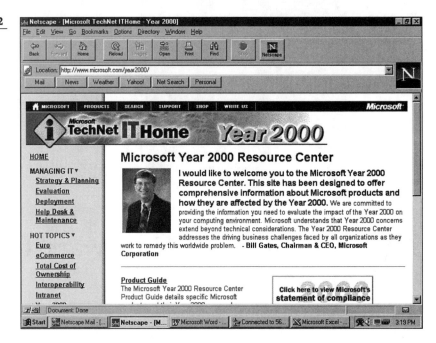

Older computers are more susceptible to Y2K problems than newer systems. Share the *PC Magazine* Virtual Lab URL with friends and colleagues that use older PCs.

4.11.3 Browse the Web for Y2K Resources

Did you know that Microsoft has a portion of their Web site dedicated to the Y2K problem? Well, now you do. Browse the Microsoft Year 2000 Resource Center (`http://www.microsoft.com/technet/topics/year2k/default.htm`) for information on Microsoft products and their status, a frequently asked questions (FAQ) page, a list of Y2K companies and services, and a very interesting online "seminar" presentation (see Figure 4.11.3).

Figure 4.11.3

*Browse the
Microsoft Year
2000 Resource
Center online.*

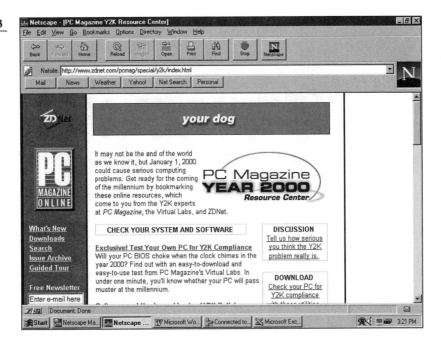

Additionally, sign up for Microsoft Year 2000 news updates from this site's
TechNet Flash service. Or, search the site for specific bugs and fixes for your
Microsoft software.

For an independent source on Y2K troubles, browse *PC Magazine's* Year 2000
Resource Center (`http://www.zdnet.com/pcmag/special/y2k/index.html`).
Here you'll find Year 2000 articles, opinion columns, and links to other resources
on the Web (see Figure 4.11.4).

Manage the Year 2000
Problem

Figure 4.11.4

Or, surf through PC Magazine's Year 2000 Resource Center.

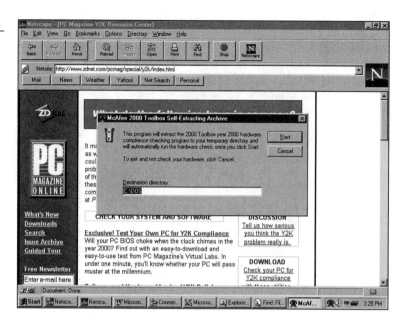

Chapter 4.12

The Windows 98 Emergency Disk

Are you prepared for a system crash? You should be. You never know when a crash might occur. In this chapter, learn how to get the most out of the Windows 98 emergency disk. I'll also mention some alternatives.

4.12.1 Load Your CD-ROM Driver onto the Emergency Disk

Unlike Windows 95, Windows 98's emergency disk includes CD-ROM drivers so that you can access your Win98 installation disc and other CDs while booting from the floppy. But the CD-ROM drivers might not work with your CD-ROM.

Microsoft uses a generic, real-mode ATAPI CD-ROM driver called OAKCDROM.SYS for the emergency disk. There's also a SCSI driver for SCSI-based CD-ROM drives. But Microsoft doesn't guarantee your CD-ROM drive will work with these drivers.

Here's a list of CD-ROM setups that Microsoft says cause problems during emergency startup:

- CD-ROM drives driven by sound cards
- PC Card (a.k.a. PCMCIA) CD-ROM drives
- Early 1X and 2X speed CD-ROM drives
- SCSI-connected CD-ROM drives where your SCSI host controller does not use the default I/O Range

If you're having difficulty getting your CD-ROM drive to work during emergency startup, you can try loading your own driver. Be aware, however, that only real-mode drivers will work in the non-GUI boot-up mode in which the emergency disk starts. If in doubt, check with your CD-ROM manufacturer about obtaining a CD-ROM driver that will work with your drive on a Windows 98 emergency startup disk.

Follow these steps to load your own CD-ROM driver:

1. Locate your CD-ROM driver. Using the Start menu, choose Start | Settings | Control Panel. Then select the System object. In the System dialog box, pick the Device Manager tab. Under the Computer heading, find the CD-ROM entry. Select it and then choose your CD-ROM drive's entry (see Figure 4.12.1) to display its Properties sheet. Pick the Driver tab and write down the driver file (.SYS) used by your CD-ROM drive. If the sheet says your CD-ROM uses no driver file, the generic driver on the emergency disk should work for your drive.

> **NOTE** When you boot from Windows 98's emergency disk, you'll see a special startup menu that asks whether you want to boot with CD-ROM support or without it. In most instances, you should definitely choose *with* CD-ROM support. You'll have access to more tools on CD.
>
> This boot sequence will most likely assign your CD-ROM drive a different drive letter than it's normally assigned. The emergency disk uses a compressed logical RAMDrive to store its disk utility files and this drive usually ends up with the old drive letter of your CD-ROM. If you ask for CD-ROM support, your CD-ROM drive will be assigned a letter farther down the alphabet from its normal position.

Figure 4.12.1
Select your CD-ROM drive's entry to display its Properties sheet.

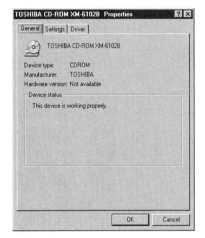

2. Copy your driver (.SYS) file to your emergency disk.

3. Change the CONFIG.SYS .configuration file on the emergency disk. Launch Notepad (under Start | Programs | Accessories) and open the A:\CONFIG.SYS file on the emergency disk. Find the [CD] heading and insert a new line below the DEVICE=HIMEM.SYS /TESTMEM:OFF line that reads:

```
device=mydriver.sys /D:mscd001
```

Make sure the mydriver portion matches the filename you copied to the disk.

Also, under the [CD] heading, modify each of the lines with MSCD001 references to MSCD002, MSCD003, and MSCD004. The completed [CD] section of the CONFIG.SYS file should look like the following when you finish:

```
[CD]
device=himem.sys /testmem:off
device=mydriver.sys /D:mscd001
device=oakcdrom.sys /D:mscd002
device=btdosm.sys
device=flashpt.sys
device=btcdrom.sys /D:mscd003
```

```
device=aspi2dos.sys
device=aspi8dos.sys
device=aspi4dos.sys
device=aspicd.sys /D:mscd004
```

Choose File | Save from the menus to save the file. Then select File | Exit to close it.

4. Now, modify the emergency disk's AUTOEXEC.BAT file. Using Notepad, open the AUTOEXEC.BAT file. Find the line reading:

```
LH %RAM%:\MSCDEX.EXE /D:MSCD001 /L:%CDROM%
```

Change it to read like this:

```
LH %ramd%:\mscdex.exe /D:mscd001 /D:mscd002 /D:mscd003 /
D:mscd004 /L:%CDROM%
```

Choose File | Save from the menus to save the file. Then select File | Exit to close it.

Try booting from your newly configured emergency startup disk and check its access to your CD-ROM drive.

4.12.2 Extract Windows System Files from the CD During Emergency Startup

During an emergency startup you might need to restore files from your Windows 98 CD onto your hard drive. SCANDISK, for example, might find corrupted system files that need to be replaced.

Microsoft included a special command-line extraction utility called EXT.EXE on the emergency startup disk. Here's how to use it.

Follow these steps to extract system files from the Win98 CD during an emergency startup:

1. When you spot trouble, write down any error messages that name missing or corrupt files.

2. Place your Win98 CD into your system's CD-ROM drive.

3. Place your Win98 emergency disk into your floppy drive and power on your system to boot from it.

4. Choose option 1 from the boot menu so that you boot with CD-ROM support.

5. At the prompt enter **EXT**.

6. The first question asks where your Windows CAB (Cabinet) files reside. Enter the path to your CD-ROM and the Win98 directory. Remember the drive letter during startup is different from the normal drive letter for your CD-ROM. You should see which letter the CD-ROM takes during emergency startup. It's probably one or two letters following the letter it normally uses. Enter the following command:

   X:\Win98 (where *X* is your CD-ROM drive letter)

7. The second question asks for the filename that you want to extract from the CD. You can enter any filename or utility name. You can even extract multiple files at once using the "★" wildcard. For example, "win★.★" extracts every file that begins with the letters "win." One example of a file you might need in a recovery situation is regedit.exe. The Registry Editor runs in real-mode as well as in Windows.

8. The third and final question asks to where you want the files extracted. Use any directory on your C drive.

The EXT utility will then go off and search the Win98 CD until it finds your files and can restore them to your hard drive.

4.12.3 Use an Alternative to the Windows 98 Emergency Disk

Some recovery situations require extreme measures. If, for example, your hard drive has completely ceased to function, you might need access to tools more powerful than the ones on the Windows 98 emergency disk.

The shelves of your local computer store are filled with crash recovery software packages. I've reviewed several for computer publications myself. Many of these products work well for bad crashes. To find the best package currently available, read recent reviews in computer publications you trust.

Iomega, makers of the Zip drive, now offer one interesting option. Their Norton Zip Rescue product features Symantec's Norton Rescue crash recovery tools stored on a 100MB Zip disk. If you own a Zip drive you might consider this alternative to Windows's emergency disk. Norton utilities are always well reviewed for crash recovery purposes.

If you choose Norton Zip Rescue, configure your Zip drive so that you can boot your PC from it. Otherwise, the product will do you no good. To do this, adjust your PC's boot-sequence setting. The latest BIOS programs include a Zip/LS-120 option for boot drives. Check with your PC manufacturer for a BIOS upgrade if you don't see this option.

Chapter

4.13

Accessibility Tools

With Windows 98, Microsoft took a big leap forward in making the personal computer accessible to people with physical disabilities. Read the hints in this chapter for information on how to customize these options, share them with others, and obtain more accessibility information.

4.13.1 Make the Screen More Visible

People with vision impairments find the standard Windows display inadequate for viewing. Windows 98's Accessibility Wizard makes it easy to customize the screen with larger fonts and high-contrast colors, but it *does not* give you access to all the display variations. In fact, it only shows you six of the 27 options.

> **NOTE**   You must have the Accessibility Tools component of Windows 98 installed for the hints in this chapter. To install this component, choose Start | Settings | Control Panel. Then select the Add/Remove Programs object. Pick the Windows Setup tab. Choose Accessibility from the Components list. Then put a check next to the Accessibility Tools entry. Click the OK button to install the files from the Win98 CD-ROM.

For the complete set, use the Custom setting in the Accessibility Options object in the Control Panel. Follow these steps to customize the display:

1. From the Start menu, choose Start | Settings | Control Panel.

2. Select the Accessibility Options object.

3. Pick the Display tab.

4. Put a check next to the poorly worded entry Use High Contrast. It doesn't matter if you don't want a high contrast screen setting. You get to choose whatever you want in the next steps.

5. Click the Settings button.

> **TIP**   If you want to toggle between your new customized setting and the standard display setup, put a check next to Use Shortcut in the Keyboard Shortcut box.

> **WARNING**   Microsoft's online technical support database has reported that a bug was found when using a high-contrast screen setup and running the Internet Connection Wizard. Some text in the Internet Connection Wizard cannot be read while in high-contrast mode. If you require a high-contrast screen, have someone else set up your Internet connection using a standard display setting. Then switch your display to high-contrast.

> **TIP** High-contrast screens are not always compatible with Web-based content, including the Web-based portion of the Windows 98 Help system. To make Web content readable under high-contrast conditions, follow these steps:
>
> 1. Open the Internet object under Start | Settings | Control Panel.
>
> 2. Select the General tab.
>
> 3. Click the Accessibility button at the bottom of the page.
>
> 4. Put a check next to Ignore Colors Specified on Web Pages.
>
> 5. Click OK, then click OK again.

6. Mark the Custom entry in the High Contrast Color Scheme box.

7. Use the drop-down box to select a display setting. To test the setting, select it, click the OK button, and then click the Apply button on the Accessibility Properties page.

> **NOTE** You can also choose these high-contrast display settings under the regular Display object of the Control Panel. In fact, the Appearance tab found there gives you a nice preview of what the resulting screen will look like before you apply it. I chose to describe this hint using the Accessibility Options object because that setting includes the HotKey capability that the Display object does not.

8. After you've chosen your setting, click the OK button on the Accessibility Properties.

These changes take effect immediately.

4.13.2 Get the Accessibility Tools Not on the Windows 98 CD-ROM

Microsoft deserves credit for providing accessibility tools in the base operating system, without the need to purchase a separate customization package. Still, they are many tools that Microsoft didn't include.

Developers have already written tools that translate text to speech, produce "flash card" views of text documents, enable shorthand typing, allow voice-control of applications, and more.

Accessibility Tools

Many of these programs are freeware, but you will find some shareware products that require a small charge for extended use. Here are some freeware/shareware sites and other accessibility resources on the Web:

Free and Cheap Windows Software for People with Disabilities (`http://www.at-center.com/windows.html`)—This site contains many useful shareware/freeware downloads for those with mobility issues and vision impairments.

Eye Tec Shareware Collection (`http://www.deicke.org/ etecshar.htm`)—Here you'll find shareware/freeware Windows screen enhancements and text-to-speech converters.

Recording for the Blind and Dyslexic (`http://www.rfbd.org/`)— Browse this site for an online catalog of audio and electronic versions of professional books and manuals including Microsoft's Win98 manuals.

Webable (`http://www.webable.com/`)—Browse this site for a massive collection of accessibility links. You find online articles from a variety of publications, non-profit organizations, and computer companies.

Trace Research & Development Center (`http:// www.trace.wisc.edu/`)—The University of Wisconsin-Madison hosts this organization. Trace has compiled a database of accessibility products and technologies that you can access online.

Microsoft's Accessibility Homepage (`http://www.microsoft.com/ enable/`)—This section of Microsoft's site offers an accessibility resource for customers and developers. Read about the upcoming Active Accessibility software model that will be part of Visual Basic 6.0.

4.13.3 Share Your Accessibility Settings with Others

Windows 98 makes it easy to configure one system with accessibility options ,and then quickly port these settings to another PC. But, they don't really tell you how to pull this off in the documentation or system help. You have to stumble across the procedure by trial and error—or you can just read this hint.

The secret lies with the .ACW settings file that you can create via the Accessibility Wizard. You'll also need a file type association set up in your Folder Options.

Follow these step-by-step instructions to share your accessibility settings with others:

1. Launch the Accessibility Wizard by choosing Start | Programs | Accessories | Accessibility | Accessibility Wizard from the Start menu.

2. On the first screen of the Accessibility Wizard, choose your font-size option: Normal, Large, or Microsoft Magnifier. Then click the Next button.

3. On the second screen, select your text-size option: Change the Font Size or Use Microsoft Magnifier. Then click the Next button.

4. The third screen is important. To save your settings to a file, you must place a check next to I Want to Set Administrative Options. You may also put a check next to any or all of the other statements that apply to you. When you've finished marking items, click the Next button.

> **NOTE**   The Set Wizard Options screen enables you to undo all your accessibility settings. Click the Restore Default Settings button if you want to reconfigure your system to use the standard Windows settings.

5. Depending on which statements you checked on the last screen, the Accessibility Wizard displays a series on screens and ask for your input to modify different accessibility settings. Make your choices and click Next to move through these screens.

6. Just before the final screen, the Accessibility Wizard displays the Save Settings to File screen (if you've checked I Want to Set Administrative Options) (see Figure 4.13.1). Click the Save Settings button. The wizard will show you a Save As dialog box. Save the .ACW file to disk in any folder you choose. Click the Save button. Then click the Next button.

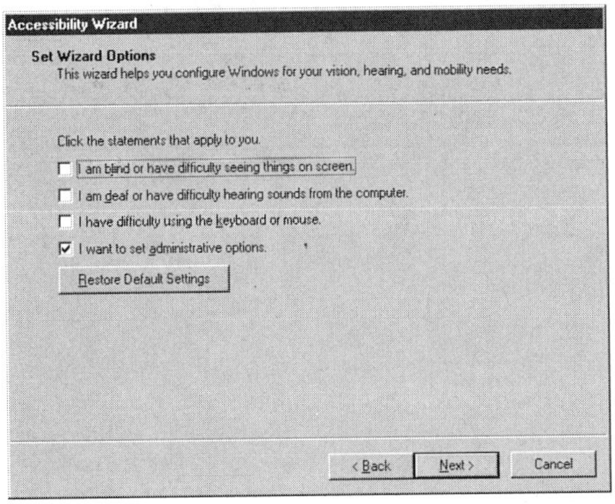

Figure 4.13.1

Save your accessibility settings using the Accessibility Wizard's Administrative Options.

7. Review your settings, then click the Finish button to close the wizard.

8. Transfer the .ACW to another computer via floppy, removable storage drive, or any other means.

9. On the destination computer, copy the file to the hard drive in any directory.

10. On the new system, check your file type associations by choosing Start | Settings | Folder Options. Then click the File Types tab. In the Registered File Types list, look for an Accessibility Wizard Settings File (.ACW) file type. If you do not see this file type listed, you must install the Accessibility Tools from the Win98 CD-ROM. See the following Note for instructions.

> **NOTE**   You must have the Accessibility Tools component of Windows 98 installed on any computer with which you want to share accessibility settings. To install this component, choose Start | Settings | Control Panel. Then select the Add/Remove Programs object. Pick the Windows Setup tab. Choose Accessibility from the Components list. Then put a check next to the Accessibility Tools entry. Click the OK button to install the files from the Win98 CD-ROM.

11. Launch the Windows Explorer and select the .ACW file that you've copied from the other computer. This loads the Accessibility Wizard with its final screen showing (see Figure 4.13.2). Simply click the Finish button to use the accessibility settings from the other computer.

Figure 4.13.2

Selecting the .ACW file launches the Accessibility Wizard with its final screen showing. Clicking the Finish button customizes your system with the accessibility settings from another PC.

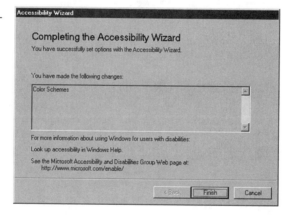

Appendix

A

Useful Web Sites

Browse these sites for additional information, tools, and tips on Windows 98.

Computer Press Resources

A few years ago, your access to computer magazines was limited to your local newsstand or the U.S. Mail. Now you'll find online outposts for all the major computer publications.

PC World

Link: `http://www.pcworld.com`

International Data Group's flagship publication, *PC World*, posts all its news, reviews, and feature stories online every month. Use the Site Search box to find articles related to Windows 98.

ZDNet

Link: `http://www.zdnet.com`

Use this site as a springboard into Ziff-Davis's computer magazines, which include *PC Magazine, PC Computing, PC Week,* and *Windows Sources.* The Search ZDNet tool explores all of ZD's publications for your topic.

CMPNet's Windows 98 Megasite

Link: `http://www.cmpnet.com/win98`

CMP, publishers of *Windows Magazine*, offers this Win98 online resource. You'll find tips, articles, and interactive forums on the operating system. Follow the hyperlinks to *Windows Magazine's* Web site.

NEWS.COM

Link: `http://www.news.com`

Browse CNET's technology news site for coverage of Microsoft's continuing battles with the government.

Tom's Hardware Guide

Link: `http://www.tomshardware.com`

At this site, find out about the very latest in video boards, processor chips, and motherboards for your Windows 98 system.

Shareware and Freeware

If you like the tools described in this book, you'll find more like them available at these Web sites. Just be aware, not all packages live up to their own hype. I've used the tools listed in this book. For other packages, you'll have to download the software and try it yourself to determine if it's any good.

FileWorld

Link: `http://www.fileworld.com`

PC World magazine stores shareware/freeware files at this section of their site. Look under the System Utilities, Desktop Utilities, Essential Shareware, Business, and Office categories for helpful Windows 98 tools.

ZDNet's Software Library

Link: `http://www.hotfiles.com`

Ziff-Davis posts shareware/freeware from third-party developers here. But they also offer "home-grown" tools that are described regularly in *PC Magazine*.

Download.com

Link: `http://www.download.com`

Check under the Utilities category of this CNET site for a list of Windows system tools.

Microsoft's Free Downloads

Link: `http://www.microsoft.com/msdownload/`

Access the Windows Update files, as well as beta programs and other free software, at this section of Microsoft's Web site.

Windows Chat Rooms

Share Windows information with other users at these sites.

Talk City: Advice and Support

Link: `http://talkcity.com/calendar/category/adviceandsupport.html`

Browse the Computer WinHelp chat room for advice from other Windows users.

ComputerChat

Link: `http://www.4-lane.com/computerchat/`

Click the WindowsChat! hyperlink for another Windows chat room.

Accessibility Resources

Point your browser to these Web sites for accessibility information and tools.

Webable

Link: `http://www.webable.com`

Page through this accessibility links clearinghouse and choose the resources that look interesting.

Trace Research and Development Center

Link: `http://www.trace.wisc.edu`

Look up computer accessibility products in the Hyper-TraceBase online database (it's in the Library section of this site).

Microsoft's Accessibility Page

Link: `http://www.microsoft.com/enable/`

The section of Microsoft's Web site provides the latest accessibility news, tools, and tips for Windows 98.

Index